W0036130

SAGE was founded in 1965 by Sara Miller McCune to support the dissemination of usable knowledge by publishing innovative and high-quality research and teaching content. Today, we publish over 900 journals, including those of more than 400 learned societies, more than 800 new books per year, and a growing range of library products including archives, data, case studies, reports, and video. SAGE remains majority-owned by our founder, and after Sara's lifetime will become owned by a charitable trust that secures our continued independence.

Los Angeles | London | New Delhi | Singapore | Washington DC | Melbourne

"Dr Ashok Sharma has given us a fascinating account of Indian lobbying in the US, a first in the history of this subject and a captivating story with drama and rich details.

The book tells of the Indian American community's efforts to consolidate its position and identity as it seeks to influence the lawmakers. And the joint lobbying with the Indian Mission in Washington that culminates in India's strategic partnership with the US.

A serious political study for scholars and the ordinary reader—to be treasured by Indian Americans."

Ambassador Lalit Mansingh
Former Foreign Secretary of India and Ambassador to the United States

"Ashok Sharma, by exploring the domestic politics of American foreign policy, opens new vistas on what could be one of the seminal bilateral relationships of the 21st century that bind India and the United States. This splendid book should be a required reading for anyone who cares about India's rise to global prominence."

Robert M. Hathaway
Public Policy Fellow and Former Director,
Asia Program, Woodrow Wilson International Center,
Washington, D.C.

INDIAN
LOBBYING
AND ITS
INFLUENCE IN
US DECISION
MAKING

INDIAN LOBBYING AND ITS INFLUENCE IN US DECISION MAKING

POST-COLD WAR

ASHOK SHARMA

Los Angeles | London | New Delhi
Singapore | Washington DC | Melbourne

Copyright © Ashok Sharma, 2017

All rights reserved. No part of this book may be reproduced or utilized in any form or by any means, electronic or mechanical, including photocopying, recording, or by any information storage or retrieval system, without permission in writing from the publisher.

First published in 2017 by

SAGE Publications India Pvt Ltd
B1/I-1 Mohan Cooperative Industrial Area
Mathura Road, New Delhi 110 044, India
www.sagepub.in

SAGE Publications Inc
2455 Teller Road
Thousand Oaks, California 91320, USA

SAGE Publications Ltd
1 Oliver's Yard, 55 City Road
London EC1Y 1SP, United Kingdom

SAGE Publications Asia-Pacific Pte Ltd
3 Church Street
#10-04 Samsung Hub
Singapore 049483

Published by Vivek Mehra for SAGE Publications India Pvt. Ltd, typeset in 10.5/12.5 pts Adobe Caslon Pro by Zaza Eunice, Hosur, Tamil Nadu, India and printed at Saurabh Printers Pvt Ltd, Greater Noida.

Library of Congress Cataloging-in-Publication Data Available

ISBN: 978-93-860-6212-3 (HB)

SAGE Team: Supriya Das, Guneet Kaur Gulati and Ritu Chopra

Dedicated to my parents
Shree Awadh Kishore Prasad Sharma and Late Girija Devi

Thank you for choosing a SAGE product!
If you have any comment, observation or feedback,
I would like to personally hear from you.
Please write to me at **contactceo@sagepub.in**

Vivek Mehra, Managing Director and CEO, SAGE India.

Bulk Sales

SAGE India offers special discounts
for purchase of books in bulk.
We also make available special imprints
and excerpts from our books on demand.

For orders and enquiries, write to us at

Marketing Department
SAGE Publications India Pvt Ltd
B1/I-1, Mohan Cooperative Industrial Area
Mathura Road, Post Bag 7
New Delhi 110044, India

E-mail us at **marketing@sagepub.in**

Get to know more about SAGE

Be invited to SAGE events, get on our mailing list.
Write today to **marketing@sagepub.in**

This book is also available as an e-book.

Contents

List of Tables

Preface

September 28, 2014, Madison Square Garden, the Indian Prime Minister Narendra Modi walks on the stage greeted by over 20,000 people of Indian origin and 42 US Congressmen. It is easy to understand why the Indian community is present in such large numbers to greet Modi, who brought a sense of hope after a resounding election victory with a convincing majority in the Indian Parliament not seen for three decades. But the presence of Congressmen tells a different story. Modi's popularity notwithstanding, their presence was more a reflection of the growing influence of Indian Americans and the Indian lobbying in the US politics, and a significant tilt of American policy toward India.

This day can be viewed as the culmination of a long process of the maturing of Indian lobbying and its role in turning the distinctly frosty American attitude toward India to one that has brought the world's oldest and largest democracies to carve a defining partnership of the twenty-first century.

American policy toward India has shifted over time from neglect to one of significant attention. During the Cold War period, the American executive and Congressional attitude were often hostile and critical toward India. Since the mid-1950s, there appeared to be a fundamental convergence of the views within the executive and legislative branches of the US Government toward India. American strategic policies and concerns, the US–Soviet rivalry, Indo-Pak hostility, and India's policy of non-alignment complicated Washington's bilateral ties with New Delhi.

In the changed post-Cold War scenario, the US–India relationship has overcome from the ideological baggage to a considerable extent. There has been a significant shift in the attitude of American policy makers, which has in turn paved the way for a robust US–India relationship. Today, the US–India relationship has entered in a comprehensive strategic partnership that includes joint military exercises, counter terrorism cooperation, defence agreement, defence commerce, and a coveted civilian nuclear energy deal. This reflects the United States' changed notion of India in the present world order and indicates that the two countries are no more grounded in obsolete conflicts of interest.

Several factors are responsible for this change. While the end of Cold War leading to a changed international scenario, increasing strategic and economic importance of India are important factors, one of the significant contributors to this change is Indian lobbying through the India Caucus, Indian–American political organizations and lobbyists and lobbying firms hired by the Indian Government, which have come on top of the increasing political influence enjoyed by Indian Americans in the US society.

The formation of the India Caucus in the House of Representative and then in the Senate is particularly notable indicator of fundamental change in the Congressional attitude toward India. It is commonly believed that successful lobbying by India Caucus has contributed to a much better image of India in the US Congress and deserves greater attention. Several variables play a role in the foreign policy decision making in the United States, the role of the lobbying is one of them.

The US governmental system, with the separation of powers, creates ample space for the lobbying activities of interest groups. The key activities of these groups in pursuit of their interests are to penetrate and influence government agencies, which are directly engaged in policy formulation. The role of lobbying in the American political life has therefore drawn the attention of American citizens, politicians, academicians, journalists, and political scientists throughout history.

Lobbying is an intrinsic part of the American political process. It is a technique adopted by many diverse interest groups, ranging from small domestic focused social, professional, ethnic groups to large foreign companies and nation states, for the purpose of putting pressure on policy makers in Congress to consider their interests favorably in policy decision making. The rights enjoyed by various groups in the United States are defined in the First Amendment to the Constitution "Congress shall make no law ... abridging ... the right of the people ... to petition the government for a redress of grievances." This very First Amendment to the US Constitution, which incorporated the freedom of assembly clause, upheld the right to organize groups, is the basis for one of the most powerful and controversial influences in the making of US foreign policy:

lobbying. Under the right to petition, domestic ethnic groups and foreign governments use favors and political skill to press their policy objectives on the legislative and executive branches of the government in Washington.

This book considers lobbying to be an effective instrument of political participation and political aggregation, which allows competing points of view to be heard. Lobbying also provides information to those who make important policy decisions, such as members of the Congress, various committee chairs, and members as well as high-level officials in the political executive bodies.

Lobbying tactics include face-to-face meetings between legislators and representatives of interest groups, grassroots campaigns, the use of the mass media, and the publication of research reports. It involves both direct as well as indirect techniques.

As American society has grown more pluralistic, and as the US Government has grown larger and more decentralized, lobbying activities in the United States have also increased. While lobbying activities of domestic interest groups are well documented and researched, the involvement of foreign interests in lobbying activities has been relatively less known. Before the 1990s, most foreign companies used the commercial arms of their diplomatic missions to promote their interests in the United States. Embassies of various countries still assist companies and provide their nationals with diplomatic and consular services, but foreign companies and countries have increasingly turned to American firms to represent their interests in Washington policy-making circles.

The history of Indian lobbying in the United States is of relatively recent origin. In fact, during the 1980s, only 5 percent of American legislators claimed that they were interested in India. If it was not for influential lawmakers like Stephen Solarz, India would have hardly figured in the deliberations. Three basic factors seem to have contributed to the increase in lobbying on issues of US–India relations:

1. the growing socio-economic and political profile of the Indian–American community;
2. the Government of India's decision to employ the help of US lobbying firms to make its voice heard in the US Capital; and
3. the increased activities of the Pakistani lobby in Washington's policy-making circles.

Although Indian Americans constitute a small segment of the total population in the United States (around 1 percent), they have acquired a respectable position for themselves in the American society. They have an influential presence in the fields of science and technology, medicine, and academia in the United States. Over 5,000 faculty members in various American universities belong to the Indian–American community. There are about 30,000 Indian–American medical professionals in the United States today and one out of every four foreign medical doctors is from India. Most recently, their presence is being felt in the software business sector throughout the country with around 15 percent of Silicon Valley's startups. Today, almost all the big US technology companies have technology pioneers from Indian–American community. With their representation of 3 percent of the nation's engineers, 7 percent of its IT workers professionals, 8 percent of its physicians and surgeons, and 15 percent of motel and hotel owners, Indian Americans have occupied a commendable place for themselves in professional and economic field in the United States.

However, for a long time the Indian community in the United States did not actively participate in the political processes and activities to voice their opinion. Their political activism was insignificant in comparison to other ethnic groups. However, the situation changed in the late 1980s and early 1990s. Increased numbers of Indian Americans began to show their interests in local political activities. Their political activism became significantly noticeable with the formation of the India Caucus in the US Congress in 1993.

In addition to reflecting the increasing influence of Indian Americans in US society, the formation of the India Caucus also reflected the increased efforts of the Indian Government. Prevailing uncertainties of the post-Cold War era and the need to engage the remaining super power induced the Government of India to adopt various means to make its voice heard in the complex policy-making process in Washington.

Formation of the India Caucus in the House of Representatives in 1993 and in the US Senate in 2004 therefore signified various developments.

- It reflected the growing importance of the Indian–American community in the United States;

- It indicated an emerging positive attitude within US legislators toward India; and
- It also provided a focused institution for lobbying by the Indian community, as well as for the Indian Government. Today the India Caucus lobby is one of the biggest of its kind in the United States.

The study focuses on two overarching developments. It looks at the professional success of Indian Americans, their political and lobbying activities, and their role in improving the relations between the United States and India. It also looks at the birth of India Caucus, its evolution, and its facilitating role in US–India relations. Concerted effort by the Indian Government to strengthen the role of the India Caucus is also a key development.

This book *Indian Lobbying and its Influence in US Decision Making: Post-Cold War* emerges from the significance of Indian–American interest groups' lobbying activities in the US political process. This work is ultimately an attempt to assess the role of Indian lobbying in the US foreign policy making toward India. It will examine the overall impact of lobbying undertaken by the Indian–American community and their organizations, and the lobbying activities of the India Caucus, lobbying firms, and lobbyists hired by the India Government.

This book has been divided into six chapters and a conclusion.

Chapter 1 is titled *Lobbying, Pressure Groups, and Ethnic Lobbying in the US Foreign Policy Making*. This chapter looks into origin and development of lobbying groups in the US political system. Different theories related to group formation advocated by David Truman, Mancur Olson, Robert Salisbury, and Jack Walker have been discussed. The factors, which have legitimized the interest groups lobbying activities in the US political system, find a detailed treatment here. It also scans the methods, techniques, and targets of lobbying. In the end, existence of some of main ethnic lobbies and their influence in the US policy process have been discussed.

Chapter 2, *Indian Americans: Immigration and Professional Advancement in the US*, deals with Indian immigration to the United States. It looks into pre- as well as post-1965 phases of immigration. The settlement pattern of Indian Americans has been explained and a comparison has been made with other Asian–American communities like Chinese Americans and Korean Americans. The current status of Indian Americans in the field of education, income, and occupational placements has also been discussed. In the end, the chapter makes an assessment of their professional success of Indian Americans.

Chapter 3, *Indian Americans and Political Participation: Growing Political Activism and Lobbying in the American Political Process*, deals with political activism and lobbying efforts of Indian Americans. The chapter divides their political activism and lobbying efforts into two phases. The first phase is before 1965 and another is after 1965 when the Immigration Act was passed in the United States. This chapter also looks into the participation of Indian Americans in direct politics, their fund-raising activities, and formation of political organizations. In the end, the chapter studies the role of the Indian–American political organizations in lobbying for the betterment of US–India relations.

Chapter 4 titled *India Caucus: Lobbying for a Robust US–India Relation* is about the events and factors that resulted in the formation of India Caucus and how it grew from eight Congressmen to 185. Lobbying by India Caucus in the US Congress for Indian Americans and for the US–India relations has been explained. The role of India Caucus in lobbying through press release, statements and resolutions in the US Congress for defending India and tackling adversary lobby on the issues such as nuclear, terrorism, Kargil, Kashmir, economic aid, and so on finds a detailed explanation in this chapter. Finally, an evaluation of India Caucus has been made by analyzing its success and failure showing its drawbacks and remedies.

Chapter 5, *The American Perception about India: The US–India Relations, and Indian Lobbying during the Cold War Period*, looks into the negative perception about India that had been dominant among the US Congressmen and executive officials during the Cold War period and how it created hurdles for developing a favorable environment or a positive platform on which they could come together and form a sound bilateral relationship. It examines the perception that was reflected during the US Congressional debate on foreign aid and nuclear issues, and how the lack of Indian lobbying allowed these negative perception to continue in the United States. Then it looks at how these perceptions further resulted into a conflicting US–India relation during the Cold War period and often harmed foreign aid prospects and denial of nuclear and defence technology to India. Finally, this chapter scans the beginning phase of Indian lobbying effort, which began to register itself at Hill during the waning days of the Cold War and early years of the post-Cold War period, that was aimed at changing perception in the United States about India.

Chapter 6 titled *Achievements and Actions of Indian Lobbying toward a Transformed and Robust US–India Relation* focuses on the lobbying undertaken with the intention of influencing US foreign policy toward India on various issues such as foreign aid, civilian nuclear deal, terrorism, and economic issues. It examines the role that Indian lobbying has played in aftermath of India's nuclear defiance in 1998 and Kargil incident, and also during the passage of the landmark nuclear deal bill in the US Congress, which marked the final arrival Indian lobbying as one of the most powerful ethnic lobbying after the Jewish lobby.

The main focus of this chapter is to show how lobbying, apart from other factors in the post-Cold War era, has played a significant role in the United States' favorable policy toward India and its integration into a major part of US foreign policy. This chapter also emphasizes on the important aspects of strategy of Indian lobbying that have been significant in its lobbying journey, such as the countering of Pakistani lobbying, aligning with Israel lobby especially for the passage of the US–India civilian nuclear deal, and hiring of lobbying firms. The chapter ends with the present status of the US–India relations.

The Conclusion looks into the significance of lobbying in the US, Indian Americans' political activities assessed in the context of various pressure groups theories, an assessment of the lobbying activities of India Caucus and the influence of lobbying on the US–India relations. Finally, despite the ceaseless efforts of both the governments to forge a robust US–India strategic partnership which is underpinned by an unprecedented convergence of interests in the changing geo-strategic and geo-economic realities of the present world which will have a considerable impact on the global order in the twenty-first century, the relevance of Indian lobbying in the US–India relationship will continue and is unavoidable.

Acknowledgments

It is my privilege to express my gratitude to a number of people who have provided inspiration, encouragement, and assistance during the course of the research activities leading to the publication of the present book.

The work described here emanates from my long-term research interests spanning over more than a decade and a half. I first became interested, in the influence of pressure groups in American politics in a course on Comparative Government and Politics, during my undergraduate studies in Political Science at Ramjas College, Delhi University. Since then pressure groups and their lobbying influence in the US policy process became a serious interest, challenging me to look more deeply into the questions such as why the lobbying groups are so powerful in the United States, what legitimizes the lobbying groups in the US society and politics, how they influence the US decision making, and so on. This interest continued when I joined Jawaharlal Nehru University (JNU) to pursue my MA in Political Science from Centre for Political Studies in 1995. Then later on the topic of lobbying groups in the US became the topic of research in my MPhil and PhD in American Studies at School of International Studies, JNU. I continued to work on this project during my stints in strategic and foreign policy think tanks in India—Observer Research Foundation (ORF), Centre for Air Power studies, and Centre for Land Warfare Studies—and then in Australia and New Zealand.

At the outset, I would like to acknowledge the contribution of the Indian–American community and of the India Caucus members whose lobbying efforts in the United States beginning in the post-Cold War era of the 1990s made this book possible. This book is an acknowledgment of the Indian–American community especially who immigrated to the United States and emerged as a successful professional ethnic group in America in the 1980s and 1990s who were eager to transcend their economic and professional success in order to participate in the American political process. I would like to acknowledge India Caucus members in both the House of Representatives and the Senate. It's been remarkable, from Stephen

Solarz, the lone vocal supporter of India in the US Congress during the Cold War period to 180 plus India Caucus members in the House of Representatives with the names such as Gary Ackerman and the first Co-Chairmen Frank Pallone and Jim McDermott to the formation of India Caucus in the US Senate in 2004 headed by Hillary Clinton and John Cornyn and their lobbying efforts which culminated in the final arrival of Indian lobbying on Capitol Hill with the passage of US–India civilian nuclear deal in 2008. Prime Minister Narendra Modi's appearance at Madison Square Garden to address a gathering of around 20,000 Indian Americans attended by some 42 Congressmen and his much applauded address to the joint session of US Congress would not have been possible without the Indian lobbying.

I would like to acknowledge Professor R.P. Kaushik, my MPhil supervisor, and Professor Chintamani Mahapatra, my PhD supervisor, at American Studies Centre, School of International Studies (SIS), JNU, for their encouragement and academic guidance to pursue the research on Indian–American lobbying. My gratitude also goes to Professor Christopher S. Raj and Professor K.P.J. Vijayalakshmi of American Studies Centre, JNU. I am thankful to Late Mr J.N. Dixit, the former foreign secretary of India and the Indian Ambassador to the United States, who as a visiting professor at American Studies Centre, JNU in 1999–2000 encouraged me to pursue research on Indian lobbying.

I would also like to acknowledge the support of the Indian Council of Historical Research Fellowship for my research at JNU, the Endeavour Fellowship for my Post-Doctoral work at ANU, India Research Fellowship at the Australia India Institute, The University of Melbourne.

The timely assistance of the Ministry of External Affairs, Government of India, and the Ministry of Overseas Indian Affairs is acknowledged. I am thankful to the former Indian ambassador to the US, Lalit Mansingh, who gave his valuable time and apprised me with interesting facts and insights on the formation of India Caucus and Indian lobbying especially on behalf of the Government of India in the United States.

I would like to acknowledge and thank Observer Research Foundation (ORF), New Delhi, where I was able to undertake interview and query a number of academics, diplomats, and ministers. Prominent among them were former Deputy Secretary of State Strobe Talbott, Robert Hathaway of Woodrow Wilson Institute, Stephen Cohen of Brookings Institutions, Amit Gupta of Air War College, Dr Praveen Choudhary of Ohio University, and Mihir Meghnani of Hindu American Foundation.

I am thankful to Professor S.D. Muni and Professor C. Raja Mohan under whom I worked for ORF-Brookings Projects on Indian Americans and US Election Watch 2004 which helped me in my research on Indian–American lobbying and India–US relations. I am also thankful to Professor Ajay Dubey of School of International Studies at JNU for his valuable inputs about Indian Diaspora.

I would like to acknowledge the former external affairs ministers of the Government of India during the Atal Bihari Vajpayee government, Shree Jaswant Singh and Shree Yashwant Sinha; Shree L.M. Singhvi, former chairman of ORF Late Shree R.K. Mishra, for their valuable time and inputs; and the writings of Dr Shashi Tharoor, whose writings brought a unique perspective as an Indian politician and as a member of Indian Diaspora in the United States. My thanks to both the Bharatiya Janata Party and the Indian National Congress Party for providing me with some valuable information on Indian lobbying efforts. My special gratitude to Shree Prabhat Jha (Member of Parliament, Rajya Sabha) for his help.

My special thanks to a number of US Congressmen, academics, the Indian–American community in the United States who have been generous enough to give their opinion via email, on the phone, and in person during the course of my research. I would also like to acknowledge the insights and suggestions I received during the April 2013 Mid-West Political Science Conference, at Chicago where I presented a paper on "Changing the Perceptions by Lobbying: The Impact of Indian–American Lobbying in the US Foreign Policy towards India" and during my stay in Washington, D.C. where I interacted with a number of academics and foreign policy experts on the US–India relations.

For this book, I owe intellectual debt to the scholarly works of Allan J. Ciglar, Burdett A. Loomis, Robert Hathaway, Arthur G. Rubinoff, Dennis Kux, Robert J. McMahon, Ramesh Thakur, Sumit Ganguly, Stephen Cohen and Tanmay Kanjilal. Their insights on interest group politics in the United States, the Indian–American community, India Caucus, the perception about India in the US Congress, and the India–US relations have informed my research.

My gratitude also goes to all my friends at JNU where I spent 10 years of a very intense and involved academic life. It would be difficult to list all of them, but I would like to thank Himanshu Shekhar Mishra and Dwapayan Bose. I would also like to thank my classmates at the Centre for Political Studies and American Studies Centre, the staff and residents of Periyar and Narmada Hostel where I lived during my stay in JNU. Also my gratitude to Professor Kanti Bajpai, then a faculty at the School of International Studies and warden of Periyar Hostel, with whom I would often discuss my research topic and his insights have always been enlightening, and Professor Harsh Pant (Kings College), my batch mate at JNU, for his encouragement for publishing this book.

My gratitude also goes to Professor Robin Jeffrey and Professor Robert Ayson at ANU during my Post-Doctoral Fellowship in 2008 and Professor Ramesh Thakur, Professor Raghbendra Jha, and Professor Rory Medcalf of ANU for their encouragement and support in my academic journey.

My acknowledgment also goes to the Department of Politics and International Relations, the University of Auckland where I was a faculty from 2012 to 2014. I would like to thank Professor Stephen Hoadley and Dr Correy Wallace for their valuable comments on my manuscript, and the support of Professor Katherine Smits and Professor Gerald Chan and all the colleagues at the Department of Politics and International Relations, The University of Auckland. I would also like to acknowledge Professor Dov Bing for his encouragement and valuable insights on Jewish lobby and support of other colleagues and friends during my visiting academic stint (2010–2011) at the Department of Political Science and Public Policy, The University of Waikato. I also wish to thank New Zealand Institute of International Affairs, especially the Gregory Thwaite and the team of NZIIA, Auckland Branch.

I would like to acknowledge the support from Professor Craig Jeffrey, Professor Amitabh Mattoo, and Mr Jim Varghese and all the staff at the Australia–India Institute, the University of Melbourne where during my research fellowship I gave the final shape to this book.

I am thankful to two anonymous reviewers of the book who accepted my manuscript for publication and their praise on the research rigor, information, analysis, and relevance of the book were rewarding for a work that I have been pursuing for a long time and that meant a lot to me.

I want to make a special mention of the team at SAGE Publications, especially Supriya Das and Guneet Kaur Gulati for their professionalism and assistance during the publication of the book.

Above all, I would like to acknowledge my brother Professor Arun Sharma (Deputy Vice-Chancellor, QUT and a past Chair of the Australia India Business Council) who was educated in the US and has been a keen observer of US politics. He has been a constant source of encouragement and inspiration throughout my academic career and his valuable insights on the impact of technology and economy on the geo-politics and international security have always been illuminating and his comments on the book have been of great help.

I acknowledge all my brothers and sisters Anil, Arvind, and Dr Amarendra Sharma, a Professor of Economics at Elmira College, United States, for his insights on Indian lobbying and India–US economic ties, and the younger ones Ajay, Anita, Abhay, Anju, and Anjali, and brothers-in-law Nalin, Abhishek, Ajit, and all bhabhis, cousins, family friends, and the next generation of "Sharma Family" of Shree Awadh Kishore Prasad Sharma and Late Girija Devi my parents to whom this book is dedicated.

1

Lobbying, Pressure Groups, and Ethnic Lobbying in the US Foreign Policy Making: Theoretical Overview

Lobbying is an intrinsic part of American political life. Across the country, lobbyists interject themselves into almost all aspects of the American political process.

Theodre Lowi has described interest group activism as "Interest Group Liberalism."[1] Charles Peter, editor-in-chief of the *Washington Monthly*, wrote, "America is no longer a nation. It is committee of lobbies"(McCutcheon, 2013, pp. 832–833). In fact, throughout the American history, from James Madison to Madison Avenue, interest groups have been central to American politics.

Many who have looked seriously at the interest group system and lobbying activities agree with James Madison, who argued in the "Federalist Papers" that interest groups are a necessary evil, best controlled rather than eliminated. Madison acknowledged the inevitability of factions, warned of their potential for tyranny, and defended the capacity of a representative republic to check and balance mischief. Scholars have focused on the potential of the interest group system to foster democratic representation through the mobilization of citizens into political life. At other times, however, commentators have dwelled upon the excessive and disproportionate power of lobbies. The dilemma for those who want to reform the lobbying system is that lobbying derives from basic American rights,

---

[1] Theodore Lowi's seminal book gives a critical insight in the influence of interest groups in the US Government (Lowi, 1979).

namely the First Amendment, and any effort to control it must avoid any contravention of those rights.

Lobbying is a technique adopted by all kinds of interest groups ranging from social, professional, ethnic, economic, and environmental groups within the US to foreign companies and even nation-states. Interest group activity is directed at the executive as well as the legislative branch of the US Government.

Lobbying has been used most often to refer to face-to-face individual meetings between legislators and representatives of interest groups. It has been used to refer to the interest group contact with the bureaucracy, the office of the president, the courts as well as within the legislature. Lobbying, however, includes grassroots campaigns, the use of mass media, and the creation of research reports, as well as face-to-face contacts. All these activities are used as instruments to influence the process of governance.

Lobbying is not a new phenomenon. It has a long history. The word lobby appeared first in the English language about the middle of the sixteenth century. It is derived from the Latin word *Lobium*, a monastic walk or cloister. Three hundred years later the word came to be frequently used in politics. It was used both to identify a hall or corridor in the British House of Commons and as a collective noun applied to all those who frequented these lobbies. It covered those who sought to influence men in office, as well as newspaper men and others looking for news and gossip.

In the United States, the term "lobbyist" came into usage in the early Nineteenth century. This was a time when corruption and conflicts of interests were commonplace, and "venal and self-seeking" methods were often used to get legislative results. By 1829, the phrase "lobby agents" was being applied to special favor seekers hovering in the New York capital lobby at Albany. By 1832, the term had been shortened to "lobbyist." Such agents became accepted in the American political process, particularly in the US Capitol Hill (Congressional Quarterly, 1982, p. 1).

Today the word "lobbyist" is used both in its narrow legal sense, and more broadly as a description of all attempts to influence not only the legislators, but also any agency or officer of government to secure or influence the passage or defeat of any legislation in the US Congress (McCarthy, 1970, pp. 200–201).

As per the estimates of the Center for Responsive Politics based on data from the Senate Office of Public Records, the number of registered lobby groups or lobbyists who have actively lobbied to influence the members of Congress and the executive administration was 11,504 in 2015 with total spending of $3.21 billion. The number of registered lobbyists was 10,405 and 14,829 with the total spending of $1.45 billion and $2.87 billion in 1998 and 2007, respectively. However, some reports contend that this is not the exact figure, the total number of lobbyists currently could be around 100,000 and total amount spend around $9 billion yearly (Li Feng, 2016; OpenSecrets.org, 2016). There have been increasing lobbying activities in Washington, and the underground unregistered lobbying activities of shadow lobbyists and their use of gradually more sophisticated strategies, which go unregistered.

Some of the most influential of them can mobilize hundreds of thousands of voters for their cause. And the groups that demonstrate the ability to carry out skilled and active grassroots campaigns wield significant influence in the policy-making circles of Washington, D.C. Apart from registered interest groups, there are probably more than 100,000 organizations engaging in interest group behavior in the US. They range from one-person outfits with almost no budget to the American Association of Retired Persons, which claims 34 million registered members. The world's largest corporations, capitalized in the tens of billions, are also prominent actors. Their number and the amount they spend on lobbying confirm that lobbying is a well-established practice in the US policy-making process and lobbies are often commanded by well-organized and well-funded lobbying firms and actors who have mastered the art of professional lobbying over many years.

DEFINING INTEREST GROUPS

Since lobbying is a technique adopted by interest groups, it is necessary to look into the views of different scholars and also the theories related to interest groups and lobbying.

Interest groups go by many names—"special interests," "vested interests," "pressure groups," "organized interests," "political groups," the "lobby groups," and "public interest groups." This varied terminology yields a diverse collection of operational definitions. Definitions, moreover, have varied over a period of time. Some have offered a normative appraisal; others have reflected the analytical goals of the scholar using the terminology. It was once standard practice to use the term pressure group; this phrase has given way to apparently more neutral "interest group" and "organized interest." Contemporary scholars use the terms that have meanings specific to that research.

Arthur Bentley defines a group as any subsection of society "acting, or tending toward action." He further argues, "there is no group without its interest. An interest is the equivalent of a group. The group and the interests are not separate" (1949, p. 211).

David Knoke provides the sociologist's definition, "A minimal definition of an association is a formally organized named group, most of whose members—whether persons or organizations—are not financially recompensed for their participation ... whenever associations attempt to influence governmental decisions, they all are acting as interest groups"(1986, pp. 1–21).

The sociologist distinguishes association and interest groups from primary groups such as the family, the corporation, and the bureaucracy. Sociologists typically begin with a definition of groups that takes the voluntary association as the base, then extend from there. As a result they typically pay less attention to corporations, land firms, cities, and other organizations that are often involved in the lobbying.

Political scientist, V.O. Key Jr., in his seminal work *Politics, Parties and Pressure Groups* (1942) defined pressure groups in terming the politics as a contest where the main players were organized pressure groups. His definition of pressure group was broad enough to include associations as well as economic interests such as firms, utility companies, and the like. He elaborated that in a political system, which values the public opinion and adheres to the principles of freedom of associations, pressure groups may be regarded as the links that connect the citizen and government. Pressure groups are differentiated in both composition and function from the political parties with the main objective focused on influencing the content of the public policy rather than the results of elections.

In the wake of Mancur Olson's (1965) *The Logic of Collective Action*, political scientists became more likely to use something closer to the sociologist's definition. Groups became synonymous with membership organization.

Salisbury shifted from increasing focus on membership organization and focused on the role of institution in lobbying. In their large study, Schozman and Tierney (1986, p. 10) were careful to use the term "organized interest" because they wanted to include organization such as corporations, hospitals, and others that do not have members as well as membership organizations.

Economists, voting analysts, and social psychologists define a group within the mind of the potential member of that group. To the extent that people believe they have shared identifications or shared interests, they are members of a group. To the extent these shared interests lead to similar behavior in the political realm, such as voting, then these groups can be considered to be interest groups. Johns Turner (1982) says no action is necessary only thought and he opines, "A social groups can be defined as two or more individuals who share a common social identification of themselves or, which is really the same thing, perceive themselves to be members of the same social category".

Among political scientists definition varies widely. Those operational in pressure group tradition have used a restrictive definition of groups focusing on active government lobbying. For them groups were corporations, industries, and hired lobbyist.

David Truman (1971) made the distinction between active groups and content interests, where latent interests exist in society but have yet to be mobilized on an organizational form. He defined interest groups as "any group that, on the basis of one or more shared attitudes, makes certain claims upon other groups in the society for the establishment, maintenance, or enhancement of forms of behavior that are implied by the shared attitudes" (p. 33).

Different scholars have tried to explain different things about interest groups. The more we go into it, the more complex it becomes. As a whole in political terms an interest group can be defined simply as any organized group of people who share common interests and goals and who attempt to influence government policy in pursuit of their goals and interests. As such interest groups share some common interests, whether it is maintenance of a strong national defence, the preservation of the environment, or the protection of the right to bear firearms. They have come together into some formal organization of like-minded individuals, and they seek to represent their common interest in the political system and try to influence public policy in the direction of their interests.

THEORETICAL EXPLANATION FOR GROUP FORMATION

The first political scientist to address the question of group formation was David Truman. He postulated in 1950s that major disturbances within the political environment produce conditions that encourage group activity.[2] He opined that people whose interests are adversely affected by these conditions will band together to improve their lot. In the process, he suggested, they would frequently turn to the government for help. He further argues that the creation and activity of political interest group spurs other people to organize to promote their interests. The process of competitive mobilization that is initiated generates additional group formation and activity. At some point a balance among groups is achieved, and the activity stabilizes. The equilibrium lasts until a new disturbance reactivates the cycle.[3]

A disturbance is some force that changes the "equilibrium" of the group with other elements in society. The purpose of forming an interest group or association is to overcome these disadvantageous forces and to stabilize relations so that a new equilibrium may be reached (Key, 1964, pp. 40–43).

Truman has suggested that increasing societal complexity, characterized by economic specialization and social differentiation, is fundamental to group proliferation (1971, p. 97). In addition,

---

[2] Truman (1971). Truman's theory was built upon the writings of another scholar of social and political movements, Arthur F. Bentley, who in his work *The Process of Government* (1908) was the first to study group behavior systematically.

[3] Truman (1971 p. 97).

technological changes and the increasing interdependence of economic sectors often create new interests and redefine old ones.

Not surprisingly, economic interests develop both to improve their position and to protect existing advantages, for example, National Association of Manufacturers originally was created to further the expansion of business opportunities in foreign trade, but it became a more powerful organization largely in response to the rise of organized labor. Mobilization of business interests since the 1960s often have resulted from threats posed by consumer advocates and environmentalists, as well as requirements imposed by the steadily growing role of the federal government (Cigler and Loomis, 1995a).

Disturbances that act to trigger group formation need not be strictly economic or technological. Wars, for example, place extreme burden on common man. Thus, organized resistance to the US defence policy arose during the Vietnam era. Likewise broad social changes may disturb the status quo. The origin of Ku Klux Klan, for example, was based on the fear that increase in the population of ethnic and social minorities threatened White, Christian America. So Truman's theory of group formation suggests that the interest group universe is inherently unstable. Group politics thus is characterized by successive waves of mobilization and counter mobilization.

David Truman's theory assumes that there exists an active and informed citizenry that has the will and the capacity to organize and pursue its interests and redress its grievances. The area that does not touch Disturbance theory is that all people do not have the same will and capability to organize themselves. Some have greater incentive to do so than others. A problem with Olson's theory of selective benefits, however, is that it does not appear to be equally applicable to all types of groups. People who join economic groups tend to be motivated more by direct economic benefits than those who join issue-oriented or ideological groups.

Thus, a prospective member of an economic group such as labor union or a business association is inclined to judge the advantages and disadvantages of belonging on the basis of financial gain. The motive for joining a pro-life or pro-choice group is very different and probably depends on how strongly a person feels about the merit of the issue. The difference in people's incentive that was not addressed by Truman led economist Mancur Olson (1968) to suggest that the principal incentives for joining a group are the selective benefits that people receive from being members. If the benefits of membership were generally available to people who did not join, there would be little incentive to join. Olson's logic is the reason that the American Association of Retired Persons, the US Chambers of Commerce, and many other groups offer their members specific benefits in addition to working for the collective good of members and non-members alike.

In fact, Mancur Olson has effectively challenged many pluralist tenets in *The Logic of Collective Action,* first published in 1965. Olson has based his analysis on the model of "rational economic man." For Olson, a key to group formation, and especially group survival, is the provision' of selective benefits (Cigler and Loomis, 1995a, p. 8). In fact unlike Truman, Olson does not deal so much with the germination of groups as he does with their ability to attract and maintain members once they have been organized (Berry, 1977, p. 37).

Robert Salisbury, a political scientist, used the concept of market place to explain why some groups prosper and others do not. He suggested that a group which has valuable product and ability to promote that product would probably succeed in creating and maintaining its organization. Salisbury gives credit of this success to the group's leader or entrepreneurs (Salisbury, 1996, pp. 20–22).

Salisbury's basic thesis is that the successful organization of potential groups hinges upon the quality of entrepreneurship. If the entrepreneur can gain profit (e.g., high salary, prestige, and personal satisfaction) and can provide sufficient materiel, solidarity, and purposive incentives, then the organization should succeed. In contrast to Truman, it is the organizer rather than the disturbing event that is the determining factor (Berry, 1977, pp. 20–22).

Another political scientist Jack Walker, in influential study of interest groups, gives importance to the resources available to the various groups that are not equal. He has argued that group formation and activity, that too in contemporary times, depends very much on the nature of groups' financial base. Start-up funds need to be sufficient to begin the group and support its operations. At least initially these funds need to be obtained from outside the membership base, although over time the membership may be able to sustain itself (Walker, 1983).

Government is no less responsible for group formation. Government action can figure prominently in generating group activity. Many interest groups are formed as a consequence of new legislation and regulations. Jack Walker pointed out in this regard that more than half of the groups representing senior citizens were organized after the passage of the Medicare Legislation and the Older Americans Act in 1965 (Walker, 1983, p. 403). Thus, not only groups try to influence what the government does, but the government itself also stimulates group mobilization and activities.

After analysing above theories of group formation, we do not wind up with a single reason that explains why groups develop. In fact, various factors seem to be conducive to the origination and maintenance of group activities. These include a discernible interest by the public, an interest that is affected by conditions in the social and economic environment; an incentive for joining and a benefit (not necessarily an economic one) for remaining a member; and leaders who are able to articulate and commercialize this benefit to those who desire it (communication task often requires a strong financial base). When these conditions are present, groups are likely to be created and sustained.

EVOLUTION OF LOBBYING BY INTEREST GROUPS

Efforts by private citizens, their organizations, and coalition of interest groups to influence the deliberations of Congress are as old as the American Republic. Throughout the nation's history lobbying groups have existed but their evolutions have occurred in the waves. According to David Truman interest group formation tends to occur in waves and is greater in some period than in others (Cigler and Loomis, 1995a, p. 11).

The first of these waves occurred prior to civil war, from 1830 to 1860. In this period, a number of significant political interest groups ranging from the anti-immigration, anti-Catholic know-nothings of the 1830s and 1840s to the anti-slavery abolitionists of the 1850s appeared.

The second phase of group activity occurred during 1880s, when industrialization and unsettled labor conditions brought about the formation of unions like the American Federation of Labor and the Knights of Labor.

Another spurt in the proliferation of lobbying activity was noticed from 1900 to 1920. This period saw the expansion of national business and trade associations like the US Chamber of Commerce, the National Association of Manufacturers, the American Medical Association, and the American Farm Bureau Federation. The formation of such large groups was made possible by technological revolution that facilitated rapid, nation-wide communication.

Further growth was seen in the 1930s. The contributor to the growth of this interest group engagement period was government itself. Early in the century, workers found it difficult to organize because business and industry used government backed injunctions to prevent strikes. By the 1930s, however, with the prohibition of injunctions in private labor disputes and the rights of collective bargaining established, most governmental actions directly promoted labor union growth. A major aim of the new deal was to use government as an agent in balancing the relationship between contending forces in society, particularly industry and labor. One goal was to create greater equality of opportunity, including the guarantee of identical liberties to all individuals, especially with regard to their pursuit of economic success (Cigler and Loomis, 1995a, pp. 11–13).

In the post-World War II period, the United States emerged as a superpower with a range of diverse international and regional interests and, as a result, there was a steady rise in level of lobbying activity directed at the Congress (Crabb, Antizzo, and Sarieddine, 2000, p. 139).

The major period of growth was from 1960 to 1980. In addition to the major growth in the proliferation and professionalization of interest groups formed to pursue economic interests, such as business, labor, and trade associations, this period also saw the rapid rise of idea and issue-specific groups focusing on basic beliefs and values (such as common cause and public citizen of Ralph Nader's organization). Cigler and Loomis argued that a "participation revolution" had occurred in the country as large numbers of citizen had "become active in an ever increasing number of protest groups, citizens' organizations and special interest groups" (1995a, p. 10).

The 1960s period of interest group activity growth has been termed by M.W. McCann as public interest liberalism (1986, p. 29). The expansion of federal programs has accelerated since 1960. In what political scientist Hugh Heclo termed an "Age of Improvement," the federal budget has grown rapidly from nearly $100 billion in 1961 to well over a trillion dollar in 1991, and has "widened the scope of federal regulations." Lyndon Johnson's "great society" in which multitude of federal initiatives in education, welfare, health care, civil rights, housing, and urban affairs were undertaken, created a new array of federal responsibilities and program beneficiaries (Cigler and Loomis, 1995a, p. 11).

The growth of federal programs and regulating activities prior to and during this period encouraged individuals and groups whose economic interests were affected by the government actions to become more involved in the political process. Since the 1960s, scores of liberal-middle-class citizen groups have sought to revitalize democratic reform politics in the United States. In most cases they have tried to protect and expand programs that have provided benefits to them.

During this period, the interest group activities were focused on the "post-industrial issues," and political movements of 1960s and 1970s were also prominent. The civil rights movement and protest movement against the Vietnam War demonstrated that an organized political activity could have an impact on the public policy. These movements further encouraged those who felt that government was not responsive to their needs and desires, such as environmentalists and consumers, and those who were adversely affected by changes in the public policy. Business groups expanded their effort to resist policies that restricted their freedom to do business. Conservative groups also became more active, influential, and successful in opposing the government's increasing economic intervention and social welfare programs.

Not only has the number of membership groups grown in recent decades, but a similar expansion has occurred in the political activities of many other interests, such as individual corporations, universities, churches, governmental units foundations, and think tanks (Salisbury, 1984). The Encyclopedia of Association (2016) has a list of approximately 23,000 organizations, up more than 50 percent since 1980 and almost 400 percent since 1955.

Apart from this, the impact of technological developments and innovations and the field of mass interpersonal communication have made it possible for organizations to reach out and broaden their membership by promoting awareness of issues, raising money, and mobilizing grassroots activities on behalf of their interests. These technological developments have also greatly facilitated lobbying activities by mass mailing and telephone campaigns, maintenance, and circulation of legislative voting records, and the compilation of reports and distribution of data related to the lobbyists' cause (Crabb, Antizzo, and Sarieddine, 2000, p. 11). Moreover, the potential membership base of many of these public interest, citizen, and consumer advocacy groups was greatly enlarged after World War II by increasing proportion having college education. College graduates tend to be more aware and concerned about the policy issues that affect them and their environment than are people with less education.

Changes in the political system, such as the fragmentation and weakening of political parties, the candidate oriental nature of elections, laws regulating contributions and expenditure, and the opening of legislative process to greater public scrutiny, have also contributed to increased interest groups activity. These changes have made candidates for office more dependent on group's support and public officials more responsive to organized interests.

The above explanations show several noticeable developments, which have marked the modern age of interest group activism in the United States. Another important factor in raising the level of lobbying activity in recent years has been efforts by a growing list of governments abroad to influence lawmakers. Beginning in the mid-1970s, one foreign government or political movement after another lobbied Congress directly or engaged in grassroots campaigns designed to influence legislative behavior, effectively overlooking the executive branch as the channel for communication between them and the United States. For example, the state of Israel has a high-level official who is viewed as its "ambassador" to the US Congress, in addition to its embassy. Today Israel, Kuwait, Saudi Arabia, South Africa, Iran, Taiwan, Philippines, China, South Korea, Pakistan, the Dominican Republic, Haiti, several countries in Eastern Europe, and now India are engaged in lobbying, designed to influence the course of American diplomacy. Frequently, these campaigns have been directed or coordinated by former members of Congress and by individuals who have served in executive agencies that play a key role in the foreign policy process.[4]

LEGITIMIZING LOBBYING: CONSTITUTIONAL, LEGAL, POLITICAL, AND ECONOMIC FACTORS

Lobbying by interest groups has a long incremental evolution, which has led to its legitimization. It is now very much integral to socio-economic and political culture of the US. Several factors have contributed to ever-increasing number of interest groups and legitimization of lobbying.

Constitutional Provisions

The first amendment to the US Constitution, which incorporates the freedom of assembly clause, upholds the right to organize such groups. The representatives of organized interest groups operate under the constitutional protection of the first amendment to the constitution. As long as the citizens enjoy the right to petition the government for redressal of their grievances, lobbyists will continue to exercise influence in making of public policies (Cigler and Loomis, 1995a, p. 5).

As political organization often parallels government structure, federalism and the separation of powers—principles, which are embodied in the constitution have greatly influenced and legitimized the existence of a large number of interest groups in the United States.

The existence of three levels of government—federal, state, and local—and the separation of powers at each level among the legislative, executive, and judiciary branches of government produces many

---

[4] According to one study, among the 91 Congressmen (both senators and representatives) who remained in Washington after they were defeated for office or retired from Congress, 81 became lobbyists, often earning two or three times their salary as public official (Gross, 1996, pp. 28–29).

points at which government policy may be influenced. This system is damaging for the political parties which try to manage and influence the government powers as a whole. But it clearly works for the benefit of the lobbyists and agencies that seek to influence specific policies. When a lobbyist is trying to block government action that it regards as detrimental, he finds that opportunity not just once but over and over again.

If a lobbyist of an interest group is not able to find a way into the house of Congress, he can try the other. Since the power in Congress tends to be personalized and scattered rather than institutionalized and concentrated, to impress just one key Congressman with the group's need may be enough. If he is a member of a committee that is considering an objectionable measure, especially if he is the chairman of the committee, he may kill the measure before the members of the house ever gets a chance to vote on it.

If the lobbyist fails to win the backing of any of the Congressmen, it may still strive for a presidential veto. But the end of the trail does not stop even there. Once a law has been passed, it is still subject to challenge in the courts, which interprets the law and has the power to decide whether a piece of legislation is constitutional or not. The interest group may succeed in having it interpreted to the group's advantage in specific cases. And when a law is put into operation, the lobbyist of group can continue to contact the administrators who interpret the law day by day.

The federal system of the United States offers another series of opportunities for interest groups at the state level. If a group cannot muster effective power at any point in national politics, it may still realize its ambitions in at least some of the states. The old saying, "If at first you don't succeed try, try again," is taken very seriously by American pressure groups. If none of these efforts to influence the government is successful, the group may finally attempt to influence nominations and elections to state or federal office with the hope that a new government may fulfill its desire (Irish and Prothre, 1965, pp. 243–245).

Legislative Acts

With the first amendment to the constitution, lobbying came to be accepted by constitution itself. When lobbying became more pervasive and sometimes appeared uncontrollable, attempts were made to regulate the activities of the interest groups. In the process, several legislations were enacted, which, in turn, contributed to the process of legitimization and acceptability of lobbying as part of the legislative and governing process in the United States.

At the federal level as early as 1852 the House of Representatives sought to protect itself from lobbyists posing as journalists (Eastman, 1997, p. 5). In 1876, the house attempted to require lobbyists to register but was unsuccessful. Since 1911 lobby regulations had been considered in almost every session of Congress. However, prior to 1995–97, only two major pieces of legislation had been passed in the Congress: The Foreign Agents Registration Act of 1938 and the Legislative Reorganization Act of 1946, which included the first general federal lobby registration laws. In 1995, the most extensive lobby law was passed since the 1946 Act.[5]

At the state level also down to 1960s and largely because of the populist and progressive movements, lobby laws were enacted in several states. Sometimes certain lobby regulations were included in the state constitutions as, for instance, Alabama Constitution of 1901 forbade legislators from accepting free railroad passes. Some of the important lobby laws related to interest group activity are given below.

Public Utilities Holding Company Act 1935

The Public Utility Holding Company Act of 1935 (PUHCA) is one of the most important federal consumer protection laws ever passed.[6] Section 12(i) The Public Utilities Holding Company Act of 1935 required anyone employed or retained by a registered holding company or subsidiary to file certain information with the Securities and Exchange Commission (SEC) before attempting to influence

---

[5] Before the 1946 Act, a 1935 law required registration of lobbyists representing holding companies before Congress, the Federal Power Commission or the Securities and Exchange Commission. Lobbyists for shipping and commercial marine interests were also required to register by a 1936 Act (Schlozman and Tierney, 1986, p. 318).

[6] PUHCA was repealed by the Energy Policy Act of 2005 due to strong lobbying by the utility industry and would be owners of utilities (Public Citizen, 2016).

the Congress. The Federal Power Commission or the SEC itself
intervened on any legislative or administrative matter affecting any
registered companies.

Section 12(i) of the Act states,

> It shall be unlawful for any person employed or retained by
> any registered holding company, or any subsidiary company
> thereof, to present, advocate, or oppose any matter affecting
> any registered holding company or any subsidiary company
> thereof, before the Congress or any Member or commit-
> tee thereof, or before the Commission or Federal Power
> Commission, or any member, officer, or employee of either
> such Commission, unless such person shall file with the
> Commission in such form and detail and at such time as
> the Commission shall by rules and regulations or orders pre-
> scribe as necessary or appropriate in the public interest or for the
> protection of investors or consumers, a statement of the subject
> matter in respect of which such person is retained or employed,
> the nature and character of such retainer or employment, and
> the amount of compensation received or to be received by such
> person, directly or indirectly, in connection therewith. It shall
> be the duty of every such person so employed or retained to file
> with the Commission within 10 days after the close of each cal-
> endar month during such retainer or employment, in such form
> and detail as the Commission shall by rules and regulations or
> order prescribe as necessary or appropriate in the public interest
> or for the protection of investors or consumers, a statement of
> the expenses incurred and the compensation received by such
> person during such month in connection with such retainer or
> employment.[7]

Merchant Marine Act

Section 807 of the Merchant Marine Act of 1936 required any
persons employed by or representing firms affected a various federal

---

[7] Public Utility Holding Company Act of 1935 as Amended. Retrieved
September 23, 2003 from http://www.aspenpublishers.com/SECRULES/
publicut.pdf

shipping laws to file certain information with the secretary of commerce before attempting to influence Congress, the Commerce
Department and certain federal shipping agencies on shipping legislation or administrative decisions. The information included a statement of the subject matter in which the person was interested, the
nature of the person's employment and the amount of the person's
compensation (Lobby, 1982, pp. 35–36).

The Foreign Agents Registration Act 1938

In the wake of the Second World War, Congress became concerned
about the propaganda activities of agents of foreign governments,
particularly those of Germany and Italy. The Foreign Agents
Registration Act, or the McCormack Act, as it was known, was an
attempt to register anyone representing a foreign government or
organization. The purpose of the Act was that it would serve as a
deterrent to the spread of pernicious propaganda. Initial enforcement
was placed in the State Department, but was deemed to be inadequate and enforcement shifted in 1942 to the Justice Department,
where it has remained since. This act was further amended in 1962
and 1966 (Clive, 1998).

The 1996 amendments sought to clarify and strengthen the act by
imposing stricter discloser requirements for foreign lobbyists. This
added to the scope of activities for which individual must register.
It required them to disclose their status, as agents when contacting
members of Congress and other government official and prohibited
contingent fees for contracts and campaign contributions on behalf
of foreign interests (Lobby, 1982, p. 36).

Federal Regulation of Lobbying Act 1946

This extremely short (four pages) act was quickly drafted and added
as an afterthought to the Legislative Reorganization Act of 1946.
Replaced in 1995, it was an important lobby law at the federal level
for about 50 years.

This act provided for the registration of any person who was hired
by someone else for the principal purpose of lobbying Congress
and for submission of financial reports of lobbying. Its key phrases
required

registration of any individual who by himself, or through an agent, or employee or other person in any manner... solicits, collects, or receives money or anything of value to be used principally to aid... the passage or defeat of any legislation by the Congress (Clive, 1998, p. 506).

This brief act suffered from many flaws, which surfaced in a federal court case...United States v. Harriss. It faced with major problems, as many lobbyists refused to register since they claimed that lobbying was not their principal purpose. Others did not register because they used their own financial resources to lobby. As a result there was a broad-based demand either to amend it or to write an entirely new law.

The 1995 Reforms (Clive, 1998, p. 509)

The 1946 Federal Regulation of lobbying Act was repealed and replaced by the new *Lobbying Disclosure Act of 1995* which was further amended substantially by the *Honest Leadership and Open Government Act of 2007*. Some of the main provisions of *Lobbying Disclosure Act of 1995*:

- Lobbyists and lobbying organizations include all those who seek to influence Congress. Congressional staff and policy-making officials of the executive branch including the President, top White House staff, Cabinet members and their deputies, and independent agency's administrators and their assistants.
- Lobbyists must register with the clerk of the House of Representatives and the Secretary of the Senate within 45 days of being hired or within 45 days of making their first lobbying contact. Lobbyists who expect to receive $5,000 or less in a six-month period, or organizations that expect to spend $20,000 or less in a six-month period on lobby with their own employees, do not have to register or make reports.
- Semi-annual reports must be filed and include the list of the issues lobbied on, a list of the institutions contacted, the lobbyists involved and the involvement of any foreign interest such as a foreign government or company, representatives of the US subsidiaries of a foreign-owned company and lawyer lobbyists for other foreign interests.

The Federal Election Campaign Act of 1971

This act and later amendments to this Act in 1974, 1976, 1979, and 2002 as McCain Feingold Act again encouraged and legitimized the participation of nonparty groups by allowing them to contribute more money to candidates than individuals are allowed to contribute. Known as Political Action Committees (PACs), these groups solicit voluntary contributions and use the money to influence political campaigns and policy outcomes. In the last two decades since federal laws and Supreme Court decisions conferred legitimacy on PACs, their numbers have increased about 660 percent, growing from 608 in 1974 to 4,210 in 1993 (Conway and Green, 1996). PACs contribute money to candidates, spend money in support of or in opposition to candidates, and mobilize and register voters on behalf of candidates. Federal Law limits PAC contribution to $5,000 per candidate per election. This means that a PAC can give a Congressional candidate up to $5,000 in a primary and up to another $5,000 in a general election. This is known as independent spending. Federal law prohibits PACs from coordinating this spending with a candidate's campaign committee. PACs can also contribute to state and local political parties in an effort to promote voter turnout. The opportunity to affect winners and losers provides a powerful incentive to PACs to participate in the electoral process. They have indeed done so in a big way. For example, during the 1991–1992 election cycle, PACs provided 32 percent of the funds received by House candidates and 20 percent of Senate candidates (Cigler and Loomis, 1995a, p. 9). Other laws also promoted PACs.[8]

Thus legislative acts regulating lobbying activities of interest groups have also legitimized their very existence at the federal and state levels of the American polity. Today four types of legal

---

[8] In fact, even without the amendments to the Federal Election Campaign Act, the largest and most sophisticated Political Action Committees (PACs) began before the mid-1960s American Medical Political Action Committee, Business Industry Political Action Committee, and American Dental Political Action Committee (ADPAC). Several Corporations also had their programs in 1960s. It was not the Federal Election Campaign Act and the Federal Election Commission that promoted the PAC movements, but it was every other regulatory body facilitated the growth of PACs (Budde, 1980).

provision related to lobby laws as a result of various lobby regulating laws exist in the United States at federal and state levels. The majority of these provisions are lobby laws, supplemented by three other types of provisions. They are as follows (Clive, 1998, pp. 501–502):

First, lobby laws provide for the registration of lobbyists and usually their employers, the reporting of expenditures. Sometimes these lobby laws prohibit certain types of activities, such as lobbying for a contingency fee, a percentage of the amount of money that the lobbyists secures of savings the group he or she presents.

Second, some laws related to conflict of interest and personal financial disclosures, generally referred to as ethical codes or laws, are intended to disclose the financial connections that legislators, elected executive officials, and senior civil servants have with individuals, groups, organizations, and big business. Prohibiting certain types of financial dealings, such laws check corruption at various levels of government.

Third categories of legislations are aimed at campaign finance regulations. These provide public disclosure, to varying extent, of contributions to political parties from individuals and organizations, that is, various interest groups. Such laws impose limits or prohibitions on certain type of contributions and in some states prohibit making of financial contributions during legislative session (Rayden, 1980).

Fourth types of laws are related to PACs. PACs are formed primarily for the purpose of channeling money to political campaigns, often circumventing contribution limits. The federal government, all state governments and some big cities have laws related to PACs.

Thus, lobbying is present in various legal provisions of the country, and it has slowly become an integral part of political process in the United States.

Weak Political Party System

Lobby groups in the United States basically function as an effective instrument of political participation and political aggregation, which allows competing points of views to be heard. Interest groups provide relevant and significant information to those who make important policy-related decisions. Lobby groups in the United States flourish also because of the weakness of the political party system. The political parties in the United States are decentralized and less unified and disciplined than parties in other countries. The resulting power vacuum in the decision-making process offers great potential for alternative political organizations, such as interest groups to influence policy (Cigler and Loomis, 1995a, p. 6).

In other words the weaknesses of political parties strengthen the efforts of these groups to promote desirable policy decisions. The failure of the major party to organize effectively in the Congress and to act with cohesion on policy matters produces a power vacuum that tends to be filled by organized interest groups (Irish and Prothre, 1965, p. 244).

Since the party exercises little control over party members, including legislators, Congressmen and Senators are accessible to whatever influences are outstanding in their respective constituency almost regardless of more inclusive claims (Truman, 1971, p. 325). On questions that are of no direct concern to prominent interests in his locality, the weakness of party structure leaves the legislators susceptible to appeals from national pressure groups that have little or no identification with his constituency.

The continued decline in the role political parties has further allowed interest groups to step in to fill the vacuum. In a political culture characterized by divided power, American political parties emerged early in the nation's history as instruments to structure conflict and facilitate mass participation. Parties through their evolution have functioned as intermediaries between the public and formal government institutions and have reduced and combined citizen demands into a manageable number of issues, enabling the system to focus upon the society's most important problems. The parties perform their functions primarily through coalition building," the process of constructing majorities from the broad sentiments and interests that can be found to bridge the narrower needs and hopes of separate individuals and communities" (Boroder, 1978, p. 3), and accordingly the New Deal coalition forged in the 1930s illustrated how this worked. Socio-economic divisions dominated the American politics from the 1930s until the 1960s. But patterns of partisan conflict are hardly permanent. Since the 1940s various social forces contributed to the creation of new interests and redefinition of older ones. This destroyed the coalition of New Deal in which Democratic and Republican Party had their own base and led to the creation of large number of political groups. Changes in the "post-industrial society,"[9] with the rise in individual expectations and class divisions, conflict did not disappear and rather got drastically transformed.

Walter Dean Burnmhan has noted that the New Deal's class structure changed, and by the late 1960s the industrial class pattern of upper middle and working class had been supplanted by one, which is relevant to a system dominated by advanced post-industrial technology. Political interest groups in the post-industrial age appear to be more liberal, cosmopolitan, and socially more permissive than the rest of the society. The traditional political party system found it difficult to deal effectively with citizen's high expectations and demands.

The economic, ethnic, and ideological positions that had developed during the New Deal era became less relevant to parties, elections, and vote preferences. The party system's inability to adapt to the changing social divisions in the post-industrial society and effectively address new issues of demands, such as abortion, the right to die, AIDS, and the death penalty, further enhanced the role of interest groups in American political process (Cigler and Loomis, 1995a, p. 19).

M.P. Petracca is of the opinion that Americans identify with various social groups as opposed to political parties. He cites the example from National Election Survey Data from 1972 to 1984, which shows a rise in identification with social groups, is a major trend in American Public Opinion, encompassing greater psychological ties to religious, class, occupational, racial, and gender groups. In another Gallup Poll, conducted in 1981, showed that as many as 20 million Americans are members of group and another 20 million gave money to such groups in 1980. Roughly 26 percent joined or contributed to group in 1980 (Petrecca, 1992).

---

[9] Affluence, advanced technological development, the central importance of knowledge, national communication process, the growing prominence and independence of the culture, new occupational structures, and with them new life styles and expectations, which is to say new social classes and new centers of power emerged (Eadd and Hedley, 1975, p. 82).

Though the political parties are trying to cope up with this environment, the weakness of political parties has helped to create a vacuum in electoral politics since 1960, and in recent years interest groups have moved aggressively to fill it.

Fundamental Changes Within the Congress

Fundamental changes within the Congress have been an influential factor in interest group activities legitimization. These changes can be meaningfully understood under the rubric of the "decentralization" of the House and Senate. As never before in the nation's history, the legislative branch has become an institution whose activities are highly fictionalized and uncoordinated, characterized by conflicting purposes, often producing deadlock and cross purposes on Capitol Hill, for instance, the old security system of determining committee assignments and chairmanship has been abandoned. Despite these measures, committees and subcommittees on Capitol Hill continue to proliferate year by year, with nearly all of them at some point claiming jurisdiction over the nation's foreign relations. Also individual lawmakers, together with their ever-expanding legislative staffs, are free to take independent positions on a variety of external policy questions (for details, see Hayes, 1981).

Political Culture of the United States

Although the Constitution of America itself has given space to pressure groups to play an important role in the political system, political culture of the country is no way less responsible for legitimizing the pressure group's activities in pluralist American society. In fact, socio-political, economic, and cultural values have considerably facilitated and legitimized pressure groups. Way back in 1830, Alexis de Tocqueville observed, "values, such as individualism and need for personal achievement underlie the propensity of citizens to join groups" (for details, see Almond and Verba, 1963). Moreover, the number of excess points—local, state, and national—contributes to American people's strong sense of political efficacy. Not only do Americans "see themselves as joiners, but they actually tend to belong to more political groups than do people of other countries" (Cigler and Loomis, 1995a, p. 6).

America is rightly known as nation of nations. In fact, half of the country's population are immigrants from other lands. On the one hand, these people have merged into large American culture but on the other, they continue to assert and preserve their identity in various ways.

Since pluralism inherent in American society is not opposed to these ethnic groups asserting for their cause. There are numerous interest groups based on ethnic composition and interests. They try to influence government decisions for their own group interest and, at times, they lobby for their mother country as well.

American–Jewish Conference, American–Arab Anti-Discrimination Committee, American–Israel Public Affairs Committee (AIPAC), and so on, are just a few examples of interest groups based on ethnicity.

Some of the interest groups in the US owe their origin and sustenance to economic reasons. Americans, who are brought up to believe that their system of government is better than that of other nations, have tolerated a political process, which is manipulated by a few well-entrenched big corporations. According to Edward S. Greenberg, big corporations acting as interest groups enjoy considerable political and public support in American society. In the recent past, majority of Americans accepted the Ronald Regan's view that big government was bad, but seemed tolerant toward the idea that big business was good. Large number of Americans, in fact, depends for their employment and financial well-being on the prosperity of giant corporations. In 1992 there were about 3,50,000 people employed by American Telephone and Telegraph, over 9,00,000 by General Motors, over 2,80,000 by Ford and about the same number by General Electric, and 5,00,000 by IBM (Sayeed, 1992, pp. 21–29).

Americans have been persuaded into believing that business ethics or business philosophy or the pressure group activities of business groups are all integral parts of social and economic system, which promotes public well-being. This also explains enormous influence that the business sector has come to exercise over American Government (ibid., pp. 21–30).

The power of gun lobby is worth mentioning in the overall context. The National Rifle Association of America (NRA) founded in

1871, the oldest continuously operating civil rights organization in the US and one of the top three most influential lobby, is dedicated to single issue of advocating for the gun rights of the American people to possess arms for their safety and security, enshrined in the Second Amendment to the US Constitution. With the membership of more than five million members, the NRA keeps informed its members about firearm-related bills since 1934 and has directly lobbied for and against legislation since 1975.

Despite the numerous spate of gun violence in the past and recent time in the US, the bids to keep deadly weapons out of the wrong hands and control sales of most lethal firearms and largest capacity arsenal have not succeeded. Congress even blocked a legislation which was meant to expand the number of gun-buyers checked for histories of crime or severe mental illness, despite 90 percent of Americans support such checks. In contrast, the Pew Research Center for the first in the last two decades found more Americans supporting gun rights than gun controls (*The Economist*, 2015). However, this can be attributed to the NRA's financial backup, the leadership, and organizational capability, support base and its extraordinary successful lobbying capability on perhaps one of the most controversial and debated topic in recent times, but it also shows the acceptance, legitimization, and the power of the lobbying in the US society and political process.

The Revolving Door

The lobbying has become as normal as activity that people hardly notice their representatives or bureaucrats playing into the hands of big corporations. Those who work in government service regularly act at the behest of corporations into whose ranks they frequently go upon after retirement from public services. Ken Silverstein in his book *Washington on $10 Million a Day: How Lobbyists Plunder the Nation* (1998) highlights the role played by lobbyists in policy making. These lobbyists work for the largest transnational corporations, for whom they buy influence in the US capital by payment of billions of dollars (in the 1996 US elections, the politicians spent $2.2 billion). Those big spenders transnational firms include the Philip Morris ($5.9 million), General Motors ($5.2 million), Pfizer

($4.6 million), General Electric ($4.1 million), and IBM ($3.1 million). The lobbyists have become so powerful that when the US Congress proposed a Revolving Door Act in 1995 to restrict the government servants from immediate employment as lobbyists the measure was roundly defeated.

Examples of this are numerous. Linda Hall Dachle was one of the principal regulators of the airline industry, she now lobbies Washington on behalf of North–West Airlines, American Airlines, and Boeing; J. Bennet Johnson, who once sat on the Senate Energy Committee, now lobbies for the Nuclear Energy Institute, a trade organization of the Nuclear Power Corporations. The top 10 lobbyists in Washington, further, once held senior government posts: Stuart Eizentstat (Carter's domestic advisor), Tomkorologos and Bil Timmons (Nixon's advisor), Patric Griffin (Clinton's advisor), J.D. Williams (aid to Senator Robert Kess), J. Jankonsky (aide to speaker Albert), and Lloyed Cutler (advisor to Clinton and Carter). The relationship between government and big corporations shows nothing but how much the lobbying has intervened US political culture.

TECHNIQUES OF LOBBYING

The lobbyists today are equipped with varied arsenal of weapons. The method and techniques used by lobbyists are almost as varied as their causes. Some appeal on a purely personal basis. Some undoubtedly use monetary or material appeals, but there is little evidence of direct pay off in lobbying activities affecting the Congress (Shaw and Pierce, 1970, p. 201).

Lobbying can take many forms: a memo or statement to a public official indicating a group's position; an organization sending influential constituents to Washington to plead its case; or a public relations campaigning in which millions of people participate and millions of dollars are spent.

There are two broad categories of lobbying techniques: direct or indirect. In direct lobbying group representatives themselves contact public officials. With indirect lobbying, representatives stimulate others to do so. Whether direct or indirect, the aim of the lobbying activity is still the same: to influence the decisions of public officials and affect public policy in a manner that accords with the group's interests.

Jeffry M. Berry in his book, *Lobbying for the People* (1977), says that a key concept governing direct lobbying is "access." A dominant goal of pressure groups or foreign governments is to gain entry to the legislative process through face-to-face meetings with law makers and their staff, through testifying before committees and subcommittees of the House and Senate (in the case of officials of foreign governments and political leaders), through addressing the entire Congress, and sometimes by drafting proposed bills or regulations for consideration (in some cases, defeating). While controversial, they also provide lawmakers with lucrative speaking engagements, vacations, contributions to their political campaigns, and other emoluments (Berry, 1977, p. 224).

Access is crucial, but knowledge and technique are just as critical as lobbyists traditionally have provided information as well as expertise to both Congressional leaders and committees. Since direct lobbying quite often begins at the committee or subcommittee level, the chances of success are substantial. After all committee decisions are frequently upheld by the full chamber. The lobbyist provides to the committee and its professional staff extensive background and technical information on issues of interest, precise legislative language for a proposed bill or amendment, lists of witnesses for the hearings, and other provides the name of a possible sponsor for the bill (Lobby, 1982, p. 8).

Examples of interest groups using direct methods to affect policy deliberations are prominent at both the national and state levels. Following the Supreme Court's Webster decision in 1989, which opened the door to legislative consideration of the abortion issue at the state level, pro-choice groups drafted bills that would protect the reproductive rights of woman, and pro-life organizations proposed legislation that would prohibit abortion after twentieth week of pregnancy. Both sides issued public statements, wrote speeches for their sympathizers, and provided officials at all levels of government with research and data to support their positions.[10]

---

[10] For details and more example, see Smith (1988); The Rise and Continuation of the Pro-Choice Movement. Retrieved 26 June 2004 from http://www.wowessays.com/ dbase/af5/dtb222.shtmland; EWTN (2004).

Interest groups have also been active within the public area as well. They have instituted grassroots lobbying campaigns to generate social support for a particular position within the general public, particularly among people who feel strongly about the issue and are likely to communicate their feelings to those in government. An example of this type of indirect lobbying is the successful lobbying by the banking industry to prevent a provision of the 1982 tax bill from taking effect. The provision would have required banks to withhold 10 percent depositor's interests for stakes, much as business withholds a part of employees' salaries. The banking industry generated 22 million letters to members of Congress, which resulted in the removal of the withholding provision (Smith, 1988, pp. 242–244). No single factor is likely to be more crucial in determining the positions of members of the House and Senate on questions of public policy than constituency influence. The dominant goal of indirect lobbying, therefore, is to create an irresistible tide of opinion within a district or state which induced lawmakers to support the lobbyist's position.

Today, grassroots lobbying, in some form, is a key tactic for many mainstream groups. For example, the American Society of Travel Agents sponsors an annual march in Washington to highlight the benefits of travel and tourism; in 1993 more than a thousand travel agents went to District of Colombia to oppose additional taxation of the industry in the Clinton budget plan (Cigler and Loomis, 1995b, p. 395).

Ricard Viguerie put together over 300 mailing lists with the names of more than 25 million contributors to various conservative causes. Not only were these individuals' likely targets for fundraising drives, but they also constituted a large number of potential activists for various conservative causes. According to Viguerie,

> Raising money is only one of several purposes of direct-mail advertising letters. A letter may ask you to vote for a candidate, volunteer for campaign work, circulate a petition among your neighbors, write letters and post cards to your Senators and Congressmen, in urging them to pass or defeat legislation and also ask you for money to pay for the direct-mail advertising campaign.[11]

---

[11] Ricard Viguerie as quoted in "New Era Group and Grassroots" in Cigler and Loomis (1995, p. 172).

The rationale behind letter writing is very simple. Public interest representatives strongly believe that government officials are quite sensitive to mail their offices receive and that members of Congress, in particular, really do listen to their constituents (Berry, 1997, pp. 233–234). Political protest in the form of street demonstrations, picketing, and sit-ins are also successful tactics to hold protest by lobbyists. As a result due to press coverage, government officials become more sensitive to issue, as press coverage creates awareness which then affects masses (Lipsky, 1968).

But today there is a change in the magnitude, sophistication, and cost of grassroots politicking. The mass efforts of travel agents, abortion activists, and dozens of other groups are only the most visible tactics. Reflecting fundamental, organic charges in American politics, grassroots efforts by organized interests now rely heavily upon mass marketing, high technology, and public relations ploys reminiscent of modern political campaigns (Cigler and Loomis, 1995a p. 395).

With the boom in computer technology, it has become easier to approach the people who are most likely to be influenced by a particular campaign. Waste in mass mailing has reduced to minimum due to targeted membership campaigns, and the use of electronic dissemination methods. The US Chamber of Commerce, for example, has opted for the use of computer-based technology to mobilize its constituents (local chambers, firms, and business-related trade associations) on legislative issues that affect them. The US Chamber of Commerce has a phone bank that allows it to contact the groups of its 215,000 members. Those who answer have the option of pressing 1 on their touch tone phones to send a personal mailgram or letter, to their legislators, pressing 2 to direct a voice mail message to the lawmakers, or pressing 3 to have a computer connect them immediately with their representative's office for a personal phone call (Cigler and Loomis, 1995a, p. 395). The NRA mailed more than 10 million letters and spent over $1.7 million in 1998 in an effort to prevent the enactment of a bill that required a seven day waiting period for the purchase of a handgun (Tierney, 1992).

There have been few instances of questionable lobbying practices to influence the Congressman. One such incident was the Koreagate scandal in 1976. In the "Koreagate" scandal, South Korean politicians tried to seek influence from 10 Democratic Congressmen by offering bribes and favors. An immediate objective of the scandal seems to have been reversing President Richard Nixon's decision to withdraw troops from South Korea largely because of the dictatorial practices of President Park Chung Hee (Encyclopedia.com, 2016). Though this was a political scandal which tarnished the image of lobbying practices and raised serious questions concerning the loyalty of the members of Congress who would accept bribes from a foreign government, Koreagate had surprisingly no long-term impact on lobbying.

In fact, despite the negative popular image of lobbying efforts, modern lobbyists rarely resort to the use of corrupt practices or unlawful pressure. Instead, they serve as conveyors of useful information, both technical and political.

TARGETS OF LOBBYING

The structure of the American system is a system of "multiple access points" and "multiple veto points", where pressure group can gain access. Among 535 members of the US Congress, for example, the odds are favorable that there is at least one legislator who will give time and attention to almost any interest conceivable. If rebuffed in the Congress, then among the 800 plus administrative agencies there may be one person. And if turned away there, the group may find it possible to make a federal case out of its interest and pursue the issues through the courts. The same pattern of multiple access points occurs at the state, and to a lesser extent, at the local level. Some pressure groups, in fact, work at two or more levels of government simultaneously, seeking the access point that will give them the most favorable results. Both civil rights and environmentalist groups have found this to be useful strategy.

To counterbalance, the multiple access points are the multiple veto points. In the American system of checks and balances, often only one person or a small number of people are institutionally placed to be able to prevent government from functioning on certain issues. The most obvious example is the veto power of the US president. It takes a simple majority (50 percent) to pass a bill in the Congress. If the president vetoes that bill, it requires a two-third majority to overrule his veto in each House. This means that the president and no more than 34 Senators can block the will of 66 Senators and conceivably, the entire membership of the House of Representatives.[12] Due to checks and balances, the multiple veto pints are significant and these give an advantage to pressure groups which are fighting "defensive battle," by trying to prevent a policy from being changed, or a new policy being adopted. This means the pressure group, which can access a veto point and maintain its access, is in a position to block the best efforts of its rivals or opponents.

LOBBYING IN THE FOREIGN POLICY PROCESS

Vice President Nelson Rockefeller observed in 1975 that foreign lobbies are guiding US foreign policies on two major foreign policy issues. Those were the Middle-East conflict between Israel and its Arab adversaries, and the crisis erupting between Greeks and Turks on the Island of Cyprus (Howe and Hott, 1977, p. 1).

On increasing interference of interest groups in the foreign policy process and proliferation of interest groups in policy process and proliferation of interest groups, President Jimmy Carter in his farewell address to the nation delivered on January 14, 1981 said, "it was a disturbing factor that tends to distort our purposes, because the national interest is not always the sum of all our single or special interest groups" (Lobby, 1982, p. 1).

The United States is expected to speak in a single voice on foreign policy issues. Foreign policy is supposed to reflect national interests that have their roots in the nation's moral principles. The stakes of foreign policy are higher than those of domestic policy as any wrong decision can lead to conflict, war, or even nuclear confrontation. Foreign policy decisions are generally based on common interest and national principles that put American interests first when looking beyond borders.

---

[12] Petracca (1992, pp. 206–207). During the 94th Congress, with Republican Gerald Ford as President, an overwhelmingly Democratic Congress was unable to override Presidential veto.

Given the scope and depth of American involvement in the world, it should come as no surprise that lobbying by interest groups in shaping foreign policy decision has become significant. Among the important examples of foreign policy lobbying are ethnic national groups, economic groups including associations of senior executives of American industry, broad-based associations such as trade and professional associations, single industry groups, labor groups, and foreign governments (Nathan and Oliver, 1982, p. 261).

Economic groups comprise a large and heterogeneous set of lobbying forces that have from time to time influenced American foreign and national security policy. It is estimated, for example, that more than 500 corporations maintain legislative liaison offices in Washington. For examples, the Chamber of Commerce and NAMs, the fisheries and associated industries lobby groups, the American Petroleum institute representing more than 300 oil industry corporations, and the most powerful industrial lobbying groups the American defence industry[13] best described as "military–industrial complex" play an important role in the formulation and implementation of national security policy and foreign policy.

Lobbying by Foreign Governments

This book also focuses on lobbying by special interest groups on behalf of foreign governments in legislative and executive branches of the US Government. This became significant with the emergence and dominance of the US as a world power in the post-Second World War era. Foreign leaders understood that lobbying in the US capital was essential to receive substantial military and economic aid to buy the US weapons, to acquire US support in the United Nations and also in multilateral lending agencies. Some undemocratic regimes around the world understood the value of US support and that failure to gain sympathy from American officials and public audiences could generate unwanted criticism and bring outside pressure on them (Newsom, 2004). Lobbying outside of the diplomatic process was therefore considered essential.

---

[13] Nathan and Oliver (1982, pp. 262–269).

Foreign governments maintain offices in Washington, and support trade councils to mobilize members of the American business community with an interest in specific aspects of foreign trade. Foreign governments have also contributed to the American universities and research institutes in an effort to develop a sympathetic hearing with the foreign policy community. As of July 1994, there were 6,308 active registered lobbyists as agents of foreign governments (ibid.). Usually foreign nations hire Washington-based lawyers to lobby for their stand and interests on foreign aid or trade laws. In many cases, former officials mainly high-ranking members of the executive branch and past Congressmen lobby on behalf of overseas interests and seek to influence the Washington policy-making establishment.

Ethnic Groups

The United States as "a nation of immigrants" with significant ethnic and racial diversity and its global involvement ensures that many ethnically based interest groups are active at one time or another in the foreign policy arena.

Arguably, foreign policy decisions increasingly reflect ethnic interests rather than an over-arching sense of national interests. Recent events suggest that ethnic groups continue to play a role. Mohammed E. Ahrari has suggested four conditions for ethnic groups' success in influencing foreign policy. First, groups must present a policy that convincingly aligns with US strategic interests. Second, the groups must be assimilated into the US society, yet retain enough identification with the old country so that this foreign policy issue motivates people to take some political action. Third, the group and its members must be politically active. Fourth, groups should be politically unified. Other criteria may include advocating policies backed by public at large, having enough members to wield political influence, and being perceived as pursuing as legitimate interest (Ahrari, 1987, pp. 155–158). Success and failure of ethnic group in promoting their cause and their positions on foreign policy issues can be gauged from these four factors which determine their strength and weaknesses.

But some ethnic groups actively or indirectly influence the country's foreign relations with their respective countries of origin. This need not always be in line with the perceived interests of the state of origin, that is, Cuba. For example, at least five ethnic groups saw the 2000 election as a chance to shape their US foreign policy goals, even though neither major candidates nor voters showed much concern for foreign policy overall. Two groups seeking to sway the election seemed to have failed; the other three may have succeeded at least in part. American Jews welcomed, while Arab Americans were worried about the nomination of the first Jewish Democratic Party's candidate for Vice President, Senator Joseph I, Lieberman. When Lieberman lost the election, the Muslim community was pleased. Cuban Americans, upset over the Clinton administration's handling of six-year-old refugee issue involving Elan Gonzalez, were probably responsible for the narrow Republican victory in Florida that gave the Presidency to the Republican George W. Bush. Latinos, especially Mexican Americans, were angry at restrictive immigration legislation enacted by Republicans in Congress and in California. Latinos established themselves as a power base in California, contributing heavily to Al Gore's victory there and helping the Democrats capture several formerly Republican House seats. Armenian Americans claimed credit for toppling a California Republican incumbent (Uslaner, 1996). While elections are generally not directly fought over foreign policy issues, except during exceptional times, ethnic groups vote or campaign against a party or a candidate on the basis of certain domestic or foreign policy issues affecting them.

In the above context, it is worthwhile here to mention the two cases of successful lobbying by ethnic community against their country and have also damaged the US national interest. One of them has been the lobbying by Shiete Iraqi Ahmad Chalabi who has been accused for influencing the US policy toward Saddam's Iraq. The diplomatic and intelligence officials charged him of misguiding the Bush administration to make case against Saddam by propagating the idea on misleading information that the Baathist regime had maintained stockpiles of biological and chemical weapons, and was poised to become a nuclear (Mayer, 2004) power; inflating the Iraqi security threat to the United States; fabricating and promoting doubtful stories linking Saddam to Al Qaeda; and overestimating the effortlessness with which Saddam could be substituted with a Western-model democracy.

Another example in this regard is of Anti-Castro Lobby—a very smart and effective lobbying formed by a small segment of Cuban–Americans against Raul Castro regime (Leogrande, 2013; Noah, 2014). Though Obama has broken the shackle of this lobby group by opening toward Cuba, this Anti-Castro Lobby stalled the US Foreign Policy to normalize the relationship with Cuba. Foreign policy experts have argued that in the post-Cold War era there was no need of containment of communism at the global level and opening toward Cuba would have promoted a free economy and better prosperity in Cuba, served the US interest, and promoted a productive US–Cuba relationship.

The Jewish lobby is regarded as the most powerful lobby groups. American Jews often successfully lobby on behalf of Israel. Greek Americans, Latin Americans, Armenian Americans, Irish Americans, and even Arab Americans at various times have followed the approach of pro-Israel lobby to gain support for their respective interests.

American Jews are distinctive in their ability to affect foreign policy. They have established the most prominent and best-endowed lobby in Washington by fulfilling each of Ahrari's conditions for an influential group. Although many Jewish–American organizations exist in the United States, the community's political activity has, since 1959, largely centered on the AIPAC, the only Jewish lobby registered under the Federal Registration of Lobbying Act of 1946. AIPAC has 150 staff, 55,000 members across all 50 states, and annual administrative budget of $15 million. It operates out of offices one block from Capitol Hill with considerable political acumen and, in a moment of perceived crisis, it can put a carefully researched, well-documented statement of its views on the desk of every Senator and Congressman and appropriate committee staff within hours of a decision to do so (Friedman, 1992). Activists can readily mobilize the network of Jewish organization across the country to put pro-Israel pressure on members of Congress. In 1991 the lobby organized 1,500 "citizen lobbyists" armed with computer printouts of their legislator's background AIPAC claims to enact more than 100 pieces of pro-Israel legislation a year through some

2,000 meetings with members of Congress (American Israel Public Affairs Committee, 2001, 2004).

Jews make up 2.7 percent of the US population, yet they are a highly motivated and organized group in the country. Since the Jewish lobby's inception in 1951, it has rarely lost an important battle. Israel receives by far the largest share of the US foreign aid, more than $3 billion a year. In 1985, Israel and the US signed a free trade pact and Israel benefits from the tax-exempt contributions from the American–Jewish community. No other nation can match the favor that Israel gets in the history of US foreign relations (Fortune, 2004).

While the US Government has its own foreign policy agenda, and the aid to Israelis motivated by its national security considerations and strategic interests in the Middle East, the influence of the Jewish Community on Washington's Israel policy cannot be underestimated.

The Jewish lobby draws its strength from a variety of factors, such as sympathy in the United States for the Jewish people due to holocaust, common biblical heritage between Christians and Jews, a shared Western value system, the democratic nature of Israel's political system and Israel's role in the Middle East as an ally of the United States. The Jewish community, moreover, is wealthy and highly educated. Jews are among the most generous campaign contributors in US politics: 60 percent of the individual contributions to former President Clinton's 1992 campaign came from Jewish donors and were among the top 20 contributors to Gore's 2000 campaign.

AIAPAC espouses clear objectives: to secure continuing aid to Israel on the most favorable possible terms; to maintain the supply of the most advanced US weapons possible to Israel; to preserve tax-exempt status to Jewish fundraising in the US; and, to oppose strongly any US measures or proposals seen as a threat to the security of Israel, including arms for Arab countries and peace proposals that might require Israeli concessions. To get a wider support in the US public, the lobby has repeatedly stressed certain themes: Israel is the only democracy in the Middle East, and it is also a strategic asset and a reliable ally.

AIPACs lobbying connections are so thorough that one observer said, "A mystique has grown up around the lobby to the point where it is viewed with admiration, envy and sometimes anger" (American Israel Public Affairs Committee, 2001).

The concentrations of AIPACs efforts have been mainly, but not exclusively, focused on the Congress. Its influences come from large contribution it makes to candidates favorably disposed to AIPACs goals and contributions to opponents of those who have voted contrary to the positions of the lobby. Significantly, it does not contribute to candidates directly; it prepares information for voters on records and positions of members of Congress. Sympathy for its cause is also generated by orchestrated visits to Israel for elected officials and candidates. When issue is before Congress, the lobby generates letters, telegrams, and telephone calls to members by circulating information on the issue to Jewish communities and sympathizers throughout the country; the flood of mail alone causes some legislators to change positions on an issue.

AIPAC opposition to US policies in the Arab world has brought it into direct confrontation with other powerful interest both in government and outside. In the 1980s, actions such as the Israel's invasion of Lebanon in 1982 created serious tensions between Washington and Jerusalem and even among many Jewish Americans.

Although AIPAC has not achieved all its stated goals, it can look back as a series of achievements. Its lobbying led to increase in US aid to Israel and betterment of terms to the point that, by 1990, most assistance was on a grant basis. It was not able to defeat selling of arms to Saudi Arabia, but it was successful in two instances of intervening   the sale of AWACS and F-15s to Saudi Arabia.

Although the Jewish population is just around 2.7 percent of the total population of the United States, 10 percent of members in both in the House and Senate are Jewish. Almost 20 percent of the Senate Foreign Relations Committee (SFRC) and the House International Relations Committee (HIRC) are Jewish and half of the members of the House Sub-Committee on the Middle East, including both the chambers and the Ranking minority member are Jewish. Pro-Israel forces were also successful in getting Joseph Liberman, an orthodox Jew and strong supporter of Israel, nominated as Vice President Candidates in the 2000 election from the Democratic Party.

The bulk of lobby is comprised of Jewish Americans who are deeply committed to making sure that US foreign policy advances what they consider to be Israel's interests.[14] According to historian Melvin I. Urofsky, no other ethnic group in American history has so extensive an involvement with a foreign nation. Steven T. Rosenthal agrees, writing that "since 1967, there has been no other country whose citizens have been as committed to the success of another country as American Jews have been to Israel" (Urofsky, 1975, p. 1; Rosenthal, 2005, p. 209).

"The attachment that many American Jews feel for Israel is not difficult to understand as it resembles the attitudes of other ethnic groups that retain an affinity for other countries or peoples with similar backgrounds in foreign lands." As the Joint Program Plan of the National Jewish Community Relations Advisory Council, a major Jewish agency, put it in 1957, "The American public accepted the American Jewish concern about Israel…as a natural, normal manifestation of interests based on sympathies and emotional attachments of a sort that are common to many Americans" (Wertheimer, 1995, p. 13).

Apart from Jewish lobby groups, there are other important ethnic groups and they have been lobbying for themselves and for their country of their origin. Greek Americans, with a US population of 2 million, have long been considered the second most influential lobby in the United States. The Greek lobby, working through the American Hellenic Institute of Public Affairs Committee has promoted the interest of the Greek Government, often at the expense of US relations with Turkey. They lobbied successfully for an arms embargo on Turkey after Turkey's 1974 invasion of Cyprus, and have since pressed for a balanced US policy toward Greece and Turkey.

Those of Irish descent, chiefly in New England, have formed an Irish National Caucus to collect aid for elements in Northern Ireland seeking to end British rule. They were successful in getting the Clinton administration to welcome Gerry Adams, spokesman for the Irish Republican Army in the United States.

Latin Americans now constitute 12 percent of all Americans and are on par with African–Americans in terms of population. This community consists of Mexican–Americans, Puerto Ricans, and

---

[14] For detail insight on Israel lobby, see the seminal work of Mearsheimer and Walt (2007, p. 115).

Cuban–American, and there is little unity among them. But they have been lobbying for their common cause and have of late become politically very active. Cuban–Americans working through Cuban American Nation Foundation, and especially the exile community in Florida, have been effective in promoting legislation and other official acts to preserve the embargo against Fiedel Castro's Cuba. Radio and IV Marti, federally financed programs aimed at Cuba, came into existence largely through the pressures of this lobby. They also contribute to the election funding.

African Americans, traditionally, have been more interested in domestic economic issues than foreign issues as most of them are not able to track their roots to specific African countries, they have begun to lobby on foreign policy issues covering Africa, especially the ending of Apartheid in South Africa. More recently, the Congressional Black Caucus has taken a firm stand on sending US troops to Somalia, lifting the ban on Haitian immigrants infected with the AIDS virus, and pushing the United States to restore ousted Haitian President Jean Bertrand Aristide to offices (*New York Times*, 2001).

Apart from these there are also other ethnic groups like Asian–American community who have established their lobby groups in the United States and have been pressurizing the Capitol Hill for their demands. Asian–Americans are second fastest growing ethnic group in the United States, constituting 3.7 percent of the population.

Indian Americans have recently become politically more active and have taken an active participation in domestic politics. They have also lobbied to influence the US foreign policy toward India. This was noticeable after India's nuclear test in 1998, and in passage of the US–India civilian nuclear bill through Congress. In fact they have come to occupy an important role in influencing and facilitating the US–India relationship. Their higher professional success in different walks of life in America has made them an ethnic group with a relatively high income. Their professional success and financial capability have given them the confidence and desire to play an active role in political life in the United States. Today their political activism is visible at all levels of American political life. Chapters 2 and 3 deal with the settlement, professional success, and political activism of Indian–Americans in the United States.

2

Indian Americans: Immigration and Professional Advancement in the US

Migration of people from India to different parts of the world is not a new phenomenon. Today, when we look at the demographic map of the world, there is hardly any country which does not have the presence of people of Indian origin (PIO). According to estimates there are over 30 million PIO and Non-Resident Indians (NRI) living in various parts of the world, particularly in the Gulf countries, Africa, West Indies, South and South-east Asia, Australia, Europe, and North America. In some countries they comprise a considerable percentage of the total population (e.g., Mauritius, Singapore, and Fiji) while in others they belong to a microscopic minority.

Human beings leave their place of origin for a variety of reasons, such as environmental deterioration, political and religious persecution, economic hardship, search for a better life, and sense of adventure. Migrational pattern of Indians can be put into three phases.

In ancient times, Indian migration was characterized by cultural expansionism. Saints and seers moved into different directions with deep knowledge of philosophy and the rich Indian cultural heritage and spread religious messages, particularly that of Buddhism. The second phase of migration took place during British rule, which was in the form of indentured labor to colonies, especially the British colonies. Humans cargo found its way to Africa, Mauritius, the Caribbean region, Fiji and, Southeast Asia. This forced migration was an exploitive and inhuman movement of people. The third contemporary phase started in the post-Independent era, and accelerated in the second half of the twentieth century. This can be characterized as voluntary migration, as people migrated for better economic opportunities and standards of living. This phase is also known as the

"Brain Drain" wave because most of the migrants are highly skilled professionals, such as doctors, engineers, academicians, technicians, and lawyers. The United States, the United Kingdom, Canada, and recently Australia are ahead of other countries as the destination for Indian migrants during the third phase. There was also noticeable large scale migration of skilled/unskilled Indian workers to the Gulf countries following the oil boom in the 1970s which has now risen to about 7 million Indians working in the region. But the United States has been the biggest beneficiary of this phase of Indian immigration, and highly skilled Indians have contributed significantly to the US economy and society.

This chapter is about the migration and settlement of Indians in the United States, the rise of the Indian professional class and the technology elite, and their journey to have a greater say in the American public life. It is imperative to have an insight into their growing number and professional success which have helped them to shape American political perception toward India through the tried and tested approach of political lobbying.

MIGRATIONAL PATTERN OF INDIAN AMERICANS

It is not an exaggeration to call the United States of America a land of immigrants. The history of the United States is a history of waves of migration. People have settled there from all known civilizations of the world. In the seventeenth century, the English Puritans settled in the New England States, even as the Spanish settled in Florida. Early in the nineteenth century came the great flood of Irish and German immigrants—2 million Irish and 1.5 million Germans came to America between 1815 and 1860. The next wave brought 10 million Western Europeans—English, Dutch, Swedes, and Norwegians to American shores between 1880 and 1890. The third wave was even bigger: 16 million migrated between 1890 and 1914. Most of these newcomers were Eastern and Southern Europeans—Sicilians, Greeks, Poles, Czechs, Italians, and Russians Jews (Goel, 2004).

The US has continued to be the primary destination for immigrants; Asian influx replaced the European in the twentieth century. Koreans, Filipinos, and Vietnamese began to join an already substantial Asian population consisting mainly of Chinese and Japanese.

A sizeable section of Asian migrants are of Indian origin, and are known as Indian Americans, who are not only a growing community in the United States, but their achievements and professional success of late have become noticeable. During various phases of modern history, diverse groups of India came to the United States in many different guises: students, scholars, diplomats, political activists, religious leaders, merchants, visitors, professionals, sojourners, immigrants, and refugees.

For the convenience of analysis, the migration of Indians to the US can be broadly divided into two phases: (a) the early immigrants till mid-1960s and (b) the post-1965 immigrants, when stricter and more detailed immigration laws were passed by the US Congress.

The Early Immigrants: Pre-1965 Phase

The Indian–American community in the US is over three million strong, but this large number has grown from small beginnings. The history of Indian immigrants in the US was conventionally thought to have begun just before 1900. This history can now be pushed back to the seventeenth century. The merchant seamen employed by the East India Company who made their way to the Eastern seaboard colonies appear to have brought slaves from India, who were almost certainly unaware that they were being taken to the Americas. These slaves married into the black population, most probably converted to Christianity, and were endowed with a new name. They were assimilated into categories such as "mulato," "dark," and "colored," and their Christian names reveal little about their origins (Lal, 2008, p. 13). But the earliest record of an Indian traveling to the Unites States is that of a young Indian man from Madras who visited Massachusetts in 1790 as a maritime worker. As Salem developed its trade ties with India during the next decade, young Indians worked on the Indian wharves at Crownshield and Derby, two of the largest shipyards. A group of approximately 200 Parsis (Zorashtrian faith) merchants devised a plan to migrate from Bombay. Isolated individuals, particularly sailors, were also brought to the United States as indentured servants by captains of merchant marine ships in New England (Jensen, 1988, p. 12).

During the period between 1820 and 1870, 196 Indians mainly from the state of Punjab migrated to the US. Indian merchants were reported to have arrived at Philadelphia in 1889 (ibid., p. 13). They traded in silk, linens, spices, and other goods from India. This period witnessed a burgeoning interest in Indian culture, philosophy, and religions among American intellectuals. Ralph Waldo Emerson and Henry David Thoreau studied Indian philosophy and religions with great zeal. Walt Whitman wrote the poem "Passage to India" in 1868. The number of people in Boston who were interested in Indian philosophy and religions grew to such an extent that soon they came to be known as "The Boston Brahmins."[1] "The Rajah's Daughter" and "Cataract of Ganges" were the name of plays performed at the Boston theater during this period. All this reached a high point when Swami Vivekananda, a fluent English-speaking Hindu monk and a thinker, addressed the World Parliament of Religions in Chicago in the year 1893. The interest he regenerated led to the establishment of Vedanta Society centers all across America.

However, Indian new comers to the US had to face the adversity. They encountered similar legal and extra-legal discrimination as other Asians. The Naturalization Act of 1870 had limited naturalization to "White persons and persons of African descent," making Indians ineligible for citizenship. Therefore, the Asian Indians were subject to the provisions of alien land, laws in California, and other states also prohibited the Indians from buying or leasing agricultural land (Kitano and Daniels, 1988, pp. 89–90).

The presence of the Indian community in the US was too small to attract attention in early decades of the nineteenth century. It was, however, not until 1880 that their total numbers crossed 200 mark in a single year. From 1820 to 1900 altogether 696 Indians immigrated to the United States. Thus, during the nineteenth century only 700 scattered adventurers, merchants, monks, and professional men mainly from northern India immigrated to the US (Table 2.1) (US Immigration and Naturalization Service, 1977).

---

[1] "The Boston Brahmins" term was used for exclusive and erudite Anglo-American upper class in the Eastern settlement of America which could be seen in the context of nineteenth-century transcendentalist writings of New England literary icons such as Ralph Waldo Emerson and Walt Whitman, and the enlightened appeal of Universalist Unitarian movements of the same period. Transcendentalism was also influenced by the teachings of Upanishads, core of the philosophy of Hinduism.

Table 2.1

Indian Immigrants to the US (1820–1900)

Year	No. of Immigrants
1820	1
1821–1830	8
1831–1840	39
1841–1850	36
1851–1860	43
1861–1870	69
1871–1880	163
1881–1890	269
1891–1900	68
Total	696

Source: US Immigration and Naturalization Service (1977).

In the early twentieth century, a noticeable group of Indians came to the West-Coast of the United States and settled in the state of California and Washington, entering from Canada. This new wave of Indian immigration—about 7,000, mostly from Punjab—took place between 1904 and 1923. Sikh by religion, Punjabis wear turbans as their religious custom. The Americans therefore termed the influx of Punjabis as the "Tide of Turbans." More than three quarters were from Punjab, while others came from Gujrat, Oudh, and Bengal. Most of them were agricultural workers, popularly described as "Hindus," in the American press.

The early Indian immigrants can be divided into two groups: (a) farmers and laborers and (b) middle-class students, elites, and political refugees.

The Indian laborers took jobs in lumber mills and the rail-road when they arrived in the Pacific North-West. However, after racial violence against Indians, perpetrated by the European labor unions in the lumber mills, a large number of Indians moved to the Joaquin Valley and the Central California alluvial plain to work as agricultural laborers. The new place suited them well as they were mostly from Punjab's agrarian society. They worked hard, saved lots of money and gradually began to purchase land. According to the 1919 census of land in the State of California, Indians owned 88,000 acres of land in California—52 percent of this land was in Sacramento Valley. However, most of these Indians were destined to lose their land under the 1915 California Alien Land Act, which held that certain aliens (specifically Japanese and Indians) were ineligible to own land, if they were not US citizens. Large tracts of Indian lands were usurped, although some Indians had American born children and lands were transferred to their name (Koritala, 2014).

A small number of early middle-class entrants, of various statures trickled in throughout the nineteenth and early twentieth centuries. Most of them settled in major urban centers on the East Coast and practiced various professions and married white women. They enjoyed high respect and power in the society because of their high socio-economic status and English language skills (Sheth, 1995).

Another group of Indians migrants to the US were students, who initially came to pursue higher studies at American universities. A number of these students at University of California at Berkley and Stanford University organized themselves into groups openly advocating Indian Independence from British dominion and formed the Ghadar Party in 1913 in San Francisco, and also published a weekly newspaper, "*Ghadar.*" The followers of the Ghadar Party had committed to liberating India by all means at their disposal. The Ghadar movement got a setback when the United States joined the First World War in 1917 and acted under pressure from the British Government to prosecute Ghadarites for conspiring with Germans against the Britishers (Jha, 1995)

The trading communities of India had been involved in trade with foreign countries since ancient times. Traders constituted another group of Indian to migrate to the United States. By the turn of the twentieth century, there were about 500 Indian traders in the United States, including several Parsi merchants in North-East and other export–import businessmen in Los Angeles. Well-known business-men like Jagjit Singh, Dalip Singh Saund, Watumal brothers, and other early Sikh agri-businessmen, also financially supported India's independence movement (Hugh, 1977, pp. 3–5).

In fact, the Indian migration to the United States at the turn of the century was motivated by a variety of factors operating at individual, national, and international levels. British colonial rule had destroyed the traditional and indigenous economies of India leading to finan-cial hardship and forcing business people to immigrate. Some argue that the opportunity to enhance the Indian Independence movement itself motivated the immigration of some earlier Indians (Mazumdar, 1984).

The increasing number of Indians migrating to the United States overlapped with rising anti-Asian sentiment, mainly against Chinese and Japanese immigrates, that was gaining ground in America. The new Indian immigrants faced a series of discriminatory measures that were taken against Indians by the US Government. White workers, trade union officials, politicians, and even the media became hostile toward Indians and pressured the state and federal governments to pass exclusionary laws against Indians. The Executive Exclusion Order of 1910 and the Congressional Exclusion Law of 1917 were the results of such pressures. Though these measures were mainly against Chinese and Japanese immigrants, Indians were no exception.

The Immigration Act of 1917, also known as "Barred Zone Act," effectively barred all Asians from entering the United States. It said that certain people from the barred zone, which included India, could not immigrate to the United States. At this time naturalized citizenship was reserved for Whites only. Now they also came under the jurisdiction of Alien Land Law 1913, amended in 1920–21, which prevented noncitizens from owning and leasing land. The Asian Exclusion Act of 1924 further prohibited Indians from immigrating to the United States. This resulted not only in a fall in the number of Indian immigrants, but also in the denial of and revocation of their citizenship (Arnold, Minocha, and Fawcett, 1987).

More than 1,700 Indian immigrants were denied citizenship between 1911 and 1917, mostly on the ground that they would need public assistance. Like the Chinese and Japanese earlier, Indians contested in court the laws discriminating against them. The lower federal courts had granted them the right to naturalize on the grounds that they were Caucasians and thus eligible White persons under the naturalization legislation of 1790 and 1870 (Hing, 1993, pp. 31–32). In these circumstances, the new immigrants imbibed their first political lessons, acquiring the skills and tenacity necessary to use the courts to their advantage, combat racism, and pursue a good livelihood among difficulties compounded by their high illiteracy rates and poor knowledge of English.

However, in the United States v. Bhagat Singh Thind Case (1923), the Supreme Court reversed its racial stances, deciding that Indians, like Japanese would no longer be considered White persons, and were, therefore, ineligible to become naturalized citizens. Naturalization certificates previously granted were subject to cancellation, and Indians fell under the harsh Asian Land Laws. In the process many Indians were denaturalized and stripped of their American Citizenship (Kitano and Daniels, 1988, pp. 93–94). Between 1911 and 1930 about 4,500 of them returned to India harboring a victim mentality. It was found in the 1940 Census that the Asian Indian population had dropped to 2,405, of whom 60 percent resided in California alone (Takaki, 1989, pp. 313–314).

Looking at the trend from 1901 to 1910, a total of 4,713 Indians migrated to the United States, while only 3,968 immigrated in the 1920s and 1930s. The number drastically decreased to a mere 496 between 1931 and 1940 but took an upward swing from the next decade to reach a total of 6,336 between 1941 and 1965 (see Table 2.2). This was possible because after World War II the United States desired entry of professionals particularly doctors, engineers, and entrepreneurs, which in turn facilitated the immigration of Indian to the United States. In 1946, the Indian Citizenship Bill was passed, which was co-sponsored in bipartisan effort of Congressman Emmanual Celler and Clare Booth Luce. It legalized the status of Indian immigrants as eligible to seek naturalization and granted India a token quota of 100 immigrants annually. Now Indians were eligible for citizenship as well as for petitioning to bring their families back to America. Although visa for entry was restricted to only 100, the actual entry was often more than that due to liberal interpretations of the law (Fisher, 1980, p. 11).

Table 2.2
Indian Immigration into the US

Year	Numbers
1941–1950	1,761
1951–1960	1,973
1961–1965	2,602
Total	6,336

Source: US Immigration and naturalization Service (1977).

In 1952, the McCarran Walter Act was passed, which introduced the special quota system for the people of Asian extraction, in effect, ending the Asian exclusion policy. Despite the introduction of these laws only few thousands students and visitors came between 1946 and 1964. This interim period remained relatively quiet. Many women in Japan, South Korea, the Philippines, and South Vietnam married the US servicemen stationed in those countries and subsequently immigrated to the US as spouses of the US citizens. They consolidated the majority of Asian immigrants during the interim period. But lack of military connection between India and the United States prevented a similar pattern of Indian immigration to the United States.

Amidst these situations the early Indian immigrants to the United States had to face problems which were further exemplified by their lack of knowledge of English, comparatively high illiteracy rates, and their lack of a wider socio-political network. However, in the pre-1965 phase the Indian diaspora had begun to learn their first political lesson and imbibed the political and legal knowledge and skills to fight against discrimination and work for the better life for their future generations.

Immigration After 1965

The Immigration Act of 1965 passed during President Lyndon Johnson's administration, brought drastic changes in immigration policy and reversed a half-century-old policy of discrimination against Asian immigrants. This Act deleted ethnicity and race as a factor of elimination; removed the restrictive Asian quota under the 1921 law; abolished the national origins quota system (as was fixed in 1924); removed the "Barred Zone" provisions of the 1917 law; set a ceiling of 170,000 immigrant visas annually for the nations of Eastern Hemisphere (with a ceiling of 29,000 for any one nation), and 120,000 for the countries of Western Hemisphere. It set up seven preference categories, favoring the entry of professionals and skilled workers which the United States needed most (ibid., pp. 19–20).

India became one of the major beneficiaries of the 1965 Immigration Act, Hart-Celler Act. The timing and the provisions of the Hart-Celler Act, especially special preference visa categories that focused on immigrants' skills, concurred with the emergence of a large number of highly educated and technically qualified persons in India mainly engineers, doctors, and business management professionals as a result of newly established institutes in the post-Independence India—Indian Institute of technology and Indian Institute of Management, All India Institute of Medical Sciences and other medical colleges. These highly skilled professionals looked for better opportunity abroad as Indian economy was not doing well in the 1960s and the 1970s.

Consequently, the 1965 immigration act facilitated the way for thousands of Indians to immigrate to the United States to have their economic desires fulfilled, and also helped them to form a distinct ethnic community of their own. Now immigrants entered from almost every Asian country, but the majority emigrated from China, India, the Philippines, Korea, and Vietnam. The trend in Indian immigration took a new turn, with Indians from Caribbean Islands, British Commonwealth countries, European countries, and about 70,000 Indian refugees from business and professional classes expelled by Idi Amin regime in Uganda in the early 1970s, entering the United States under a special clause (Sheth, 1995, pp.172–173).

Table 2.3 indicates that from 1966 to 1975, altogether 96,153 Indians immigrated to the United States, with surprisingly high number was in 1972 despite United States–India relations becoming

Table 2.3
Number of Indian Immigrants to the US(1966–1975)

Year	No. of Immigrants
1966	2,458
1967	2,642
1968	4,682
1969	5,963
1970	10,114
1971	14,310
1972	16,926
1973	12,256
1974	11,863
1975	14,939
Total	96,153

Source: Sheth (1995).

very strained in the wake of the 1971 the India–Pakistan war that led to the creation of Bangladesh. By 1979, the seven leading exporters of manpower to America were all from the third world, and India ranked sixth after Mexico, the Philippines, and China (including Taiwan and Hong Kong). In the 1980 census, the Indian–American community accounted for 387,223. In five year, from 1976 to 1980, a total of 291,070 had immigrated to the US. The 1990 US Census recorded the number of Indian Americans at 815,447 and between the 1980 and 1990 Census, the annual growth rate of the community was 8.5 percent (U.S. Department of Commerce-Economic and Statistics Administration, Bureau of Census, 1990).

According to the estimate of the Population Reference Bureau, the growth rate of Indian–American population was 103 percent between 1980 and 1990, a growth rate second only to Chinese migrants, among Asian–American ethnic groups, and by 55 percent in 1990–1997, second only to the Vietnamese. The Indian–American population numbered 1.215 million in 1997, making it the third largest Asian–American ethnic group in the United States after the Chinese and the Filipino Americans, leaving behind the Japanese (The U.S. Embassy in India, 1999). As of the Census of 1990, of all the Asian population, Indians ranked fourth after the Chinese (1,645,472) (U.S. Immigration and Naturalization Service, 1990).

The Filipinos (1,406,770) and the Japanese (842,562) both outnumbered the Koreans, the Vietnamese, and others (see Table 2.4). While Asians represented 2.92 percent in total, the Indian immigrants

Table 2.4
Immigrants from India and Other South Asian Countries, 1970–1990

Year	Total	India		Pakistan		Bangladesh		Sri Lanka	
1970	11,884	10,114	85.1	1,528	12.9			226	1.9
1975	19,297	15,773	81.7	2,620	13.6	404	2.1	432	2.2
1980	27,912	22,608	81.0	4,265	15.3	532	1.9	397	1.4
1985	33,469	26,026	77.8	5,744	17.2	1,146	3.4	553	1.6
1989	42,112	31,175	74.0	8,000	19.0	2,180	5.2	757	1.8
1990	42,624	30,667	72.0	9,729	22.8	1,252	2.9	976	2.3

Source: Immigration and Naturalization Service (1965–1977, 1978–1989; Statistical Year Book, 1990).

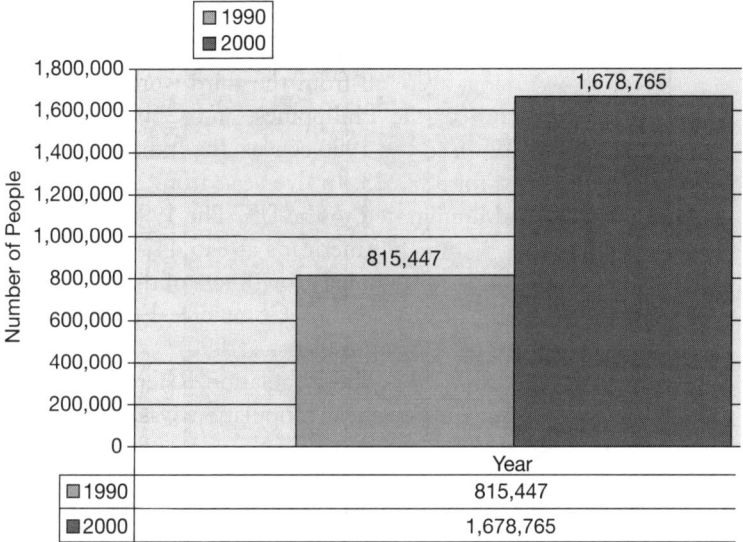

Figure 2.1
Population of Indian Americans, 1990–2000
Source: http://www.iacfpa.org/census2K/census.htm

represented 0.33 of the total US population of 248 million in 1990, and comprised 11.21 percent of total Asian and Pacific Islander population of 7 million (1990) (Tables 2.4 and 2.7).

When compared with South Asian countries, Indian immigration to the United States is far ahead of its neighbors. But Pakistan, Bangladesh, and Sri Lanka's immigration patterns show that their share has been increasing since the 1970s (see Table 2.4).

According to the 2000 US Census, the Indian–American population was 1,678,765 out of a total US population of 281,421,906 (Figure 2.1). Between 1990 and 2000, the overall population growth rate for Indian Americans was 105.87 percent, which is the single largest growth among the Asian–American community, which stands at 7.6 percent (Figure 2.2). According to the 2000 Census, Indian Americans became the third largest ethnic group among the Asian–American community after Chinese American and Filipino American. According to 2000 US Census, Asian–American community grew at a rate of 48.26 from 1990 to 2000 (Figure 2.3). Above 10 million Asian Americans constitute 3.6 percent of the US

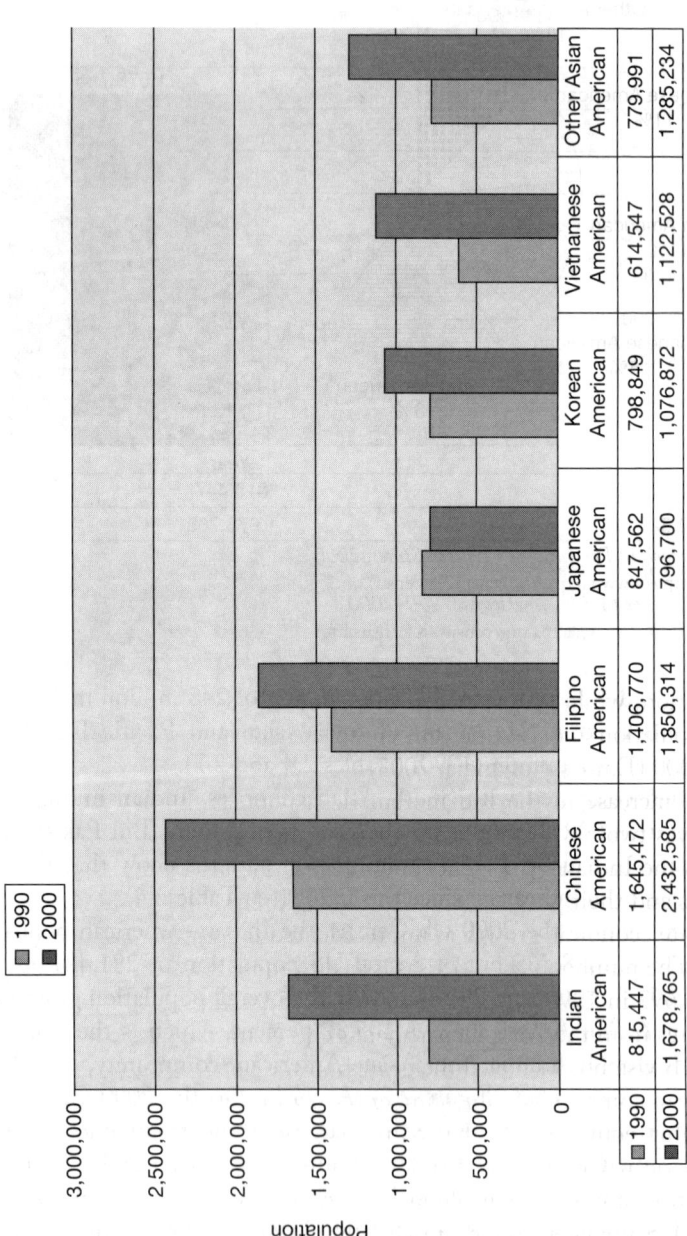

Figure 2.2
Asian–American Groups Population, 1990–2000
Source: http://www.iacfpa.org/census2K/census.htm

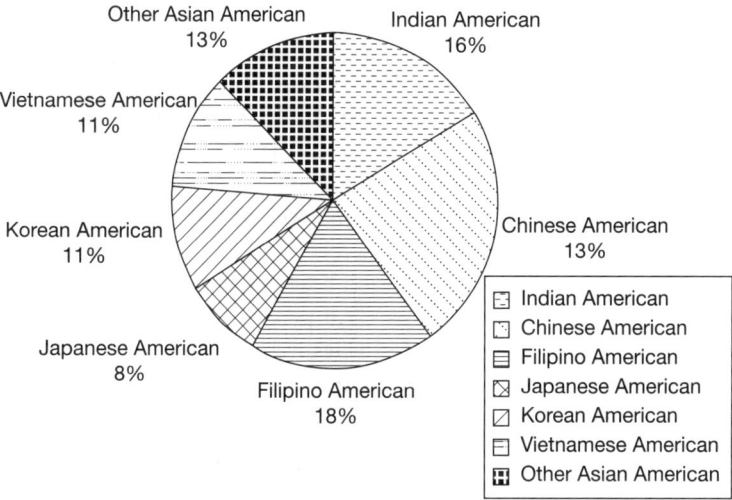

Figure 2.3
Asian American Percentage in United States, 2000
Source: http://www.iacfpa.org/census2K/census.htm

population, while Indian Americans represented 0.6 percent of the US population and 16.4 percent Asian–American population in the year 2000 (Embassy of India, 2003).

The increase in the Indian–American population from 1990 to 2000 was twofold. A key factor that accounted for the rising numbers in the Indian–American community is the influx of H-1B visa holders and their families (spouses and children). They have helped stimulate economic growth at unprecedented rates in the last several years. The number of H-1B visas issued to those from India jumped from 2,697 in 1990 to 15,228 in 1995 to 55,047 in 2000, according to figures from the State Department. This sharp rise in the number of H-1B visa holder fueled the growth in the population of Indian–American community. The number of Indian–American population is roughly equivalent to that of the state of Nebraska. According to American Community Service Data, in 2010 Indian–American population stood at 3.18 million people constituting about 1 percent of the US population and are country's third largest Asian ethnic group after Chinese Americans and Filipino Americans.

In terms of foreign-born population category, the Indian population has surged since the 1990s to become the second largest immigrant group in the country after Mexicans, and ahead of those born in China, the Philippines, and Vietnam. In 2013, more than 2 million Indian-born immigrants resided in the United States, accounting for 4.7 percent of the 41.3 million foreign-born population (Zong and Batalova, 2015). In fact majority of Indian Americans are new immigrants to the US 87.2 percent of Indian–American adults in 2010 were foreign-born, the highest percentage among the six largest Asian–American groups; 37.6 percent of those had been in the United States 10 years or less (Desilver, 2014).

Indian nationals have become the top recipients of temporary high-skilled worker H-1B visas, accounting for 70 percent of the 316,000 H-1B petitions (initial and continuing employment) approved by US Citizenship and Immigration Services in fiscal year 2014. The announcement by the Obama administration for reforms in the immigration policy which will allow the spouses of H-1B visa holders skilled workers to legally work in the United States will further see increase in Indian–American population, as eventually they will be able to apply for the permanent residency in the United States (Rajghatta, 2015).

In addition to the skilled workers, the Indian-born students will further add to the growing population of Indians in the United States. About 103,000 Indian-born students were enrolled in US educational institutions in the 2013–14 school year, which makes Indian students the second largest foreign students in the United States after China.

The immigration to the developed countries from the developing countries is likely to continue. India's young demography, especially the age group of 16–34 years, will continue to move to the United States as one of the most preferred destination for studies and for better opportunities (White and Subedi, 2008). Furthermore, the presence of a large number of Indian immigrants in the United States is likely to maintain the flows of information and remittances that encourage further migration. The presence of the educated and skilled Indians is going to be further accelerated by the growing synergies in the United States–India relationship, especially in the economic and trade relationship which have become the focus of present Modi government.

In fact, the US Government created the necessary conditions for brain drain from India to take place, and now its India that is too getting benefits of this out-migration of their highly skilled immigrants and students (for detail insight, see Sahay, 2009). The old immigration laws were reformed and the new immigration legislative initiatives have been taken in the United States to facilitate the immigration since 1965. The Indian–American community in the United States has experienced a remarkable transformation from modest beginnings. They left their homelands to settle in America in the hope of better economic opportunities and a better life style. But at the same time it is also true that the US desired, welcomed, and hosted them in its national economic interests. The early immigrants catered to the American needs for laborers and in the post-1965 phase skilled workers, engineers, doctors, scientists, educationists, software computer experts, information and technology experts, contributed to other sectors of American life and society.

SETTLEMENT PATTERNS OF INDIAN AMERICANS

The Indian-American population today is more or less evenly distributed throughout America, although the early Indian immigration, like other Asian immigration showed a kind of ethnic concentration in the American West-Coast, especially in California. The early Indian immigrants were ghettoized because they had many common traits, such as agrarian orientation, illiteracy, poor knowledge of English, and willingness to get married to non-Indians, especially poor Hispanic. They generally belonged to North-West region of India, and most of them belonged to Sikh community and were dependent on each other (Jain, 1993, pp. 37–38).

In post-1965 phase, Indian Americans' residential pattern has been remarkably widely distributed as compared to other Asian groups. This is obvious from the residential patterns of Indian Americans that show they have been staying only in the West-Coast region of America. In fact for Indian Americans, proximity to other Indians seems to be on low priority and desirability of a given residential area on grounds such as property, value, and location are on a high priority. Table 2.5 shows that nearly 20 percent of Indian Americans have settled in California and only 3 percent reside in

Table 2.5

Distribution of Indian Americans by Region and Major States in 1980 and 1990

	1980		1990		Increase	
	N	Percentage	N	Percentage	N	Percentage
US Total	361531	100.00%	815447	1000.	453916	125.6
West	71992	19.9%	188608	23.1	116616	162.0
California	57901	16.0	159973	19.6	102072	176.3
Midwest	85175	23.6	146211	17.9	61036	71.7
Illinois	35749	9.9	64200	7.8	28.452	79.6
Michigan	14690	4.1	23845	2.9	9155	62.3
Ohio	13106	3.6	20848	2.6	7742	59.1
Northeast	120758	33.4	285103	35.0	164345	136.1
New York	60505	16.7	140985	17.3	80480	133.0
Pennsylvania	15212	4.2	28386	3.5	13184	86.7
New Jersey	29510	8.2	79440	9.7	49930	169.2
South	83606	23.1	195525	24.0	111919	133.9
Texas	22231	6.1	55795	6.8	33564	151.0
Florida	9144	2.5	31457	3.9	22313	244.0
Virginia	8483	2.3	20494	2.5	12011	141.6
Maryland	13705	3.8	28330	3.5	14625	106.7

Source: US Bureau of the Census (1983, Table 62, 1993a, Table 253).

other West-Coast states. By contrast, the largest proportion 35 percent of Indian Americans have settled in the north-east and mostly in two States, New York and New Jersey.

New York and New Jersey, home to more than 30 percent of Indian Americans, can be considered the capital of Indian Americans in the United States. The high concentration of Indian immigrants in New York and New Jersey is due to the fact that these two states absorbed a large number of Indian immigrant medical professionals in the late 1960s and the early 1970s, following the pattern of chain migration, many other Indian immigrants settled in these two states. A good number of Indians have also settled in such states as Illinois, Texas, and Florida.

In fact, a large Indian–American community exists in every state of the United States, the five largest states—California, Texas, New York,

New Jersey, and Illinois—are home to Indian–American populations of over 200,000 each. New York City is home to the highest Indian–American population of any individual city in North America, with more than 200,000. Washington, DC metropolitan areas has a community of over 60,000 people. Indian Americans are the largest of Asian–American ethnic groups in New Jersey, the second largest (after the Chinese Americans) in New York and Maryland, and (after Filipinos) in Illinois, and the third largest (after Vietnamese and Chinese) in Texas (Indian Embassy, 2014; NRI Online, 2014; America's Asian Population Demographic Patterns & Trends, 2015).

One can find Indian grocery stores and other ethnically oriented business flourishing in Flushing and Jackson Hights (in the Queen Borough of New York City) in Edison and Iselin (in Central New Jersey), and on Devon Street (in Chicago). However, they have not established India town in any city comparable to China town in many cities and Korea town in Los Angeles. In the post-1965 phase, Indians have been able to create symbolic communities. They have settled around workplaces, such as high technology firms, hospitals, universities, and hotels/motels in or around metropolitan areas or along state highways. They have also developed places of worship, stores, and other services around their residences (Helweg and Helweg, 1990; also see Takaki, 1989). Selection of the residence of the Indians rests on pragmatic criteria such as access to work, proximity to the best schools in their neighborhoods for their children's education, property values, and proximity to relatives and friends.

The residential pattern of Indian Americans shows that they have not formed a little India or India town as ecological ghettos. Unlike Chinese Americans (they have Chinatown in many cities) and Korean Americans (they have formed Koreatown in Los Angeles) the recent Indian Americans and also Filipino Americans have not established ethnic ghettos.

Chinese immigrants in San Francisco, New York City, Los Angeles, and other cities established segregated communities known as Chinatowns. Chinese created Chinatowns somewhat involuntarily in response to racial oppression and violence against them, in late nineteenth century. Because of the convenience of employment in ethnic business, ethnic food, and language a large number of recent immigrants from China have resided in Chinatowns. Consequently, a significant proportion of Chinese Americans in each major Chinese Community still live in Chinatown. In the same manner, Koreans in Los Angeles have also established an ethnic ghetto named Koreatown which is the only officially recognized as Korean enclave in the US.[2]

Although Indian Americans are highly represented in suburban residential areas, they have not formed ethnic concentration leading to ghettoization of the community. There are number of reasons for this. First, the Indian–American community, though apparently homogeneous to the outsiders, but in reality lack cultural homogeneity and are divided on the basis of religion, language, and region of origin. Second, Indian Americans are characterized by higher educational and occupational levels than other Asian immigrants. Immigrants from middle class and professional background generally do not need an ethnic ghetto. Third, their fluency in English language enables them to comfortably live with other Americans. Yet another reason may have to do with Hindus and Hinduism. Hinduism, unlike Christianity or Islam is not a congregational religion. Moreover, Hindu temples have significant influence in language-based group identification (Jain, 1993, pp. 37–40). However, the lack of ethnic concentration should not be taken as if there is no pan-Indian–American organizations. Residential pattern of Indian Americans has not negatively affected their political activism and related lobbying activities (Sharma, 2011b). The principles of "Unity in Diversity" work among Indian community in the United States too. The belongingness to India and sense of Indianness largely in terms of religion, culture, family values, popular culture, Hindi language, and other primordial identities provide enough ground to come together and form pan-Indian–American organizations and lobbying groups in the United States.

---

[2] Min, Pyong Gap. "An Overview of Asian American," in Min, n. 9, pp. 22–23.

CURRENT STATUS: EDUCATION, INCOME, AND OCCUPATIONAL PLACEMENT

The Indian–American community continuously outsmarts every ethnic group in the field of educational, economic, and professional category and tops the US Census charts. Though relatively a small segment in the total population of the United States, Indian Americans have made a niche for themselves in American society. They have achieved a respectable professional status for themselves in the United States in comparatively shorter time than several other ethnic immigrants who took several generations to achieve the same. They have found a congenial atmosphere for pressuring their cultural identity in the United States and have remarkably higher achievements in the field of education, compared to other ethnic groups.

Indian Americans form a section of high-quality human capital comprising educationists, scientists, engineers, doctors, and the United States is home to the largest number of outstanding Indian talent outside India (Sami, 1990, p. 301).

Education

The 1990 US Census published some revealing information about the Indian–American community and shows that their educational levels are extraordinary. According to the Census, 85 percent of Indian Americans have graduated from high school and 58 percent of them hold a bachelor's degree or higher. This is an impressive level of higher education, especially when compared with the 20 percent of the total population in the US, who hold a bachelor's degree or higher.

When compared with other Asian–American groups, educational standards of Indian Americans are still higher. According to the 1990 US Census, 41 percent of Chinese Americans were graduates or with higher degree, 40 percent of Filipino Americans were graduate degree, 35 percent of Japanese Americans have completed 4 years of college or more. When compared to the US population, of whom 20 percent had completed college or more, the Asian–American ethnic groups' education level figure high but in comparison with

Indian American, of whom 58 percent holds a bachelor's degree or higher, they lag behind.[3]

However, unlike other immigrant to the United States, the majority of Indians migrating to the United States had high educational qualification and professional degree, and came from an upper middle-class or middle-class strata of the society. Table 2.6 illustrates the percentage of Indian Americans with bachelor's degree and master's degree based on the 1990 US Census.

It is obvious from Table 2.6 that over a period of time Indian immigrants coming to the US did not have a higher degree in comparison to the early Indian immigrants of 1970s and 1980s. The immigrants who came in 1980s were having lesser percentage of higher degree than Indian who immigrated to the US in 1970s. The pattern also shows that Indians who went to the US in 1980s did not have the higher levels of degree than those who entered in 1970s, but in comparison to the national average of the US, Indians were more qualified. The explanation for this considerable declining trend of Indian immigrants with less educational qualifications in the 1980s can be seen in the context of 1976 revisions of the immigration law. For example, in the year 1992 only 6 percent of the Indian immigrants were third preference professional immigrants and 86 percent immigrants entered the US on the basis of family reunification. The Indian professional such as medical practitioners, nurses, pharmacists, and other medical-related professionals entered the US before 1980 (Sheth, 1995, pp. 177–178). However, the declining trend of Indian immigrants with high educational and professional qualifications has not affected the inclination toward higher degrees among the second-generation Indian Americans who are born in the United States. Considerably, the new generation of Indian Americans has shown a strong commitment and inclination for higher degrees and professional qualifications. According to the 2000 US Bureau of the Census, out of 16,873 US-born Indian Americans, there were 14,776 US-born Indian Americans (between the ages 18 and 24 years) had graduated a least from high school and 10,965 had a college education. This means that more than 65 percent of this new generation of Indian Americans received some college education (United States

---

[3] Min, n. 9, pp.79, 119 and 147.

Table 2.6
Percentage of Bachelor's and Master's Degree Holders for Indian and White American 25 Years Old and Over, 1990

	Immigrants	Immigrants	Immigrants	Native Born	US Population
	Before 1979	1980–1984	1985–1990	1985–1990	
Bachelor's degree holders	71.1	67.8	42.2	44.0	20.3
Masters' degree holders	44.9	27.5	21.7	20.7	7.2

Source: U.S. Bureau of the Census (1993 b, Table 3)

Census, 2010). Another example of the new generation of Indian Americans making their presence in the US is Indian–American spellers winning streak at the National Spelling Bee for eight years in a row, with 2014 and 2015 featuring Indian–American co-champions (Shankar, 2015). This can be seen in the context of status and prestige attached to winning such competition, but it clearly shows that young Indian Americans have followed their parents and value education. Today the new generation of Indian Americans is putting their best efforts for achieving a better education and a professional career, and is well supported by their families who have resources and know the value of education.

According to the 2010 US Census (US Census Bureau, 2010), 71 percent Indian Americans with bachelor's or higher degree were placed at second to the Taiwanese Americans with 73.6 percent and far ahead of 53 percent Chinese Americans and 28 percent US national average. However, according to a more recent finding of the American Community Survey, 40.6 percent of Indian Americans 25 years and older have graduate or professional degrees, and 32.3 percent have bachelor's degrees; an additional 10.4 percent have some college education. This puts Indian American ahead of Taiwanese American average figure of 74.1 percent 2010 US Census. This is attributed to the immigration of a large segment of Indians to the United States under the H-1B visa program, which permits highly skilled foreign workers in designated "specialty occupations" to work in the US.

Occupational and Professional Placement

Indian Americans have become a productive section of US society and high level of education has significantly helped the Indian–American community to achieve this status. The productive segment of Indian Americans were obvious form the facts that 72.3 percent of Indian Americans were involved in work force, in which men constituted 84 percent. In this work force, 43.6 percent Indian Americans were involved in jobs related to managerial and professional specialization. Another 33.2 percent of Indian Americans were doing jobs related technical sales and administrative support and the rest 23.3 percent of the population work in other areas, such as operators, fabricators, laborers, and precision production (see Table 2.7).

Table 2.7

Percentage Comparison of Indian Americans with White Americans in Occupations (1990)

| | *Indian* | | | |
	Total	*Native Born*	*Foreign Born*	*White*
Professional	29.6	22.2	30.0	19.4
Managerial	14.0	10.8	14.1	12.8
Technical and sales	20.0	22.5	19.9	16.1
Administrative support	13.2	17.9	13.0	16.0
Service	8.1	12.1	7.9	12.0
Farm	0.6	0.8	0.6	2.5
Precision production crafts	5.2	5.3	5.2	11.9
Operatives and labors	9.4	8.5	9.4	14.3

Source: US Bureau of the Census (1993b, Table 4; 1994, Table 4s).

Figure 2.4 shows a continuing trend in share of workforce of Indian Americans in which managerial and professional skills remain high in the 2000 US Census too.

Both the data clearly show that Indian Americans are well placed in the production segment of US society. Indians represent the largest foreign medical professional groups and also include a large number of engineers and scientists who hold academic positions.

Indian Americans surpass other Asian-American groups. In matters of holding professional or managerial jobs, Indian Americans are ahead of Chinese Americans, Japanese Americans, and Korean Americans. In 2010, according to Pew Research Center, 28 percent of Indian Americans worked in science and engineering fields; according to the 2013 American Community Survey, more than two-thirds (69.3 percent) of Indian Americans of 16 years and older were in management, business, science, and arts occupations (ibid.).

Most of Indian immigrants in the US have continued with their old occupation that they had in India. However, in case they are not able to find employment in their specialized occupation, they move to small business and entrepreneurship. Eventually, they become successful entrepreneurs. As of 2010, 66.3 percent of Indian Americans are employed in select professional and managerial

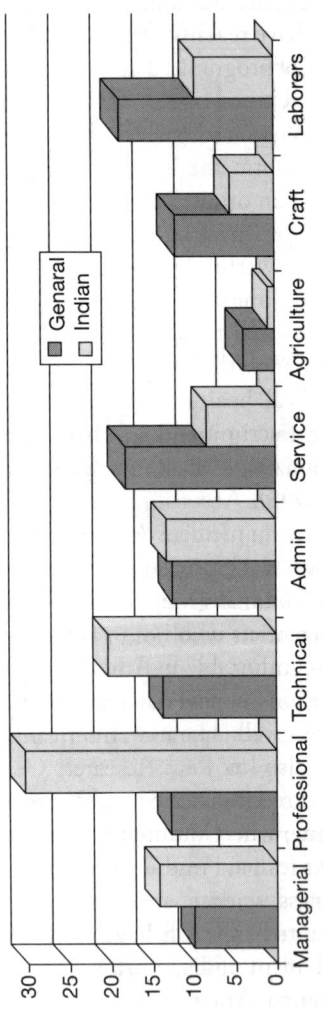

Figure 2.4
Occupational Distribution Data: US 2000 Census
Source: http://www.iacfpa.org/census2K/iadem.htm

specialties compared with the national average of 35.9 percent (The US Census Bureau, 2010).

The community's achievements in the field of science and technology, medicine, and academia are praise worthy. Over 5,000 faculty members of Indian origin are teaching in the various American Universities. Many of them have reached the level of chairman of the departments or coordinators of programs. The first Indian to graduate from a medical school in the United States was a woman, Anandibai Joshi, who graduated from Women's Medical College, Pennsylvania, on March 11, 1886. Indians form the largest single ethnic medical group. The physicians of Indian origin have formed an organization called American Association of Physicians from India (AAPI). This has acquired the status of a powerful professional group with a full-time legislative office in Washington, DC, since December 1995. It has enabled the Indian doctors to better promote their interest. AAPI is particularly concerned with the future of Indian–American physicians and Indian medical health management organizations, where they may face subtle discrimination. It is also reportedly the first Indian–American organization to set up a legislative office in Washington, DC (Arora, 1995). According to the AAPI, there are close to 35,000 Indian–American medical doctors, the second largest group of medical doctors after non-Hispanic White medical doctors (US-India Political Action Committee, 2012).

Thousands of Indian Americans involved in academic institutions have traditionally felt most comfortable in fields of science and technology, but the new generations of this community are increasingly attracted toward liberal arts as well. The new and the latest rush is in the so-called new economy also known as IT sector. The computer software business is spread throughout the country. This is the largest sector of the US economy, when one fourth of programmers are Indians. One third of the wages paid in the entire IT industries goes to Indian infotech technicians working in the US. About 300,000 Indians work in technology firms in California's Silicon Valley. They account for more than 15 percent of high tech set up in that region. The median income of Indian Americans in the region is about $125,600 a year.

According to the findings of a joint Duke University—UC Berkeley study, Indian Americans have founded more engineering and technology companies from 1995 to 2005 than immigrants from the United Kingdom, China, Taiwan, and Japan combined (Assisi, 2007). A University of California, Berkeley study came out with findings that one-third of the engineers in Silicon Valley are of Indian descent, while 7 percent of valley hi tech firms are led by Indian CEOs.

The importance of Indian IT professionals for the information industry in the United States was reflected in President Bill Clinton's decision to support the bill to increase the quota for Indians who wanted to work for the US high-technology companies. The US Department of Commerce report which estimated a shortage of over one million programmers, particularly in the light of dangers from the Y2k problem, influenced the Clinton administration to improve ties with India in this sector, despite its ire over Indian nuclear tests. Within two months of imposition of sanctions against India, the US Congress passed a bill increasing the quota of H-1 work visas from 65,000 to 90,000 in 1999 and to 115,000 by the year 2002, a large part of which benefited Indian infotech experts (Jha, 1999, p. 7). The contribution and the importance of Indian American in IT industry can be summed up by Senator Harry Ried: "Silicon probably perhaps would not exist but for the fact that these young men, and now women, are coming to do the scientific things that only could be done by very smart people" (NDTV Profit, 2012).

In the last three decades, a large number of Indians and Pakistanis have found career opportunities as taxi drivers and taxi owners in the nation's large metropolitan centers. They are visible particularly in the New York City. The newsstand business in New York City is also dominated by the Indian community. There are also a large number of Indian-owned gas stations and car repair shops.

Another industry where the Indian–American community has achieved remarkable success is the lodging industry. At least 50 percent of the independently owned hotels and motels in the United States are owned by Indian Americans. The Asian Americans Hotel Owners Association (AAHOA), established by the Indian Americans, has membership of over 4,000. It looks after their business interest and functions as a center for co-ordination. AAHOA members together own over 50 percent of the business in the lodging sector managing approximately 640,000 rooms. In 1996, AAHOA own around 12,500 hotels, with a total market value of their properties estimated at $31b.[4] The organization continues to grow. Today AAHOA is an influential conglomeration of Indian–American hoteliers and the fastest growing hospitality organization in the United States. However, this success has not been easy. Their success story is full of struggle which shows the life breaming with long hours, low wages, and intense dependence on family network. It is very well depicted in the award-winning sociological work done by Pawan Dhingra in his recent book, *Life behind the Lobby*.[5]

Indian Americans have made their presence felt in every walk of life in the United States ranging from genes to Jeans. Har Govind Khurana was the first person to synthesize a gene in a laboratory. Mohan Majrani put Gloria Vanderbilt's name on the blue jeaned derrieres of millions of American Women. Jaydev Patel became the best of New York Life Insurance Company's 9,000 odd agents. Didar Singh Baines turned out to be the biggest peach farmer in America. Sankar Chatterji is the paleontologist who discovered the fossil bones which may prove that dinosaurs evolved into birds. Raj Reddy was elected the president of the American Association for Artificial Intelligence. Subrahmanyam Chandrashekhar was the astrophysicist who discovered "black holes" and "white dwarfs" in a Universe of dying stars. Zubin Mehta achieved the distinction of being the director of the New York Philharmonic Orchestra. Narendra Karmakar became famous as computer scientist of the Bell Laboratories. Srijan Lal Tandon, the founder of Silicon Valley's Tandon Corporation; Amar G Bose, who reinvented stereo speakers; and Bharti Mukherjee and Vikram Seth, who have emerged as internationally recognized writers and have been awarded prestigious American literary awards for their best sellers *Middleman* and other stories and the *Golden Gate*, respectively; and Amartya Sen, Noble Prize winner, are the latest addition to this growing list of Indian Americans, who have demonstrated their talent and ability in the United States. The professional advancement and entrepreneurship

---

[4] AAHOA Information Broachers, 1996.

[5] There are number of studies on the professional aspects of Indian American community. In his recent book, Pawan Dhingra deals with the rise and the struggle of Indian motel and hotel owners, majority of whom almost 70 percent belong to the Patel community from the Indian state of Gujarat (for details, see Dhingra, 2012).

of Indian Americans further gets reflected from the fact the in the last two decades the United States has seen CEOs of Indian origin heading major US companies such as Rajat Gupta at Mckinsey & Company and Gangwal at USAir in the mid-1990s to Indra Noovi at PepsiCo, Vikram Pandit at Citigroup in the 2000s, Sanjay Jha of Motorola Mobile Company and now of Global Foundries, Satya Nadela of Microsoft, and Sundar Pichai of Google are among the list of a dozen of Indian CEOs in US companies (*Hindu*, 2015).

Income

Given their high education levels and professional success, it is not surprising that Indian Americans top the chart of median household income too, and have emerged as one of the most affluent community in the United States. The former US President Richard Nixon once remarked "The average Indian immigrant to the US has higher income than the average American."[6] The average annual income of Indians today is indeed higher than that of any other ethnic group in the United States, and Indian Americans record the highest median family income as well.

The higher level of education and excellence in the professional and business activities appear to be main factors for higher per capita income of Indian Americans (Ghose, 1990). According to the 2010 US Census, Indian Americans had the highest household incomes of all ethnic groups in the United States. The average median household income in the United States is $50,046 and that of Indian–American community $90,711 (U.S. Census Bureau, 2010). The 1980 data showed that while the overall poverty rate was 12.1 percent, it was 9.9 percent for Indian Americans. Their household median income was $25,644 compared with $18,544 of Chinese households and $16,841 for all US households.

According to 1990 Census, only 9.7 percent of adult Indian Americans live in poverty, which is lower than 12 percent of Asian Americans' overall average and 13 percent of the US population. It is estimated that the annual buying power of Indian Americans is $20 billion annually (Asian Indians a Success Story, 2011). The

---

[6] The mean earnings of Indian American household in 1989 was $56,438 (Nixon, 1988, p. 273).

average Indian–American family has 3.83 people and 89.2 percent of this population is married couple families. This also indicates the importance of Indian family values is intact in the US and their life is centered around family and children.

In 2002, there were over 223,000 Asian Indian-owned firms in the United States, employing more than 610,000 workers, and generating more than $88 billion in revenue (U.S. Census Bureau, 2012). The image of the wealthy Indian American further got enhanced following estimates from the investment firm Merrill Lynch that there are 200,000 millionaires of Indian origin in the United States which means that one in every nine Indians in the United States is a millionaire, considering their total population is 1.8 million. For the record, the United States has an estimated 2.1 million millionaires, which is less than 1 percent of its population compared to the nearly 10 percent of Indian Americans making it the wealthiest immigrant group in the US.

The remarkable success of Indian Americans in professional and economic fields cannot be attributed to a single factor. In fact a number of factors have played their role. At the outset, their desire and ability to pursue upward mobility is due to moving from one socially, economically, and educationally higher strata of society in India to another society in the United States. Then the language proficiency is another advantage that Indian Americans have over other Asian immigrants. Unlike other Asian immigrants, most of the Indian immigrants do not have serious language barriers and thus have been more successful in maintaining their original professional occupation and expertise than other highly educated Asian immigrants. A large proportion of Indian immigrants have adjusted their status to permanent residents after completing their graduate programs in the US. The high education, professional status, and economic advancement of Indian Americans have facilitated cultural emergence of Indians in America which have helped them in their political activism too.

RETAINING INDIANNESS AND CULTURAL CONTRIBUTION

Indian–American community in the United States not only has very well assimilated in the American society, but they have retained their

Indianness, family values, and contributed toward spreading Indian culture in the United States too.

The spread of Yoga and Ayurveda among Americans is another achievement of Indians in the US. Yoga has become immensely popular in the United States and people are not only practicing it but they are earning by teaching Yoga in America. Yoga is already a multi-billion dollar industry in the United States, with 18 million American practitioners, with revenues of $27 billion per year revenues (from classes, videos, books, conferences, retreats) and over 10,000 studios/teachers. Over 98 percent of yoga teachers and students in the US are non-Indians. America's yoga centers are potential retail outlets for Indian culture. Ayurveda rakes in $2 billion a year and is part of the high growth international market for plant medicines. Indian Americans have significantly contributed in the spread of Yoga and Ayurveda in the US. In 2012 the total worth of Yoga industry in the US was estimated at $6 billion (Thomas, 2012).

But when it comes to retaining Indianness in a strict sense of family values and culture, it can be aptly illustrated in the professional success of Indian Americans. The success in different walks of life of Indian Americans in comparison to other ethnic community and Native Americans is very much attributed to the family values and structure, which Indians have been able to retain in the United States. Indians in America help their kith and kins by helping each other and this has helped in small business too. Indian families are closely knit. Parents and elder members of the family make sacrifices for their children, and brothers help brothers. Indian grocery stores, motels and hotels, and other businesses usually are the product of pooling together of extended family resources. This is absent in many other communities. For Indian Americans this is a common practice for parents or parents-in-law to arrive for lengthy stays, or for nieces, nephews, or the children of cousins to be informally adopted into US households for the duration of their college-going years. The open expansiveness of the Indian family may not be its most unique feature, but it is one of the most enduring and admirable features. The children of Indian Americans can look forward to their parents to be involved in their lives, to pay college tuition and living expenses, to assist them find marriage partners, help them set up new homes, and assist them with new babies. For example, in Queens, New York, entire villages from Punjab state in India have re-established them-selves and maintain their traditional family values (Sharma, 2007). Another example of Patel community from Gujarat, who own three-fourths of motels in the United States, is a population that prides themselves on autonomous professions, working for themselves, but with a very strong community and family values.

The belief that close contact with relatives should be cultivated is shared by most Indian families, where the definition of a relative is broad, and includes not only immediate and distant blood relatives, but friends from the same town/village/city and so on. When contact with immediate relatives is not possible to maintain, surrogate family relations are assiduously developed. New immigrants to the commu-nity are often given material and emotional support; at celebratory or other events like deaths, it is this circle that serves as the immediate family.

The traditional music and dance, religious and ceremonial prac-tice, regional food-joints, ethnic clothing or ornamentation, popular culture, films, media, and special summer camps have helped in retaining Indianness in the community. However, the challenges for Indian Americans have been to imbibe and inculcate Indian values, norms, and culture. This is disturbing for the first genera-tion of Indian immigrants as home and family figure significantly in their definition of Indian consciousness. There are differences among Indian Americans on the idea of Indianness and how it can be imbibed into their new generation.

The Indian–American community is also facing challenges in retaining their Indian values. For example, the Indian immigrants of the 1960s, after 40 years in the United States, are finding it hard to differentiate family and cultural roles in a multigenerational and aging immigrant population. This complexity of cultural identity is reflected in how Indian immigrant seniors adopt American ideals of self-reliance and independence in their own lives and yet simul-taneously emphasize on passing on Indian values such as family loyalty and cultural traditions for their grandchildren (for details, see Dave, 2013). Also, the Indian families are finding it difficult to absorb dominant norms, like the nuclear family. They find it tough to reconcile these changing norms and end up differentiat-ing between work life and home life. As a result, they follow the prevalent work ethics of the United States at workplace and maintain their Indianness at home. Women's role is pivotal in putting up and retaining extended family structures, and in the socialization of their US-born children. By maintaining religious tradition and extended family structure women often find themselves under stress. Also, maintaining Indianness at times leads to sticking to the older, static, and rigid image of India as the outlook of Indians long settled in the United States have become static in time, even as India has progressed and changed. Despite all the odds, Indian community has flourished and retained their Indianness in multicultural America. Sticking to their family values has helped Indian Americans in establishing their businesses and in their professional success.

Food

Indians have introduced Indian cuisine to the United States, and it has become established as a popular cuisine in the country, with hundreds of Indian food-joints nationwide. After the Immigration Act of 1965 with the increase in the Indian population in the United States and with its the prevalence of Indian cuisine, especially in San Francisco, Los Angeles, Chicago, the New York City neighborhoods of Murray Hill, Jackson Heights and East 6th Street, and in Edison, NJ. All-you-can-eat buffets with several standard dishes are typical in some Indian restaurants in the United States. At present, there are many Indian markets and stores in the United States. Some of the biggest Indian markets are in Silicon Valley, Chicago, New York City, the Philadelphia metropolitan area, and Edison, New Jersey. Areas with a significant Indian market presence also include Devon Avenue neighborhood/market in Chicago and Pioneer Blvd. in the Los Angeles region. Other predominantly Indian neighborhoods are Journal Square in Jersey City, New Jersey, Jackson Heights in Queens, New York, Hilcroft Avenue in Houston, Texas and the SE Maynard Road/Chatham Square area in Cary, North Carolina (Indian Cuisine, 2011).

Recreation and Entertainment

Indian Diaspora have maintained their cultural bonds by sticking to their literature, films, and other entertainment and recreational practices and at the same time have left their mark in their adopted land.[7] In the field of entertainment, Indian Americans have preserved their likings. There are Hindi radio stations in areas with high Indian populations, including Radio Humsafar, Radio Salaam Namaste, and FunAsia Radio. There are also Tamil radio stations in the United States. The cultural emergence of Indian Americans and their contribution to popular American mainstream culture are now being noticed and visible in Hollywood movies and television shows. For instance, director Manoj Night Shyamlan, two time academy award nominated Indian–American filmmaker and scriptwriter, got international fame when he directed and scripted "The Sixth Sense." Based on the lives of slum dwellers of Mumbai, the movie *Slumdog Millionaire* is a big hit around the world, but particularly in the United States, having just won eight Academy Awards and grossing over $120 million dollars in North America symbolizes the cultural emergence and influence of India and Indian Americans in popular mainstream American culture (Sharma, 2011; also see MTVDesi, 2011).

Model and cooking author Padma Lakshmi's "Top Chef" TV season and then became the celebrity face for many products, Anoop Desai, dubbed "Noop Dogg," drew fans with his singing on "American Idol," and Aziz Ansari was in TV's medical comedy "Scrubs" before moving to a regular role in the upcoming comedy series "Parks and Recreation." Indian Americans have shown their presence felt in the field of TV journalism too. For instance, Fareed Zakaria, editor of *Newsweek International* and Sanjay Gupta, a neurosurgeon and medical correspondent, have their own weekend shows on CNN. Indian music and themes are gradually occupying its place in popular American culture. Indian dance and music as a fusion with genres such as hip-hop, house, and reggae, and in such forms it became popular in the United States as well as in the United Kingdom. These aspects of Indian Americans have made them noticeable in the larger American society, helped in creating a good image of India, and helped in the interest of Indian Americans and in the betterment of the United States–India relations.

---

[7] For details on the cultural practices of the Indian Diaspora in their adopted land, see Gamez-Farnandez and Dwivedi (2015).

Religion

Communities of Hindus, Buddhists, Zoroastrians, Sikhs, Jains, Muslims, and Christians from India have established their religions in the country. As of 2000, the American Hindu population was around a million, if all are taken as Indian origin, this would make around 62.5 percent of Indian Americans (1.6 million in 2000) as Hindu (Adherents.Com, 2014). There are many Hindu temples across the United States. ISKCON, Swaminarayan Sampraday, BAPS Sanstha, Chinmaya Mission, and Swadhyay Pariwar are well established in the United States.

According to Pew Research's 2012 Global Religious Landscape report, 18 percent of Indian Americans were Christians and 10 percent were Muslims. The religious demography of Indians in the United States noticeably differs from those in India, where an estimated 80 percent of the population is Hindu (Desilver, 2014). There are many Indian Christian churches and Indian Muslims' organizations such as the Indian Muslim Council—USA (Indian American Muslim Council, 2014). A large percentage of American Muslims are of Indian origin. Most Indian Muslims, however, are affiliated with larger mainstream Muslim population of the United States. The large Parsi community is represented by the Federation of Zoroastrian Associations of North America (Federation for Zoroastrian Association of North America, 2014).

Swami Vivekananda brought Hinduism to the West in the 1893 Parliament of the World's Religions held at Chicago. Today, Hinduism is among the fastest-growing religions in the United States and many Hindu temples, most of them built by Indian Americans, have emerged in different cities and towns of America. Hindu philosophy and spirituality has found its space in American society. More than 18 million Americans are now practicing some form of Yoga. In particular, Kriya Yoga was introduced to America by Paramahansa Yogananda. In addition, A.C. Bhaktivedanta Swami Prabhupada initiated a popular ISKCON also known as Hare Krishna movement while preaching Bhakti yoga. Rajan Zed, Hindu chaplain, delivered the first Hindu prayer in the United States Senate in 2007.

Started during George W. Bush presidency, Diwali was celebrated in the White House on October 14, 2009, by President Barack Obama by lighting the ceremonial lamp at the White House amidst chanting of Vedic mantras, seeking world peace, tranquility, and happiness. This was the first time that any US president attended and celebrated Diwali at the White House, giving official recognition to this festival celebrated by many Hindus. This marked the cultural influence of India and Indian Americans in the United States.

Retaining one's cultural identity is important for forming a group or an organization based on ethnic identity. This has eventually helped Indian–American community to form a large number of organizations and pressure groups and some of them have been involved in the political activism and work for political rights of Indian–American community as a whole and of late for advancing a better United States–India relation. Indian Americans' contribution in expanding India's culture in the United States has helped India's attempt to leverage soft power in advancing its relation with the United States.

Summing up, Indians have made their mark in the United States by demonstrating their hard work, entrepreneurship, and intelligence in various walks of life. It can be attributed to many factors. To begin with, one of the best explanations for the success of Indian success story is perhaps the psychological factor. Like previous immigrants, the Indian immigrant brings with him drive and motivation to succeed at all costs. The psychological, social, and economic support that a strong Indian family and community network provide to Indian Americans has helped them in their success story. The Indian family structure and well-developed work ethics have been helpful. Indian families are closely knit. Parents and elder members of the family make sacrifices for their children, and brothers help brothers. Indian grocery stores, motels and hotels, and other businesses usually are the product of pooling together of extended family resources. Their community network too has helped them in their family and professional life. Indian Americans are also known for their strong work ethics in the United States. Unlike the earlier European mass migrations, which originated from the poor working class, the post-1965 Indian immigrants were neither poor nor illiterates but were highly educated, skilled, and techno-savy with a good command over English language. The next chapter explores the material and professional success of Indian Americans and its culmination into the political activism in the US politics as well as the formation of various political pressure groups that have lobbied for the Indian–American community and for the advancement of the United States–India relationship.

3

Indian Americans and Political Participation: Growing Political Activism and Lobbying in the American Political Process

For a long time, Indian Americans were not active participants in the political process and activities and had no avenues to voice their opinion. This is particularly true in comparison to other ethnic groups with a political consciousness in the US. However, this situation changed in the late 1980s and early 1990s. More and more Indian Americans began to show an interest in domestic politics. Today there is an "India Caucus" in both the House of Representatives and the Senate. Organizations such as Indian American Forum for Political Education (IAFPE), Indian–American Centre for Political Awareness (IACPA), US–India Business Council (USIBC), Indo-American Chambers of Commerce (IACC) and its regional forum in cities such as Dallas, Houston, and US–India Political Action Committee (USINPAC), and so on are actively promoting and undertaking lobbying on causes of interest to Indian Americans. And crucially, Indian Americans are actively taking part in the electoral process through voting, putting up candidates, or through activities like fund raising for the candidates.

This chapter examines the Indian–American community's involvement in American political process and assesses the extent of their involvement, the factors motivating their lobbying activities, and hindrances to their political activism.

Indian Americans as a community have proved their mettle in the United States in different walks of life. They are one of the most well-educated groups and are well placed in professional jobs. Overall, they are a relatively affluent community in the United

States. They have resources as well as an increasingly mobilized political network in the form of active and visible political associations. They are also a significant voting bloc in some of the Congressional districts in the United States. According to the 2010 US Census, the Indian–American population in the United States grew from almost 1,678,765 in 2000 (0.6 percent of US population) to 2,843,391 in 2010 (1 percent of US population), a growth rate of 69.37 percent, one of the fastest growing ethnic groups in the United States, although it is still one of the smallest communities in the United States, not even 2 percent (Nasser and Overberg, 2011).

Up until the contemporary period, however, a low level of political representation despite political resources was a feature of the community that puzzled political analysts. According to the US 2000 Census figures, Indian Americans constituted 0.6 percent of the US population, and this should have proportionally resulted in the Indian–American community having at least 45 state legislators of Indian origin (as opposed to the maximum of four at a time) out of the 7,424 state legislators nationwide. Their success in other fields was not commensurate with their political representation. They have not shown the same level of political assertiveness that Hispanics, Jews, and African Americans have shown in the US political process.

There are many factors responsible for the lack of political assertiveness and the low level of political representation of the Indian community in the US political system. The non-White culturally alien status of Indians might have introverted them from becoming active in the American political system as their acceptability to other groups might have deterred being assertive. Another great impediment comes from within the community itself in that it was not well organized, especially given that Indians are diverse and even within the US divisions on the basis of language, religion, region, and caste are not unusual. Perhaps paradoxically, as a relatively prosperous community, most Indians in the United States appeared quite content with the status quo.

This lack of assertiveness and representation is, however, increasingly becoming a thing of the past. Discrimination in employment and potentially more restrictive immigration policies in particular have galvanized the concern of the community. There is a realization that political activism needs to be embraced and Indians need to have representation proportionate to their population in the United States. There is a greater awareness that without a greater assertiveness Indian Americans may fail to protect their rights as a minority and put at risk their interests, especially in competition with other groups with a strong ethnic consciousness and political focus. Leaders and opinion makers in this community therefore are now engaged in educating their community to actively participate in the American politics.

Political activism and lobbying activities by Indian Americans were not all that significant, however, before 1965. Their real political involvement started only after 1965 when a new immigration law was passed by Lyndon Johnson as part of the "Great Society" reforms. Indian–American political activism and lobbying gained impetus with the increasing number of Indians in the United States. Before examining the prevailing pattern of political activism at present, it is necessary to delve into the historical background of the politicization of Indian Americans in pre-1965 phase.

PRE-1965 PHASE INDIAN–AMERICAN POLITICAL PARTICIPATION

During this phase, the number of Indians coming into the United States was very low in absolute and relative terms. To the degree that there were political activities, these were generally limited to protest against restrictive US immigration and naturalization laws. Nevertheless, the politicization of Indian Americans during this period provides useful background and a powerful historical analogy.

The first notable group of Indian immigrants, Sikhs who settled in California in the early twentieth century, was similarly politicized by discrimination meted out to them in America. In 1907, a series of race riots were directed against the "rag heads" as Sikhs were demeaningly called (Jenson, 1988). There were also a few Indian political activists who used the United States as a base and launching pad for their movement against the British rule in India. Their main goal was to liberate India from the British colonialism. Some of the eminent leaders were Taraknath Das, Hardayal Singh, Dhan Gopal Mukherjee, and others, who conducted activities aimed to liberate

India through different organizations. Taraknath Das founded the publication of *Free Hindustan* in 1908. While these protests did not result in any changes, real political lobbying started in the 1910s.

One of the most thoroughly documented political movements was of the Ghadar Party, a militant organization that emerged in San Francisco in response to British colonialism in India and to the discriminatory and exclusionary practices against Indian immigrants by Canada and the United States. It was founded in 1913 by Lala Hardayal Singh and others, and lasted until 1917 (Kitano and Daniels, 1988, pp. 48–49). Indian Americans across all the sections were attracted by the revolutionary messages of *Ghadar*, a weekly mouthpiece of Ghadar Party. The purpose of the Ghadar Party was to inform, build anti-British propaganda, and thereby elicit international empathy and support for the Indian freedom movement.

The Ghadar leaders received financial aid and other help from Germany and also sympathy from Irish Americans, who held the British as a common enemy. The Ghadar Party, it is claimed, was credited to have had fomented a spirit of nationalism among Indians, made them more indignant regarding British rule, and helped develop awareness and interest about the prevailing political situation, problems and priorities of India and Indians. Despite these developments, the Ghadar Movement failed. Many revolutionaries were arrested, convicted, imprisoned, and even executed in the United States and in India by the British Government. As a memorial, the Ghadar Hall still stands in San Francisco (Takaki, 1989, pp. 300–301; also see Banerjee, 1969; Kanjilal, 2000, p. 75).

The Home Rule League, another US-based Indian revolutionary outfit, was also dedicated to organizing Indians and mobilizing their support for Indian Independence. Prafulla Chandra Mukherjee founded "The Friends of Freedom for India" in 1915 in New York (Fisher, 1980, p. 13; Kanjilal, 2000, p. 75). Its aim was to expose the undemocratic and exploitative nature of the British rule in all its colonies. There were several other Indian groups, which were not revolutionary and did not support the Ghadar Party, yet endeavored to inspire the Indians in the United States and promote ideals of Indian nationalism. Indian Americans clearly have a historical background of being active politically in the United States during the birth of India's national self-determination and independence movements inside India and beyond, even though their numerical strength was not so large. During this period, the Indian immigrants tried to influence the American political process from outside the political system.

All these activities were to various degrees curtailed by severe politico-administrative hurdles and strains (Takaki, 1989, pp. 300–301). The fact is that they had to face twin menaces—they were not eligible to become American citizens, and, second, the colonial status of India made them suffer from an inferiority complex. The effectiveness of their pro-liberation activities began to diminish with the disapproval of the US Government. That was in a sense fatal blow to their hope of the respect that an independent India could fetch them (ibid., pp. 300–301; also see, Kanjilal, 2000, p. 75).

These lessons led to a refocus on political activism which started with efforts to obtain US citizenship. Such lobbying activities started in 1920s in the form of protest against the ill treatment inflicted upon them. The "Barred Zone Act" of 1917 and the "Thind Decision" of 1923 put any further Indian immigration to the United States into a deep freeze. The US Supreme Court ruled in 1923 that Indians were not considered Caucasians and therefore not eligible for citizenship. More outrageously, Indians who had formerly naturalized were subsequently deprived of their citizenship. Early Indian leaders decided to fight denationalization and the effective creation of "stateless persons" through the courts with limited success. Sakharam Ganesh Pandit, a lawyer, won his citizenship in 1927, Bhagat Singh Thind, a US educated agribusiness man, received his citizenship soon after. Indian Americans were in no mood to give up their rights to citizenship.

In the 1930s, a few extremely successful Indian professionals and businessmen re-started interactions with American politicians. Some of the notable Indians who provided leadership to the movement were D.S. Saund, the first president of the India Association of America (California), Mubarak Ali Khan who founded the Indian Welfare League in 1937, and Sardar Jagjit Singh who founded the League of America in 1938. The Indian Welfare League and the India League of America (ILA) led by Jagjit Singh continued their lobbying efforts in support of both independence for India and naturalization rights for the Indians in the United States. They also capitalized on American commitments to the rights of people and national self-determination announced in the Atlantic Charter (Clymer, 1997, pp. 203–284; Takaki, 1989, p. 368).

While in the early 1940s President Franklin Roosevelt attempted to suggest dominion status for India, but British Prime Minister Winston Churchill refused to entertain even the idea of Indian freedom. Furthermore, thousands of American troops had been stationed in India for the Second World War to fight Japan. The resentment against American troops in India grew because of the United States' hypocritical policy of supporting British colonial hegemony over India. Nevertheless, at home there was some progress in terms of addressing the interests of Indian Americans. Republican Clare Booth Luce and Democrat Emanuel Celler introduced bills to lift restrictions on Indian immigration as previous bills had done for the Chinese and the Japanese.

The committee on immigration and naturalization initially stonewalled it until President Roosevelt sent William Phillips in March 1945, his personal representative who had visited India, to testify secretly for the bill. Finally, the famous Luce-Celler Bill, restoring the citizenship rights of Indians in the United States, was approved by Congress and was signed by President Truman in July 1946. This bill allowed Indian immigration and naturalization (Takaki, 1989, p. 368; also see Clymer, 1997, pp. 203–284; Venkatramni and Srivastwa, 1983). While a long process, this represented an initial first attempt at political and lobbying activities for Indian Americans where they organized themselves, mobilized the support of influential Congressmen, and finally got a favorable bill introduced in the Congress. This was a noteworthy achievement given the very limited numerical strength of the Indian community and its lack of voting power.

Subsequent to this, there is some evidence for a low level of political activism within the Indian community. There were series of public relations efforts, Congressional, and Senate hearings and court cases in which immigrants consistently sought to represent their views through offering testimony, bringing legal suits, raising money, and supporting lobbying efforts. Given their small number and formerly disenfranchised status, it may not be surprising that as a group Indian Americans never commanded much serious political influence in the power structure of that day. But the declaration of

Indian Independence in 1947 brought a new enthusiasm and zeal among Indians and boosted their confidence in the United States.

The 1946 Congressional law had already made them eligible for consideration for American citizenship. Not surprisingly Indian Americans took the initiative to participate in the American political process as insiders. This confidence was reflected in the career of Dalip Singh Saund, who was elected as a judge of a Justice Court, Westmoreland Judicial District, in 1953. Then he was elected to the House of Representatives in 1956 from California, thereby gaining the distinction of being not only the first Indian, but also the first Asian to be elected to that post. Few days after taking his seat in the House, he was appointed to the House Foreign Affairs Committee— an honor for a first term Congressman. He was elected twice to the House of Representatives as a Democrat candidate (Jha, 2003).

What is notable about these approaches is that political activity and lobbying by Indian Americans in the pre-1965 phase reflect an approach that was not carried by any unconstitutional means nor by any seditious recourse either, but through working within the system. It is evident that they sought to achieve their aims not by defying the political system of United States, but by participating in it. A look at Saund's career shows that while the cause of minority rights needed to be raised, it was also necessary for Indians to associate themselves with mainstream American issues so as to make their presence felt in a democracy. Two inter-related strategies used by Indian Americans had become quite evident. The first was their effort to assert the distinctiveness of the community in order to extract benefits from the system which minority groups are generally entitled to and had started to fight for in the pluralist tradition of US interest group-based politics. The second strategy involved participating in the country's mainstream politics by contesting elections or by raising funds for presidential and congressional campaigns.

POST-1965 PHASE INDIAN AMERICAN POLITICAL PARTICIPATION

The passing of the Immigration and Nationality Act of 1965 represents a significant watershed moment in Indian American history.

Reversing decades of systematic exclusion and restrictive immigration policies, the Act resulted in unprecedented numbers of immigrants from Asia, Mexico, Latin America, and other non-Western nations entering the United States. In the process, the new arrivals, particularly from Asia, have transformed the demographic, economic, cultural, and, more recently, political characteristics of many urban areas, the larger Asian American community, and mainstream American society in general.

The Indian–American community subsequently evolved in many ways. In the 1960s and 1970s, a first generation of Indian immigrants dedicated themselves to earning a living through their chosen professional fields to support their children and families and set the stage for their next generation. They achieved success in many fields, including medicine, engineering, computer sciences, hotel and motel ownership, law, education, and small businesses ownership.

Arguably, a large number of the recently migrated Indians were politically inactive at first. Indian migrants came to the United States in search of employment opportunities, and by 1975 their number had risen to well over 175,000. While most of them focused on professional accomplishments, some of them started to realize that the next stage in the overall process for the Indian community was to assert themselves in political fields and achieve their political goals without which their success in other fields could be undermined.[1] As the number of Indians grew, Indians in America often faced racial discrimination and ethnic violence, and were marginalized in the wider political community, which caused worries and anxiety in the Indian–American community. Nonetheless, the community leaders continued to organize themselves to fight against racial discrimination and for minority rights. A desire for self-representation and an urge to protect the community's interest and sense of ethnic security motivated Indian Americans to better organize and to get involved in lobbying and political activities and forge a sense of Indian identity. Although professional lobbying and high-level political activism by Indian Americans started in 1990s, the beginning of this new era can be located at around this time.

---

[1] Indian American Center for Political Awareness. Retrieved 23 January 2004, from http://www.iacfpa.org/progs/2003.html

For instance, in 1980 a study of Indians in New York City was conducted, which reported that his informants variously described themselves as Aryan, Indo-Aryan, Caucasian, Oriental, Indian, Asian, Mongol, and Dravidian. Other Americans, however, generally labeled the Indian immigrants, as "Hindus" and slowly they came to be called "Indians." The term "Asian American" was referred primarily to those from the Far East and Indians were classified as East-Indians to distinguish them from Native Americans. This was seen as unsatisfactory by the Indian community and after successful lobbying by the Association of Indians in America (AIA), the US Government began to classify Indians as Asian Indians in 1980 Census, which also established their eligibility for Affirmative Action Program (designed for the advancement of ethnic minorities). According to Vinay Lal, AIA argued that "Indians are different in appearance, they are equally dark skinned as other non-white individuals and are therefore, subject to the same prejudices" (Lal, 1999). The lobbying by AIA to preserve the minority status of Indians, allowed them to publicly assert a distinct identity, and "yielded results when the 1980 Census Bureau classified Indians in the US as Asian Indians" (ibid., pp. 42–48).

Traces of racial violence, hatred, and discrimination against the Indians in the US, however, persisted. In 1986–87, racism against Indians, which had taken a violent turn on previous occasions, first appeared in a systematic form. A group of Americans calling themselves DOT BUSTERS indulged in a number of violent incidents against the Indian women who wore cosmetic dots on their foreheads between the eyebrows. This was particularly prominent in New Jersey. Indian males were also subject to taunts and violence from Whites, African Americans, and Hispanics. In one incident a group of Hispanic youths killed Nawaz Mody belonging to the Indian community. These incidents of racial attacks targeted against the Indian community compelled them to protest against the issue of rising anti-Indian violence and harassment. Quick action was demanded to halt those violence and taunts.[2] Eventually, these hate crimes were protested by the Indian–American Community leaders. They lobbied and responded politically by organizing marches and

---

[2] Kanjilal (2000, p. 103); *New York Times*, 8 October 1987, 12 October 1987.

holding meetings and sit-ins to stop the racial attacks and called for introduction of new laws in New Jersey for the protection of the minorities. Their lobbying led to some restructuring and changes in the department of police by the New Jersey state authorities in March 1988.

Growing experience of discrimination in employment also made Indian Americans aware of the need to join politics. Many professionals who arrived in the US in late 1960s and early 1970s found jobs for which they were actually overqualified. Yet they accepted sacrifices in status and responsibility because they were able to find some employment, which entailed prospects for further mobility and improved working conditions with higher salaries, compared to their previous jobs back in India. But they did not acquire the sought after higher positions and had because of discrimination in promotion. Indian Americans complained about a "glass ceiling," meaning that they did not get the kind of status and rewards received by the Whites professionals of similar levels of accomplishment. This effectively resulted in the shutting out of a large number of Asians from the top level of management posts in various organizations. A study conducted by Rober Oxnam in 1986 indicated that occupational discrimination and disappointment was common for Asians in America (Daniel, 1988, p. 51).

Here it is worth mentioning some of the examples. The cases of discrimination against Indians include a radiographer named Johnson at the University of Illinois, who was denied promotion on the basis of his national origin and color. In Elmont City, a predominantly White Long Island suburb, 200 Indian Christian families from Kerala suffered racial attacks on their houses and verbal abuse by teenagers for years. The AAPI claimed that Indians educated in foreign medical schools were denied opportunities for licensing, residencies, and staffing privileges. Also negative propaganda and misinformation were spread against foreign medical schools. As a whole, they were discriminated on flimsy grounds, like speaking English with an accent, and were hated as they grew in prosperity and achieved in various economic and professional fields.

Among the Indian–American community, doctors organized themselves to fight against the discrimination meted out to recently arrived physicians from India who faced discrimination in jobs in the form of the "glass ceiling", which restricted promotion and salary rises. Their efforts led to the reduction of discrimination against the Foreign Medical Group.

Indian Americans consistently lobbied against these discriminations. While their immediate response led to protest, sit-ins, organized meetings and marches against these crimes, they soon realized that their safety and well-being would not be possible without active involvement in the formal American political process. As a result, Indian Americans began to organize themselves into various groups and formed over 1,000 Indian–American organizations across the country. They began to participate not only in cultural and civic activities but also to act as a pressure group and get involved in political activities. They took to lobbying activities for the Indian–American community's interest in domestic affairs and for the better relations between the US and India. Today, one witnesses small associations of Indian Americans coming under larger unifying umbrella organizations such as the National Federation of Indian–American Association (NFIA), the AIA, the IAFPE, and the National Association for the Defense of Indian Americans, IACPA, Federation of Indian American Association (FIA), Indian American Democratic Organization (IADO), and the USINPAC. All these organizations have enabled Indian Americans to lobby for their interest in a more cohesive and effective manner. More detailed description of these associations is provided at the end of this chapter.

DIRECT PARTICIPATION IN POLITICS

The 1990s saw considerable growth in political activism by Indian Americans with an influx of Indian immigrants to the US in the field of software and information technology industry. After Saund, there was no Indian member of Congress for over 40 years. The year 1994 marked the resurgence of such a presence. Peter Mathews, an Indian by race and origin, ran for a Congressional seat from California in 1994 as a Democrat. Although he lost the election, it reflected direct participation in national level politics by the Indian Americans. In the same year Ram Uppulari and Kunwar Sunil Singh Dhillon sought tickets for contesting Congressional elections from the State of Tennesse and Maryland, respectively. Both of them lost in primaries, but once again their participation was important from the community point of view. Similarly, Kanak Dutt fought for a seat in the legislature of New Jersey and Ram Higorani of Connecticut, but did not win the election (Pais, 1994).

Neil Dhillon opines, "As *success begets success* this trend of increasing office holders from the community, further encourages others in the community." Dhillon believes that if a member of a community formerly inactive runs for office it inspires the community to mobilize and get active. According to Dhillon, "The community's main fault was that no one followed up Dalip Singh Saund after 1956, but the community as a whole has been more involved and active than when I was on the Hill twenty years ago" (NetIP Atlanta, 2002). Success soon came and Indian Americans participating in and elected to municipal, state, and national positions increased. Indians have increasingly been participating in elections at local municipal level. Several Indian Americans hold or have held the position of Mayor; for example, Balak Srinivas in Hollywood Park, Texas; John Abraham in Teaneck, New Jersey; and Arun Jhavari in Burien, Washington (Anand, 1992). There are many candidates who have been contesting for these posts.

At the state level, Ash Bhatt (D), Chonchol Gupta (R), Swati Dandekar (D), Sreenivasa Dandamudi (D), and Nikki Randhawa Haley (R) made their presence felt in the 2004 elections, although the only success was Swati Dandekar, who was re-elected in the 36th State House district of Iowa. The prominent Indians participating can be seen in state legislatures such as State Representatives Upendra Chivukula in New Jersey and Kumar Berve in Maryland, Swati Dandekar in Iowa, and one senator in Minnesota named Satveer Choudhary. Kumar Berve has been in the House for over 10 years and is one of the most respected representatives in Maryland. Satveer Choudhary, whose parents migrated to the United States in 1960, was elected to the second chamber of the Minnesota and became the youngest senator in Minnesota's history. The community now has an unprecedented number of persons running for office, from Ven Challa who ran for the Republican seat for US Senate in North Carolina to Renu Lobo who ran for a seat in the New York City Council.[3]

---

[3] Indian American Center for Political Awareness. Retrieved 12 February 2005 from http://www.iacfpa.org/southasia/office.htm

In the 2002 elections a good number of Indian Americans made their presence felt in the national political arena. Viz Pawar was a nominee for New Jersey's 11th Congressional District; Ayesha Nariman for the US Congress, Professor G. Nanjundappa from the 72nd District of California for assembly seat on Democratic Party nomination for the second time; Shawn Aranha on Democratic Party ticket for the 41st District of Illinois House of Delegates, and Rahul Mahajan, author and anti-war activist of the Green Party, ran for the office of Texas Governor.[4] The 2004 national election also saw increased participation. Chiranjiv Kathuria made a bid for the Republican nomination for the US Senate seat in Illinois. Rohit Khanna, Peter Mathews, Ayesha Nariman, and Arjinderpal Singh all tried for Democratic nominations from their Congressional districts. They lost but they received good percentage of votes. Bobby Piyush Jindal, Tim Philips, and Inam ur-Rehman ran the for the Republican Party nomination from their Congressional districts. Bobby Piyush Jindal from the first Congressional District of Louisiana in the US election won in 2004, making him the first Indian to be elected to Congress since Saund in 1956.

Indians are also becoming more prominent within the executive branch of government. For example, Bobby Jindal became the Assistant Secretary of Health and Human Services and Neil Patel held the position of Staff Secretary to Vice President, Dick Cheney. Prakash Khatri was appointed in July 2003 to serve as the first Citizenship and Immigration Services Ombudsman at the Department of Homeland Security (Department of Homeland Security, 2005). The most prominent examples of Indians gaining nation-wide recognition in the United States can be seen in Bobby Jindal and Kamal Hariss. Kamala Harriss' victory as District Attorney of San Francisco is another feather in cap. Bobby Jindal, whose parents belong to first-generation immigrants, is even more notable. He contested the Louisiana governorship in 2003 on a Republican Party ticket, and although he lost to his rival Catheleen

---

[4] U.S. Embassy in India. Retrieved 12 February 2005 from http://www.usembassy.state.gov/posts/in1/wwwhspjfaind.html

Blanko, it was a close election.[5] Leaving his Congressional position, in 2007 Bobby Jindal contested the Louisiana governorship again and was this time elected, making him the first person of Indian descent to be elected Governor of an American state. He was sworn in on January 14, 2008. He was re-elected to the post of governor in 2011 with a landslide majority. Bobby Jindal was one of the candidates for the Republican nomination in the 2016 US Presidential election. In 2010, the State Representative Nikki Haley was the first women to be elected as Governor of South Carolina, and became the first Indian American woman and second Indian American to become Governor of an American state.

The number of Indians that were successful in winning election in the above cases is of less significance than how many of them came forward to participate in the election. Indian Americans in the 1990s and 2000 onwards have shown increasing interest in playing a direct role in politics. Finally, Indians are working within all levels of the political spectrum, and their efforts particularly in direct politics and grassroots movements are growing. There have been initial successes, and with persistence, patience, and experience, more success is sure to follow. This will be the case as more Indians engage in political fundraising activities and lobbying activities become more professional and effective.

However, there has been a tendency among some influential Indian Americans to deny or stay away from their Indian roots and identity for their political ambition. The particular case is of Bobby Jindal whose statement that "My parents came to become American not Indian American" in an article in *Washington Post* on June 23, 2015, which posted a Tweet also "There's not much Indian left in Bobby Jindal." This invited widespread criticism from the Indian–American community (Gowen and Bridges, 2015). This was during the beginning of his bid for the nomination for 2016 Presidential candidate from the Republican Party. Jindal was criticized for calling

---

[5] Bobby Jindal's initial close defeat may not have even been due to mainstream resistance to Indians but due to the Pakistan lobby. In this election the Pakistani Americans Congress (PAC) and Patriot Muslim Americans (PMA) asked its supporters to defeat Jindal and they collected about $50,000 for his rival Balcano's campaign, showing the salience of inter-interest group rivalry between ethnic groups in the U.S. (Rajghatta, 2003b).

people to follow his path and denounce their roots for completely assimilating in the American culture. Bobby Jindal is seen as an Indian American who has spent whole life in distancing himself from his Indian roots. Bobby Jindal, whose parents immigrated to the United States in the 1970s, born and raised in the United States, grew up Hindu but converted to Christianity and changed his first name from Piyush to Bobby in his teenage, has been criticized for his deliberate attempt to dissociate from his Indian roots. Many attribute this to his strong belief in Catholicism and his political ambition in an ultra-conservative constituency. His constituency is in the South of America where being a staunch Catholic and adhering to an ultra-conservative and far-right nationalistic view is considered as a necessity for winning the election.

The contrasting example is of another Republican Governor General Nikki Haley of the South Carolina, who also converted to Christianity from Sikhism is at ease with her Indian roots and parental faiths. To be an American one does not need to give up his roots. In the late 1960s and 1970s, many Indians who immigrated to the United States to pursue the "American Dream" were welcomed by America and have imbibed American values. They are not only proud Americans and hold top professional and public offices but also have retained their Indian roots and have actively pursued the cause of Indian Americans and the US–India relations. Above all not to forget the first Indian–American Congressman Dalip Singh Saund, a Sikh by religion, who became the first Asian American/ Indian American elected as voting member of the US Congress in 1957 and actively lobbied and fought for the cause of the Indian American community.

FUNDRAISING

Despite being a small voting bloc, Indian Americans' growing political influence and lobbying clout can be seen in the context of their fundraising ability and campaign contributions.

Their fundraising capability is not confined to just one party. At first glance, it appears that Democrats may have an advantage in gaining the attention of the Indian American electorate in terms of

both votes and fundraising. Indian Americans have been traditionally more associated with Democratic Party. It may be because of
their opinion that the Democratic Party does a better job in coordi-
nating and organizing the Indian Americans, in advocating the cause
of the minorities, and caring more for them.

The Republican sample survey of August 1972 asked Asians
to state their party affiliation. In that surveys, around 52 percent
Indian Americans were Democrats, and 23 percent were affiliated to
Republicans (35 percent Japanese Americans and Filipino American
were Democrats and around 25 percent were Republicans). In the
presidential election of 1988 about 57 percent Indians voted for
Michael Dukakis, the Democratic candidate, and 23 percent voted
for George Bush, the Republican candidate. The Democratic
candidate Bill Clinton had also a large share of Indian-Americans
support. According to unofficial data, the breakdown of Democrats
to Republicans in the community is roughly 60:40 (Kanjilal, 2000,
p. 76).

Indian Americans also lobby through their campaign contributions and are active in fundraising efforts for political candidates on
the federal, state, and local levels. This has been one of the most
successful methods of political influences. When George H.W. Bush
became a presidential candidate in 1988, he attended a fundraiser at
the home of physician and activist Raj Bothra. Bothra coined the
slogan "Dukakis Means Doom Bush means Boom," which Bush
supporters liked so much they used it. Perhaps more importantly,
this one Indian physician had collected $600,000 from fellow physi-
cians in one night alone; this was said to be the largest contribution
by any individual (Shenoy, 2004). In the 1992 Presidential and
Congressional races, as well as at the state and local levels, the Indian
community supported both Democratic and Republican parties and
contributed substantially, particularly to the latter. During the presidential election of 1996 a group of Indians contributed $500,000
for the Democratic Party Campaign. They organized a fundraising
function for which President Clinton himself attended. Perhaps for
the first time a serving President attended a function organized by
Indian Americans. During Clinton's presidential tenure, Indian doctors paid $100,000 to the Democratic Party so that they could have
President Clinton as the keynote speaker at Doctors' Convention in

Chicago.[6] In the 2000 presidential election, Indian Americans contributed over $7 million to various campaign funds. The community
has come to be seen as a "cash cow" willing to fork out donations to
political campaigns without asking for much in return. The impres-
sion has begun to change with the growing demands and assertiveness
of Indians (Chatwood, 2005; Prasad, 2004). But in recent elections
there has been a shift in their party affiliation and they have shown
tilting toward Republicans too. Indian Americans raised funds for
both the parties in 2000 presidential election in which Republicans
are said to have got larger share than Democrats. Indians also run
for the Republican Party ticket to contest election. For instance, both
governors of Indian–American community, Bobby Jindal and Nikki
Haley are from the Republican Party.

The reasons for this shift can be attributed to the fact that Indian
Americans have become successful in professional and economic
fields and so they want to have presence in both the parties to serve
their interests. They do not like antagonizing any of the parties.
Moreover, if they were to assert politically as a community, rallying
behind one party would not serve the purpose. At the same time
Republican Party's tax cut policy, and its pro-life stand on abortion
rights and its opposition to same sex marriage have attracted the affluent but traditional Indian–American community. The Republicans
too seem to have worked hard on Indian–American community to
take them into confidence. Today, Bobby Jindal, Raghwendra R.
Vijayanagar (Chairman of Indian American Republican Council,
IARC), Zach Zachariah (co-chair of the George W. Bush-Dick
Cheney Florida Campaign Committee), and Nikki Haley are the
prominent and leading Republicans among the Indian–American
community.

The Indian–American community, which wields considerable
clout in Silicon Valley, until recently had not been visible on the
political front. But according to PNS commentator Richard Springer,
a staff reporter for Sanleandro, CA-based *India-West* magazine, this
is changing in a significant way. Indians are now making their presence felt in lobbying and other political activities, such as engaging
in fundraising for the candidates contesting for the Presidency and

---

[6] *The Telegraph*, September 21, 1996, p. 4; also see Kanjilal (2000, p. 40).

for Congressional seats. Making a powerful statement, a small but influential group of Silicon Valley Indian–American entrepreneurs and their wives donated about $600,000 to Vice President Al Gore and the Democratic Party on June 23, 2000. Al Gore was the featured guest at a $5,000 per couple intimate dinner fundraiser hosted by Hotmail founder Sabir Bhatia's at his condominium overlooking a stunning panorama of San Francisco Bay.

Al Gore was faced with several tough questions from the Silicon Valley entrepreneurs and executives. They pressed him about need for better relations between India and the United States. They also complained about the sanctions that were still in place against India because of its nuclear tests, but not for Pakistan despite its aggressive moves, and pointed out that China had been granted Most Favored Nation (MFN) status. Questions were also raised about the possibility of India getting a permanent seat in the UN Security Council. In reply, Gore, sidestepped the China issue and the issue about India's possibility of getting a permanent seat in the Security Council, saying it depended upon India's future nuclear policy. However, he strongly favored the increase in the H1-B visas for Indians and emphasized deeper relations between the United States and India. Bhatia said he hosted the dinner because he thought it was important for Indian Americans to make a dent politically and send a message that the community was a lot more powerful entity than just its individual numbers. Dinesh Shastry, a board member of Democratic leadership in 2000 and an organizer of the event, argued that this notable event signified that the era of Indian–American political apathy was over.[7] Financial contributions by Indian Americans to American politicians in recent years have substantially increased. Although no total tally exists, campaign finance records show the four top Indian donors alone contributed nearly $850,000 during the decade to many candidates and donations went to both the national parties.

Indian Americans also played an important role in 2004 US Presidential election. Both Democrats and Republicans responded in a positive manner and welcomed the Indian–American community

---

[7] Indian American Dinner Raises More than Half A Million for Gore. Retrieved 28 October 2004 from http://www.comebackkid.com.html

like never before. As electoral victory margins diminished, both the Democratic and Republican parties have turned their attention to immigrant vote blocs for a much-needed boost to their race for the White House and set their sights on the Indian–American community. New Republic Online reported that all the attention paid to the Republican Party's courting of the Jewish vote "obscures an important trend: Democrats might have an answer in the increasingly powerful, wealthy and energized Indian American community." The Far Eastern Economic Review added: "Other Asian communities... are stepping up their involvement in US politics, but none are as organized as the Indians" (Sen, 2004). The USINPAC was actively involved in a "policy dialogue" with both President George Bush's and Senator Kerry's campaign. The committee planned to send delegations to both the Democratic and Republican Party National Conventions "to make sure that the Indian American viewpoint is heard." While USINPAC does not endorse candidates, its members are bipartisan, and during the 2004 Presidential contest formed "Indian–American Support Groups" for both President Bush and Kerry.

"Most Indians are Democrats at heart," asserts Vikram Chatwal. The New York-based hotelier, a prominent supporter of Senator John Kerry said that community's support for the Democratic presidential candidate had been "very strong and positive." During the primaries, Democratic presidential candidates, including Senator Kerry, sent policy papers to USINPAC. "[As president] I will nurture the important relationship between the United States and India and ensure that the rights of Indian Americans are protected here at home," Kerry said in his letter (ibid.). SAKI was formed in March 2003 to mobilize the resources of the South Asian American community to support Senator Kerry's run for the White House. It was also an effort to invigorate the South Asian presence in the political process and tap into potential supporters. SAKI worked closely with the Kerry campaign with chapters in Boston, Washington, D.C., New York, and the San Francisco Bay Area. The group focused on fundraising, voter registration, and policy initiatives throughout the South Asian community. The Indian–American community has realized that in order to have its views represented it needs to become a part of the democratic process, says Congressman Joseph Crowley,

New York Democrat and Co-Chair of the Congressional Caucus on India and Indian Americans.[8]

Virginia-based Inder Sud, coordinator of a John Kerry Support Group, said the community had been very energized by Kerry's candidacy. "In part, it is because of their natural Democratic leanings; and in part because of dissatisfaction with the policies of the Bush Administration, particularly with regard to his approach to foreign policy," said Sud. He expected Indian Americans to vote overwhelmingly for Kerry in November 2004 election. However, Kerry's public opposition to outsourcing of jobs annoyed many Indians who were expected to switch loyalty to the Bush camp. "We support Kerry's goals of creating jobs in the United States, so that anyone willing and able to work has a job," said Sud. However, he added,

[W]e are opposed to any attempts at creating artificial barriers. Senator Kerry has assured us that he favours free and fair trade. We are also concerned that the rhetoric on outsourcing does not translate into prejudice against immigrants generally, and the Indian American community specifically.

Joseph Crowley, Co-Chairman of India Caucus, shared these concerns. "I want to make sure that the issue of outsourcing isn't vilifying India," he remarked. "India has been receiving some of these contracts but the issue should not be where these jobs are going but why they are going abroad."

Year 2004 was ultimately an important year for the relationship between Indians in America and the Republican Party. Traditionally, the majority of Indian Americans had identified themselves with the Democratic Party. However, since 2000, there has been a greater number of Indian Americans registering with the Republican Party (Sharma, 2004). In fact, their economic advancement and their closeness to social conservative values have made them natural Republican supporters in many ways, even if Democrats are more in tune with the social justice agenda of minorities. This was also a

---

[8] History making fundraiser by 'South Asians for Kerry' and 'Kerry Victory 2004. Retrieved 2 February 2005 from http://www.iacfpa.org/p_news/nit/iacpa-archieve/2004/07/23/elec3-23.html

period when India–US relationship was being redefined by Prime Minister Atal Bihari Vajpyee and President George W. Bush. Their views on strategic and security issues were converging, and the Bush administration had a very positive view about emerging India, which was expressed publicly.

Joseph Melookaran, a member of President Bush's Advisory Commission on Asian Americans and Pacific Islanders, admitted that the community has made "considerable progress in establishing itself throughout the American political spectrum." The latter part of the Clinton administration and certainly the George W. Bush presidency greatly valued the Indian Americans participation in the country's political process and serving the administration. Melookaran co-chairs the Indian–American Network for Bush-Cheney. The network worked toward development of an "Indian–American agenda" to address issues pertaining to the community's interests and bringing them to the attention of the 2004 Bush–Cheney campaign and the Republican National Committee.[9]

"I see a deeper and more meaningful relationship developing between Indian Americans and Republicans in the future," said Joe Wilson (Sen, 2004), then India Caucus Co-Chairman. This was his way of pointing out that successful professionals and people who share strong family values were welcomed into the Republican Party—a description that could be applied to many Indians.[10] The greater Indian–American community seems to have supported President George W. Bush in particular on the ground of strengthening the US–India relations, tax cuts, and the "family values" agenda. But there were some deep reservations expressed regarding the "War on Terror", Iraq, the Patriot Act and the growing federal deficit. For weeks leading up to the election in 2004, there was a great deal of discussion concerning which political party best suited the Indian–American community.

---

[9] Indian American Center for Political Awareness. Retrieved 26 October 2004 from http://www.iacfpa.org/p_news/nit/iacpa-archieve/honors/honors290504-on.html

[10] Sen (2004); Former Assistant Secretary in the Department of Health and Human Services, Bobby Jindal's Congressional bid on Republican Party ticket energized Republican supporters in the community. Jindal has become a potent symbol of the party's success in ethnic outreach.

The Bush campaign featured an elite class of fundraisers for the 2004 election cycle. The "Rangers" raised at least $200,000 individually, and the "Pioneers" pledged to gather $100,000. Florida cardiologist Zach Zachariah, was a Ranger, and his brother Mammen Zachariah, also a cardiologist, was one of the Pioneers. Other Indian Americans in this elite group included Raghavendra Vijayanagar, chairman of the IARC, and Texan Sharad Lakhanpal, president of the AAPI, both of them were pioneers.[11] Indian Americans were also "serious movers and shakers" in the Bush Administration, said Dr Vijayanagar. "President Bush has shown that if you are intelligent, hardworking and dedicated to conservative principles, the White House and [Republican] congressional leaders want you on their team…. Indian Americans are turning to the Republican Party… the GOP is embracing us," he said (Sen, 2004).

During the 2012 US Presidential election, the Indian American community again generously contributed and raised funds for both the candidates. But President Obama seems to have done better in comparison to Mitt Romney in getting support from the wealthy Indian–American community. While the Mitt Romney campaign at the Republican National Convention wooed the community by inviting a record number of Indian Americans to address the event, he was unable to exceed the Indian–American money laid out for President Barack Obama (*The Hindu*, 2012; Raj, 2012). This could be explained by the factors such as the presence of some of the Indian Americans office bearers in Obama administration and in the Democratic Party, his inclusive approach toward ethnic minorities in the United States, and some of the steps such as giving nod to India's inclusion in the United Nations Security Council (UNSC) during his 2010 India visit, and as a President, it was easier for Obama to energize the Indian Americans, who traditionally have been supporter of Democratic Party, to work for his re-election for the top post of the country.

After the departure of Bush, Obama's Presidential tenure seems to have brought Indian Americans in Democrats fold again. According to survey done in 2012 by Pew Research Center, the leaning toward

---

[11] Bush took time out for Indian Americans. Retrieved 21 February 2005 from http://in.rediff.com/news/2004/aug/30gop.htm

Democratic Party among Indian Americans increased and 65 percent of Indian Americans were Democrats or leaned toward the Democrats. A similar percentage of Indian Americans endorsed Obama's performance in 2012 (Desilver, 2014). Coming to fundraising, while it is difficult to track the exact figure, both the contributions and fundraising efforts by the Indian–American community for both party candidates have become increasingly significant and reflect the bipartisan affiliation of the community. The community's ability to raise money has been undoubtedly a factor that attracted politicians from both sides. Former President Bush, and former candidates for the US President Kerry and Romney appear to have taken particular note of the Indian–American community's political potential and they have had their share of vote. The overall effect of both parties competing for Indian attention is that issues of importance for the Indian–American community will remain on the agenda for both parties, as they cannot afford to risk alienating the Indian community in terms of both competition for votes and competition for financial resources.

Some have raised doubts over whether these fundraising activities are having an impact in terms of lobbying and getting the community's agenda on the political radar. Political contributions by Indians have never been the norm. As per the year 2000 Census data, only about 10 percent of Indian Americans donate to political campaigns or causes. Mike Patel has lamented this aspect of not donating to political candidates and has advocated that by donating Indians could turn a candidate's attention toward their community's issues and interest. Again Aneesh Chopra, a member of the political advisory council at the newly formed Indian–American Policy Institute, pushes back against the widely held criticism that the community throws money at politicians that do not support Indian Americans or work for their cause. This, according to Chopra is an unfair expectation. He believes that funding should not be strictly tied to reciprocity in short term and that relationship building is not about buying a candidate's loyalty. Chopra believes the goal of donating and fundraising should be to build a long-term friendship with those at the Capitol Hill who matter regardless of their stance on specific issues at specific points in time. Chopra also notes that alienating influential Congressman just because they do not agree on issues prevents the Indian–American community from ever being able to change their stances (Contractor, 2002).

One example in this case is the experience of North Carolina-based Swadesh Chatterjee, a former President of IAFPE, who was instrumental in influencing Senator Jesse Helms, Chairman of the powerful US Senate Foreign Relations Committee (SFRC). It is believed that Chatterjee turned him from an India basher to a friend and an ally. Earlier, Helms was a highly vocal critic of India's nuclear testing, and it would have been tempting to dismiss him as an adversary not worthy of contribution from Indian Americans. But Chatterjee recognized Helm's important role in the Senate and lobbied by educating him on why India could be a valuable strategic partner to the United States, and why India's nuclear testing was critical for its "strategic autonomy". Chatterjee's work in building such relationships and his general contribution toward the India–US relationship earned him a Padma Bhushan Award from the Indian Government. Thus lobbying through political contribution should be viewed more as a part of a long-term and broad relationship building strategy rather than narrow, immediate, issue-based effort.

Indian Americans also lobby by playing a significant role in the organizational and policy matters of the political parties. This helps them in becoming familiar with the political process in the United States. Party activists are involved in political activities such as the selection of candidates, campaigning for them, fundraising, and influencing public opinion to their favor. In addition, they act as secretaries, organizers, and campaign managers. By holding these posts they can push their community's issues and interests more effectively. Ramesh Kapur was a prominent man in Michael Dukakis's election campaign team in 1988 (Pais, 1994, pp. 4–8). Dinesh Shastry was a prominent member of the Democratic leadership in 2000 and active in lobbying for Indian Americans and for better US policy toward India. Nikore worked as a budget coordinator for Al Gore's presidential bid. There are also a good number of Indian Americans who hold influential posts in Republican Party. Akshay Desai for Republicans was a prominent fund raiser for Mitt Romney in 2012 US Presidential election.

In addition, some examples of intense lobbying activities by the Indian–American community are also seen at the local level. These lobbying activities are done through organizations as well as activists themselves. Indian Americans have not been always successful in their attempts at the local level. While the Little Chamber of Commerce, in the partly Indian neighborhood of Artesia outside Los Angeles, was unable to persuade the municipality to put up signs guiding visitors to "Little India", Indian Americans in New Jersey City succeeded in naming a school after Mahatma Gandhi. The same town recently renamed a portion of one of its street after Dr Babasaheb Ambedkar, an architect of the Indian Constitution (Lal, 1999, pp. 42–48). The Indian–American community's activism has ensured that Mahatma Gandhi's message of nonviolence and tolerance finds its place in the United States through artistic portrayal which is visible in Gandhi's statues in several American cities, including outside the union Square Park in New York City, the Martin Luther King, Jr. National Historic Site in Atlanta, in San Francisco Embarcadero Neighborhood, outside the Bellevue Library in Washington state, a wax statue at the Madame Tussaud's wax museums in New York, and a Mahatma Gandhi Memorial on Massachusetts Avenue in Washington, D.C. in front of the Indian Embassy in Washington, D.C. unveiled by the former Prime Minister Atal Bihari Vajpayee during his visit to the United States in September 2000. This memorial to Gandhi in the diplomatic enclave in Washington, D.C., is not far from the hallowed grounds where memorials dedicated to Lincoln, Roosevelt, and Washington can be found.

INDIAN AMERICAN POLITICAL ORGANIZATIONS

In addition to the direct political participation and fundraising activities, Indian Americans have also resorted to political participation through a number of their political organizations. They have sought to protect the special interests of the ethnic group through forming over 1,000 Indian–American organizations across the country. These pressure groups and associations have lobbied and persuaded the decision makers to take certain decisions in the community's interest. These pressure groups perform a variety of roles including acting at times as Indian socio-political think tanks, working in the normal political process, and concentrating on the betterment of US–India relations. Some of the broad-based political organizations of Indian Americans and their lobbying efforts are worth discussing here.

The earliest Indian–American associations like AIA and ILA have been highlighting the causes and interests of Indian Americans from the early twentieth century under the leadership of D.S. Saund and Sardar Jagjit Singh, respectively. In response to the denial of the citizenship right in 1923, these two organizations lobbied intensely based on the objective of regaining this right. While there were many roadblocks in the way, these organizations' vigorous and sustained lobbying efforts succeeded in obtaining the right in 1946 leading to the passing of Luce Celler Bill in Congress (Dutt, 1980). The AIA was responsible for having Indians recognized as a separate category and "Minority Status" in the US Census. The lobbying effort for "Minority Status" by AIA was backed by belief that gaining a minority group status would be a benefit for Asian Indian in employment, housing, education with respect to loans and health services. But the problem from the federal government and Bureau of Census was that the PIO were "Caucasians" and for that matter Whites and also US Census Bureau had no statistics of the precise number of Indians. The AIA did not accept this position of equating race with color and in the meeting with the Bureau (First time Indians were invited in a meeting sponsored by Government), the AIA submitted recommendation for providing a separate category for self-identification of Indians and recognizing their color as "brown" instead of White and their race as "Asian Indians" instead of "Caucasians." But ILA opposed the drive toward the minority status, believing that such a designation would provide hostility from Whites, Blacks, and Hispanics against Asian Indian, who among all immigrant groups were the most highly educated and skilled. The ILA held several conferences, debates, and conducted surveys too and had challenged the AIA over its claims, and challenged the AIA's authority to represent the Indian community. But finally, consistent lobbying effort by the AIA won the Indians a separate category, Asian Indians, won the Census of 1980. The obtaining of "minority group" status still remains close to AIA's agenda (Fisher, 1980, p. 131).

Insecurity among Indian professional due to racial discrimination that they were facing in 1980s, every professional felt threatened and this feeling acquired urgency in 1980s and gave impetus to formation of number of important professional organizations. As the laws governing the admission of doctors from overseas into the American medical profession were tightened, the AAPI was formed to represent doctors. Since its inception AAPI has lobbied for medical professionals and for the Indian–American community. They have raised funds for the American politician and presidential candidates and lobbied for a favorable policy for India too. President Bill Clinton addressed the Annual Convention of AAPI in 1995 (Lal, 1999, pp. 42–48).

The AAPI has been active in lobbying for the Indian–American community. AAPI has been prominent in fighting for the community's cause. Many reasons can be cited for this. First, since the immigration of Indians to the United States, there have been always a substantial numbers of medical professionals. At present around 35,000 medical professionals are officially registered with AAPI. Second, medical professionals constitute the affluent and richest section of the American society. Their money power makes them more influential as economic strength is very significant in American political life. Finally, the physicians got used to mobilize politically early because they had to fight against the discrimination meted out with foreign medical students in the United States.

The need of active political participation led to the formation of IAFPE in 1982–83. IFPAE has been working to empower Indian Americans politically by raising civic consciousness and increasing participation in community affairs and the mainstream political process and to enhance, facilitate, and promote the US–India relations. The forum has successfully lobbied by establishing bipartisan liaison with the Democratic and Republic National Committees and opened communication channels between Indian Americans and the White House and executive agencies, including the US State Department. IAFPE leaders have held meeting with the US Presidents starting from Ronald Reagan to discuss issues of importance to Indian Americans and the US–India relations and testified before Congressional Committees to preserve the second and the fifth preferences relating to family re-unification issues in the immigration law. The forum has also used lobbying techniques of grassroots participation in local government election campaigns, and raised funds for Congressional and Presidential candidates (Indian American Forum for Political Education, 2005). IAFPE lobbied against the Simpson-Mozibill, mobilized support for the Civil Rights Act of 1984 (*The Telegraph*, 1997).

The FIA of Northern California, an umbrella organization of over 50 Bay Area organizations representing over 100,000 Indian Americans, has been providing a strong and effective voice for the Americans of Indian origin in the cultural, social, political, academic, and economic fields. By providing a forum for all Indian Americans to communicate among themselves, the FIA has helped in assimilation of best aspects of Indian culture in mainstream America, effectively represented the common interests and goals of community, lobbied in public policy through active participation in political process to protect the civil and human rights; charitable and humanitarian cause and forge links with other FIA organizations (Lal, 1999, pp. 42–48).

Another pan-Indian organization in the United States which has been active is NFIA, formed in 1971 and a federated body of 60 associations. The NFIA, together with the IAFPE and AAPI, agitated against proposed legislation in 1985 that would have deeply cut Medicare funding to hospitals employing doctors with foreign medical degrees. NFIA was also one of the organizations which had shown the way to Indian Americans that how they might further the interests of India, when in 1987 it mobilized the Indian community, with apparent success, to persuade Congress to withdrawal the sale of sophisticated AWACS planes to Pakistan (ibid.) its recent political work includes organizing voter registration drives, encouraging Indians in US to act as a bridge between the US and India and help better the relations between two,[12] and has been in the forefront of activities in the US–India relations by organizing Congressional lunches, White House briefings, lobbying for the betterment of the US–India relationship, and has prepared position papers on this relationship for the US Congress and the Senate. The IADO, founded in Chicago in 1980, has lobbied the government on various issues such as to establish fair immigration laws, to improve the US–India

---

[12] National Federation of Indian American Associations. Retrieved 12 March 2005 from http://www.nfia.net/delhi%20press%20release.html

relations, and improve the representation of Indian Americans and Asian Americans in government, and worked in coalition building with other ethnic groups to achieve goals in areas of common interest.[13]

The formation of IACPA founded in 1994 for the purpose of creating political awareness among Indian Americans and a year later, the *Washington Leadership Program* (WLP), through which it has placed several young interns in Congressional offices since 1994 for the better understanding of legislation on the community, is yet another example of the political participation and lobbying to achieve community goals and interest by the Indian–American community.

IACPA has led successful national campaigns addressing hate crimes, immigration, voting rights, and defamation.[14] Through the WLP young Indian interns partake in a specially designed speaker's series, discussion groups, and attend dinners and events organized by the Indian Embassy and others. The added benefit is that Congressmen also get to learn the issue closest to Indian–American community (Nurnberger, 2005).

One of the noticeable problems that the Indian–American community has been facing was that their substantial campaign contribution could not fetch them much return. They realized that for the successful lobbying for the community they needed to increase their presence in Congress. To address this concern the *Indian–American Leadership Incubator (IALI)* was launched in 2003. Through its leadership initiative program the IALI has tried to encourage, recruit, train, and fund a fresh cadre of Indian–American political leaders (Chea, 2003).

It is worth mentioning here some of the prominent organizations dedicated to business interests of the Indian–American community. For example, the organizations such as the USIBC and IACC-USA have been prominent in promoting the business interests of the community and for the betterment of the US–India relations with strong focus on economic and commercial aspects. Formed in 1975, the

---

[13] Indian American Democratic Organization. Retrieved 12 March 2005 from http://wwwiado.org/history.html
[14] Indian American Center for Political Awareness. Retrieved 12 March 2005 from http://www.iacfpa.org/aboutus/aboutus.htm

USIBC is a business advocacy organization which has been working to enlighten and encourage the private sectors of both the countries to increase investment flows by creating an inclusive bilateral trade environment by serving as the voice of industry, connecting governments to businesses, and supporting long-term US–India commercial partnerships that will nurture the spirit of entrepreneurship, create jobs, and successfully contribute to the global economy.[15] The USIBC's lobbying role during the passage of the US–India nuclear deal has been commendable, which is discussed in Chapter 6. With establishment of its USA Mission in 2003, IACC-USA has focused itself to cater to the needs and growth of Indian and American businesses and professionals at local, national, and international levels (Indo-American Chamber of Commerce USA, 2016). With its regional chapters, such as in Houston, Detroit, and Dallas, IACC-USA has provided networking, marketing, information exchanging opportunities for the business professionals to develop economic, commercial, and financial relationships in overall objective of facilitating the economic and business ties between Indo-American business communities.

The formation of the USINPAC has proved to be a significant step in consolidating the voice of Indian–American community at Capitol Hill. The USINPAC, the first and only Indian–American Political Action Committee registered with the federal commission,[16] has not only given the community an access to decision makers, but also has influenced policy on issues of concern to the Indian–American community and supported all candidates for public office who address the concerns of the Indian–American community. The formation of the USINPAC can be seen in the fact that most of the Indian–American organizations were formed along the professional lines and there was a need of an organization, totally dedicated to foreign policy and domestic issues concerning Indians and the US India relations. It was the first Indian–American organization which established itself in "K Street Neighborhood" in the capital with a comprehensive organizational structure required for lobbying.

---

[15] For details, see U.S.-India Business Council. Retrieved 15 April 2016 from http://www.usibc.com/home

[16] USINPAC. Retrieved 15 April 2005 from http//:www.usinpac.htm

A conduit for the Indian–American community to raise and effectively resolve their issues, the USINPAC has been working to ensure that their individual contribution is recognized by the candidates who receive their contribution, and also by the community at large. By providing candidates for political office with financial support and a united voice of the Indian–American community, the USINPAC has tried to give the Indian–American community 'Brand' recognition on Capitol Hill.[17] The USINPAC in alliance with India Caucus has lobbied for India and has blocked some of the anti-Indian measures in Congress, thus inflicting severe setback to Anti-India Lobbyists Campaign. Its lobbying efforts in relation to the US–India relations have been commendable. (This has been dealt in Chapters 4 and 6).

The USINPAC is at present the strongest organization representing the Indian–American community and India on Capitol Hill. It is also the first and at present only PAC representing the Indian–American community on Capitol Hill. USINPAC's mission is to ensure that they have an impact on policy related to issues of concern to the Indian–American community and Indian on various issues.

Since its formation in September 2002, the USINPAC lobbying effort has influenced on policy issues related to the Indian–American community and for a comprehensive US–India relation. In pursuit of its mission, USINPAC has aimed to support all the candidates for public office who address the concerns of the Indian–American community and India. Its approach has been bipartisan.

In the beginning years of its formation, one of the main goals that the USINPAC focused was to diminish Pakistani lobbying presence on Capitol Hill. It inflicted a severe setback to the Anti-India Lobbying Campaign and was able to postpone the hearings indefinitely. The hearings were supposed to be on the so-called atrocities being perpetrated by India against the people of Kashmir hatched by Robert Giuda and Dan Burton in March 2003. Along with other lobbying groups for India, it made a call to defeat the candidacy of Dan Burton to the chairmanship of the House Subcommittee on South Asia in January 2003. Lobbying in collaboration with the India Caucus the USINPAC had success in getting House

---

[17] Ibid.

International Relations Committee (HIRC) to pass a landmark Anti-Terrorism Amendment in the month of May 2003. The House of Representatives passed the amendment by a wide margin of 382–42. This landmark vote marked the first time that Congress acknowledged the role of Pakistan in abetting terrorism and in the proliferation of nuclear weapons technology (USINPAC, 2003).

When the House took up the $3 billion aid package to Pakistan for its support to US war on terror in Afghanistan, USINPAC delegates urged lawmakers to link US aid to Pakistan with that country's pledge to permanently end infiltration of armed terrorists to India. Joe Crowley and Joe Wilson, the co-chairmen of India Caucus in the House, strongly advocated the need of stopping the terrorist's infiltration permanently to India and urged that Pakistan's actions need to be monitored carefully (Mitra, 2003).

Further exposing Pakistan's role in abetting terrorism, the USINPAC succeeded in bringing the noted counter terrorism expert of India, B. Raman to review US counter terrorism policy in South Asia, on October 29, 2003, before the House International Relations Subcommittee on Asia and the Pacific and the Subcommittee on International Terrorism, Nonproliferation and Human Rights.

The executive summary of B. Raman's statement reads:

India has been the victim of the use of cross-border terrorism by the State of Pakistan and its intelligence agencies since 1956 to achieve their strategic objectives, which are three in number. First, to create a religious divide between the Hindus, who are in a majority, and the Muslims, who are in a substantial minority. Second, to keep the Indian State destabilized and preoccupied with internal security tasks in order to hamper the economic development of the country. And third, to annex the State of Jammu & Kashmir (J&K), which is an integral part of India (Raman, 2003).

The USINPAC has been actively lobbying for India cause on a wide range of issues, be it supporting Frank Pallone's signature campaign in the US Congress for a permanent membership for India in the UN Security Council or Senator Orrin Hatch (R-UT) recommendation of an Indian American for Federal Judgeship in February 2003 resulting into nomination of an Indian American for a federal judge-ship or blocking of the Congressman Tancredos bill to kill the H1-B visa program which was aimed at stopping the entry of Indian skilled workers in the United States. Its lobbying efforts have been across the spectrum of the issues related to India.

Another significant lobbying initiative by the USINPAC was related to India's security concern because of China–Pakistan military nexus. On June 9, 2005, the USINPAC and India Caucus coordination was reflected when the HIRC voted to pass the State Department Authorization bill. A provision in the bill added by Congressman Brad Sherman (D-CA) for the first time acknowl-edged the dangers of the ongoing close military partnership between China and Pakistan and also the fact that the nuclear technology peddled by the father of Pakistan's nuclear bomb to rogue countries originated in China.

A second provision, added by Congressman Tom Lantos (D-CA) and Congresswoman Ileana Ros-Lehtinen (R-FL), conditions mili-tary sales to Pakistan on that country's full compliance on terrorism and proliferation of weapons of mass destruction. Congressman Tom Lantos (D-CA), who has also praised USINPAC's work, emphasized that "this measure is not aimed at any specific country, but addresses the global threat of nuclear black market activities because it is in our vital interest to shut them down" (US India Political Action Committee, 2005).

The role of USINPAC in mobilizing support for the passage of historic US–India civilian nuclear deal has been commendable. The USINPAC coordinated with other individuals and lobby groups for India and ensured the successful clearance of the nuclear deal legisla-tion on Capitol Hill. (The lobbying for the nuclear deal is dealt in Chapter 6, in detail.) Of late, USINPAC, with its organizational strength, coordination, leadership, and resources, has become the strongest voice for Indian Americans and the US–India relations.

Unlike the above Indian–American political organizations, there are organizations which are directly linked to the ideologies and programs of their original party in India, and have been working for the Indian–American community and as a bridge between the US and India. Though Congress party began to engage Indian Americans during the freedom struggle in 1922 and *Indian Overseas*

Congress—USA directly aligned with the Indian National Congress Party was formed in 1969, it lost its base among the Indian Diaspora in America in the liberalization phase of 1990s when India actually began lobbying in the United States (Guha, 2014). Instead, majority of Indian Americans in the 1990s became more attracted toward the Bharatiya Janata Party's (BJP) revisionist and revivalist ideology grounded in India's ancient Hindu civilization, its foreign and economic policy, stand on nuclear and security issues, social issues, and the clean image of its leaders when most of the Congress Party leaders were tainted in corruption and scam cases in the early 1990s. As a result, though the reaching out to the Indian Diaspora for lobbying started by the then Prime Minister Narsimha Rao-led Congress Government, it was the BJP aligned *Overseas Friends of BJP-USA* (OFBJP-USA) which has been able to connect strongly with the Indian–American community. Overseas Indians are not immune to the Indian political developments. From two seats in the Lower House of Parliament in 1984 to an absolute majority of 282 in 2014 General Election shows that there has been an expansion in BJP's base across the various segments of social, regional, linguistic, rural, urban, gender, age, and class in India. Not surprisingly, this has manifested in the expanding base of the OFBJP in America too.

The OFBJP-USA, with its main objective to project a positive and a 'correct' image of India and its people in the United States, have been actively playing a bridging role between the United States and India. Its various local chapters in America have organized the Indian community on social, economic, and political issues concerning Indian Americans and India, and actively played their role during India's lobbying efforts on the issues of Pakistan's unprovoked military incursion in Kargil and India's nuclear test (Overseas Friends of BJP, USA, 2016). The OFPJP-USA works in coordination with various Indian–American organizations, such as the US chapter of Rashtriya Swayamsevak Sangh and Vishwa Hindu Parishad, Hindu American Council and the Friends of India Society International and credited with its role in reaching out to Jewish lobby in America.

During his second visit to the United States in a bid to reactivate the Indian lobbying, Prime Minister Modi, in addition to his busy schedule of meetings with a number of delegations, made it a point to meet a 50-member delegation of OFBJP and listened to their concerns and issues. A re-energized OFBJP-USA in the wake of PM Modi-led BJP victory, had organized its first-ever US convention to mobilize the Diaspora for the better future of the country too. With the emergence of the BJP as the leading and dominant political party, the OFBJP-USA will further add to the lobbying efforts of India and Indian Americans.

INCREASING CONNECTION BETWEEN INDIAN DIASPORA AND INDIA

Today Indian Americans are no more brain drain but they have become a brain gain for India. Not only by sending money to India, by investing in India, by transferring technical knowhow to India, but the most significantly transforming their professional and economic achievements into lobbying for India. The efforts of the Indian–American community toward the US–India relations have been welcomed in India and reciprocated by the Indian Government as well.

On a more popular, mass level, communications technology is helping to connect India to the United States through the Indian Diaspora. The India media establishment has recognized the need to establish a web presence globally to appeal and influence Indians living overseas and ensure they are invested in the latest relevant Indian news and issues. It has been rightly observed in one of the works on Indian Diaspora,

> Since these new technologies of representation became available, the relative isolation of expatriate South Asians in their discrete locations in Northern countries (Canada and the United States) has been effectively offset by the presence of a large, visual, instant community that may be geographically scattered but is electronically and sometimes epistemologically and ideologically-connected and contiguous (Bahri, 2001).

An example of this, during the emerging phase of Indian–American lobbying, can be seen in the Gujarati–American community's rapid and effective response to the 2001 Bhuj earthquake. They were also able to convince former President Bill Clinton to help raise contributions for the earthquake relief effort.

The Indian–American community began to find their voice on issues relating to the US–India relationship. It was not inevitable that the Indian–American community would become advocates for the combined national interests of India and the United States. There are a number of Diaspora groups, such as Scandinavian groups in the United States, which remain passive in terms of domestic and international politics and do not form distinct group view around these issues. Critical events that raised concerns about the treatment of this Diaspora's former homeland in the US foreign policy played an important role as a catalyst of engagement in the political process on behalf of India by the Indian Diaspora in the US. Some of the major events can be identified in particular as being responsible for raising political awareness and mobilizing the wider Indian American community. The first event was the growing tension between India and Pakistan in the 1990s which culminated with the India–Pakistan Kargil conflict because of the infiltration of Pakistani soldiers and Kashmiri militants into positions on the Indian side of the Line of Control (LOC). As India–Pakistan relations deteriorated leading to the Kargil conflict in 1999, Indians in the United States with support from the Indian Government started getting involved in lobbying for India due to the perceived US tilt in favor of Pakistan during the early years of Cold War.

India's nuclear test in Pokhran in May 1998 invited the imposition of economic and military sanctions by the US Government. As a result, Indian Americans lobbied actively to have these sanctions rolled back. Since that point, there has been an active lobby advocating an increase in US–India cooperation. This has also resulted in the Indian lobby forging a strategic relationship with Jewish Americans to curbing radical Islamic terrorism and to counter Pakistani lobbying efforts in Washington. Lobbying activities during India's nuclear test and the Kargil intrusion by Pakistan were watershed moments for the way India sought to cultivate the US Government to defend India's nuclear test on the grounds of security threat from Pakistan and China, and to highlight Pakistan's unprovoked armed intrusion in India's Kargil region.

The terrorist attacks of September 11, 2001, in the United States and the backlash that followed against the Indian–American community also accelerated the Indian–American political activism and lobbying as the Indian Americans were attacked physically, particularly Sikhs (for more information, see, South Asian American Leaders of Tomorrow, 2012). Additionally, according to one estimate, 15,000 lost their jobs because of new federal regulations specifying that only US citizens can become airport security checkpoints personal (Gupta, 2004). The affluent Indian Americans realized that being wealthy and law abiding did not prevent an individual from being pulled out of line at an airport or being ejected from a plane because a pilot felt uncomfortable with an Indian onboard.

The Indian Government's decision to acknowledge the contributions of Indian communities abroad by awards such as *Pravasi Bharatiya Samman*, and by India's civilian Honors *Padma Bhushan* and *Padma Vibhushan* have also helped them to connect well with the Indian community abroad. The announcement by the then Prime Minister Atal Bihari Vajpayee on January 9, 2003, that India would grant dual citizenship to certain group of persons of Indian origin, including Indian Americans, added to the already growing lobbying activities and political mobilization of the Indian–American community. Vajpayee's move was a key component of a new and three-pronged strategy to raise the consideration of the interests of India in the US foreign policymaking process. First, India would engage in direct government-to-government diplomacy by pursuing a closer strategic relationship with the United States. The foundation for the US–India strategic partnership was laid during the George W. Bush administration and the Vajpayee government during the period 2000–2004 which finally culminated in May 2004 with the signing of the Next Step in Strategic Partnership (NSSP) which would set the direction for the US–India engagement in the field of defense, civilian nuclear energy, space and high-technology cooperation. Second, India would also support the setting up and restructuring of professional lobby organizations. Indian American organizations such as USINPAC, IAFPE and IACPA began to work on the lines of AIPAC, the most successful lobbying group of any ethnic community. Third, it would make use of the Indian Diaspora in the United States and take advantage of pre-existing political mobilization networks. In addition to groups that have lobbied for Indian American representation and interests in the domestic policy sphere, political interest groups such as IACPA, IAFPE, and USINPAC have lobbied for consideration of the interests of India and the US–India relations.

Summing up, ethnic-focused associations get involved in lobbying activities and political activism for a number of reasons. Ethnic security has always been a key motivating factor. Given their hyphenated identification in a multicultural poly-ethnic land, any ethnic community, and related associations primarily aim at securing and protecting their socio-economic interests and fighting against racial discrimination. The Indian associations assume the responsibility of championing and protecting community's ethnic interest. Protesting against the racial violence and discriminatory practices in professional and other spheres and drawing the attention of the politicians and the government officials are some of their activities.

The Indian–American associations have clearly increased their political and lobbying efficacy in a relatively short period of time. They have balanced their status as minority subject to discrimination while trying to maintain the perception of them being a model minority. Their model minority status is not simply because of high level of education and influences, but because of their approach toward American political system, where they have lobbied for their community interests and India within the system, and have always shown a respect for the democratic norms prevalent in the United States. They have lobbied through institutional channels and exercised moderation, which, coupled with their affluent status, has resulted in greater influence for Indian associations in the American political process.

Indian American community has emerged as one of the most prosperous and affluent communities in the United States. Their economic prosperity, educational achievements, professional accomplishments, and entrepreneurial performances have been impressive. They have made their presence felt in the information technology field in particular. These successes have resulted in their gaining political clout. They are now actively participating in American politics on all levels. They have successfully lobbied on different issues and influenced decision makers and have protected their interests.

The second generation of Indian Americans is similarly engaged in politics and it is likely that their collective political clout and importance as voters will continue to draw the interest of Congressmen from both the parties. Since the 1990s, in particular, the Indian–American community has gained some experience in politics and has become politically aware. Indian Americans through their political organizations are now better organized and well coordinated, politically aware, and they have gained the understanding of American political process and how to lobby at Capitol Hill. The next chapter looks at how connections between the Indian–American community and the nation of India over the last two and half decades, in particular, have driven a particular type of interest group lobbying surrounding the relationship between India and the United States, that is a concern of this highly successful Indian Diaspora.

4

India Caucus: Lobbying for a Robust US–India Relation

Several variables play a role in the US foreign policy decision making, and the role of the lobbying is one of them. The previous chapter showed that the US political mainstream has become more tolerant of Indian Americans, and they are now an increasingly vibrant part of the US body politic. They are sought out as voters and as sources of human and financial resources during elections. The growing influence of the nation-state of India in international politics and its emphasis on professional lobbying activities globally has piggybacked on the success of the Indian–American community to create an even more robust concern with the issues of the Indian ethnic community in US politics. Most noticeable is the formation of the India Caucus. Despite initial US suspicion of the Indian nationalist movement leading up to independence, the formation of a robust India Caucus is a clear indication of fundamental change having taken place in the terms of how the US sees Indian interests. The attitude of Congress in particular toward the nation of India is noticeable, and successful lobbying by the India Caucus in the US Congress has contributed to a much better image of India in the US.

This chapter deals with the origin of India Caucus, its expansion, its aims, and objectives and lobbying done by the India Caucus members on various issues related to Indian Americans and the US–India relations. It places the increased interest in US–India relations in the context of changes in the post-Cold War period which has seen India reach out to the West and the United States, including the naturalized Indian citizens already in the United States. The connections and complementarities between the Indian–American community and the Indian Government's increased activism on the international stage are discussed. This is followed by a description of the formation of the India Caucus as a recognizable entity. A detailed discussion is presented on the lobbying done by the India Caucus on the various issues, which helped in creating a positive image of India and setting the stage for a robust US–India strategic partnership. In the end, this chapter evaluates the effectiveness of the India Caucus focusing on its drawbacks and positive contributions.

INDIA'S OUTREACH TO THE INDIAN DIASPORA AND THE INDIAN–AMERICAN COMMUNITY'S INCREASING INTEREST IN INDIA

As discussed in the last chapter, coupled with rise of Indian Americans political activism there has been shift in the policies of the Indian Government toward its Diaspora. In the past, India did not pay much attention toward the Indian Diaspora. It was only in the early 1990s, when India embarked on economic liberalization and pursued market economy reforms that NRI investment in the country became a factor. A citizen of India who holds an Indian passport and has temporarily migrated to another country for six months or more for employment, residence, education, or any other purpose comes in the category of NRI. Since then there have been efforts from both the central as well as state governments to attract the Indian Diaspora and particularly affluent and highly qualified Indian Americans to work, invest, and do business in India itself. A sizeable section among the Indian–American community now acts as guardians for the relatives of the native Indian elite class. Indian businessmen, bureaucrats, military personnel, academics, and politicians often send their children to study or live in the United States. They are a politically conscious group with influence as they have connections to the important elites in the Indian decision-making apparatus.

The Government of India's High-Level Committee Report on Indian Diaspora on January 8, 2002, provides a succinct and revealing insight into the increased interest that the Indian Government has taken in the Indian Diaspora in the United States,

A section of financially powerful and politically well-connected Indian Americans has emerged during the last decade. They have effectively mobilized on issues ranging from the nuclear tests in 1998 to Kargil Conflict, played a crucial role in generating a favourable climate of opinion in Congress and defeating anti-India legislation there, and lobbied effectively on other issues of concern to the Indian American community. They have also demonstrated willingness to contribute financially to Indian causes, such as relief for the Orissa cyclone and the Latur and Gujarat earthquakes, higher technical education and innumerable charitable causes.... For the first time, India has constituency in the US with real influence and status. The Indian community in the United States constitutes an invaluable asset in strengthening India's relationship with world's only superpower (Government of India, 2002).

In the year 2000, highlighting the role of Indian–American community in lobbying for India in the United States, the then India's External Affairs Minister, Jaswant Singh, said, "Americans of Indian origin have acted as a catalyst to Indo-US relations that even I did not see 10 years ago." Prime Minister Vajpayee in same visit to the United States echoed the same sentiment when he spoke to a group of Indo-Americans at Blair House, saying, "You Indian–American entrepreneurs have shown with your success in information technology that East and West cannot only meet but they will meet on agreed terms" (Chaudhari, 2000).

However, one of the most significant developments as a result of the professional success of Indian Americans and increased political activism could be seen in the formation of India Caucus in the US Congress. As a result of these activities, together with the growing commercial interest and strategic interest in India, the India Caucus in the House of Representative increased to around 185 members. The India Caucus is an inner group within the US Congress that serves the interests of the Indian–American community and works for the betterment of US–India relations by attempting to influence US policy toward India. Indian Americans have lobbied for Indian

Americans and the US–India relations through India Caucus in US Congress.

THE ORIGIN OF INDIA CAUCUS

Overall, American policy toward India has shifted from one of neglect during the Cold War period to a positive attention. The American attitude toward India has over time been shaped by a variety of complex factors. The executive and Congressional attitude had formerly often been hostile and critical toward India, especially during the long years of the Cold War. The United States by and large neglected India during the Cold War years in comparison with other areas of the world. This was despite its growing economic, political, and strategic importance. As recently as the mid-1980s, only about 5 percent of the members of Congress had an interest in South Asia. Legislative activities were confined to a cluster of related issues, such as human rights and nuclear proliferation. Due to absence of significant South Asian population, there was inconsistency in Congressional concern about the region, and members of US Congress had great discretion in their activities. As a result, high-level decision makers were not involved in the foreign policy process for South Asia. It was also the era when the prominent critics of India at Hill, such as Dan Burton (R-Ind), Dana Rohrabacher (R-Calif), and Robert Dornan (R-Calif), used the foreign affairs and intelligence committees as platforms to criticize India.[1]

India was mainly criticized in the United States due to concerns about human rights, India's close relations with the Union Soviet Socialist Republic (USSR), its independent foreign policy, and its willingness to confront the United States on international issues and criticize US foreign policy. Dan Burton, a prominent Republican Congressman from Indiana, used to bring a bill almost every year to cut aid to India, which was already very low, on the ground of human rights violation and low voting record of India in United Nations in favor of the United States. He used to be very critical of

---

[1] *India Today*, "Think before you Knock India", 15 November 1993, pp. 207–209.

India and contributed to a very negative image about India in the United States.

The genesis of Indian lobbying in terms of international issues can be traced back to 1980s. It was also during the 1980s that the lobbying firms too approached the Indian Embassy in the United States. The debate within the Indian Government took place on hiring of lobbyists for India. But, no final decision could be taken on proposal for hiring lobbyists and lobbying firms for India in the United States. It was during the Sidhartha Shankar Rai's tenure as Chief of the Indian Mission in the United States in early 1990s that the idea of hiring of lobbying firms for India got a push. They studied general lobbyist hired by the countries like Israel, China, Taiwan, Pakistan, and so on. China and Pakistan had for long hired multiple lobbies.[2]

Nonetheless, at the end of 1980s and the start of the 1990s, India still had a command economy and was still seen as a pro-Soviet country. Furthermore, there was little substantial US and India cooperation. The Soviet withdrawal from Afghanistan, the lessening of Soviet–US tensions, and finally collapse of the Soviet Union encouraged US lawmakers to break out of their habit of viewing the subcontinent through a Cold War prism. There were still issues, nonetheless. For example, Robin Raphel was the Assistant Secretary of State for South Asia at a time when the Kashmir issue had gained in salience with rising terrorist violence and numerous reports of human rights abuses coming out of the valley. Robin Raphel got on the nerves of many Indians in India and in the United States because of her negative remarks toward India on the Kashmir issue. All these events seemed to have activated Indians in the US. The IAFPE and other organizations started actively trying to enhance India's profile in the US.

In addition, India's economic liberalisation and market opening program in 1991 began to change the perception about India as it abandoned socialist dogmas to embrace and engage with the international economy. Capitol Hill seemed to discover an enlarging South Asian market for US goods. Congressional thinking about India slowly began to shift and the US–India bilateral relationship started

---

[2] Interview with former Indian Ambassador to the US, Lalit Mansingh, 24 May 2005, New Delhi.

to free itself of the ideological baggage to a considerable extent. There has been a considerable shift in the attitude of American policy makers, especially in the legislative branch. This has in turn paved the way for improved perceptions of India, which has resulted in the development of a robust India–US relationship. The US law-makers have also moved away from the generally pro-Pakistan stance that had prevailed throughout much of the Cold War. The War in Afghanistan in particular saw a more favorable tilt toward India take place (Hathaway, 2001). The US had engaged Pakistan to fight against Soviet Union in Afghanistan War, but at the same time the US started the opening of its policy toward India as it did not want to push Indian further toward the Soviet Union. Also, as the War in Afghanistan came closer to the end with the withdrawal of Soviet troops from Afghanistan, the disintegration of the Soviet Union became clear and with that end of the Cold War ideological baggage which had halted the United States' close relationship with India. Simultaneously, Pakistan began to lose its strategic utility in the eyes of the US lawmakers with the disintegration of the Soviet Union.

Apart from these strategic factors, the change in perception among the US lawmakers toward India has nonetheless been part of a slow process for which several factors and actors are responsible. In the final days of 1992, Representative Stephen J. Solarz (D-N.Y.), an American Jew, lost his Congressional seat. Stephen J. Solaraz, the influential chairman of the House subcommittee on Asia, had been widely regarded as India's most energetic advocate in the Congress, and over the years had, almost single handedly, raised large sums of money in the Indian–American community. Stephan Solarz, was not only a strong supporter of India who took up India's causes despite prevailing negative sentiments regarding India, he also helped India to establish cordial relations with Israel.[3] Solarz's defeat opened the door for a junior New Jersey Democrat, Frank Pallone, who up to this time had displayed no particular interest in either American foreign policy or the Indian–American community (Hathaway, 2000).

This led to great concern about the need to give a voice for Indian–American community and from where this would come from now

---

[3] Interview with Former Indian Ambassador to the US, Lalit Mansingh, 24 May 2005, New Delhi.

that Solarz had been defeated. The idea of creating a Congressional Caucus on India was raised. This would be modeled along the lines of Black Caucus that already existed then in the Congress. The main focus was to counter India's opponents in legislative and executive branch, improve the US–India bilateral relations and to inform members of the Congress on the issues concerning India.

The areas with concentration of Indian–American population were identified and their representatives were targeted by IAFPE and other Indian–American organizations, which resulted in the formation of India Caucus in 1993. Frank Pallone, a farsighted politician who due to redistricting had a large Indian–American population in his new Congressional district, persuaded six other Democrats and Republican Bill McCollum (R-FL) to join him in organizing a Congressional Caucus on India and Indian Americans. One of the first Congressional Caucuses devoted to promoting relations with a single country, the group grew more rapidly than Pallone envisioned. The Indian–American press gave considerable coverage to the fledging group and encouraged its readers to urge their Congressional representatives to join the Caucus. Seeing no downside to enlisting in the Caucus and sensing an easy way to please constituents, House members readily complied. The bipartisan Caucus of India and Indian Americans in the US had a membership of 50 in the House by the end of 1993. It was co-chaired by Frank Pallone (D-NJ) and Bill McCollum (R-FL)—a critic of Pakistan's record on narcotics and terrorism (Congressional Caucus on India and Indian Americans, 2004a).

AIMS AND OBJECTIVES

The Congressional Caucus on Indian Americans and India has become an important institution for the Indian–American community and India. The Caucus was formed with the dual mission of advocating for the concerns and needs of the Indian–American community and to promote a better US–India relation. The intended role and objective of the Caucus and the range of issues that Caucus members planned to envisage are explicitly mentioned in two documents: the "Statement of Purpose" and the "Statement of Issues."

According to the "Statement of Purpose," the Caucus will make its presence known by writing regular and frequent letters to members of Congress, sponsoring lectures and events featuring experts on issues of interest to Indian Americans, and "disseminating news articles and scholarly articles to Congressional offices." It also envisions "members of Congress presenting testimony at hearings, offering statements in the House of Representatives, and monitoring public statements made by prominent officials concerning Indian issues" (Parekh, 2000).

The second document, a "Statement of Issues," is a far-reaching document that envisions the Caucus playing a "prominent role in identifying priorities and shaping debate on domestic issues of concern to the Indian–American community and furthering better ties between the US and India." The domestic issues to be addressed are racial violence and hate crimes, education, small and minority businesses, immigration and family reunion, political empowerment (of the Indian–American community), the glass ceiling, health, and human services. And other issues include foreign aid and development issues, trade and investment in India, intellectual property rights, human rights, and nuclear proliferation (ibid.).

LOBBYING BY INDIA CAUCUS

For years, India did not even employ a lobbying firm in the United States, until it contracted one for the first time in 1993. But with the formation of India Caucus in the House of Representatives dedicated toward the betterment of ties between the two countries, the lobbying for Indian cause registered its presence on the Hill. India Caucus members not only enthusiastically participated in cultural activities organized by Indian Americans but some of them began to actively lobby for changing old perceptions about India and influencing the US foreign policy in India's favor.

Ever since the inception, the India Caucus has been active in a wide range of activities encompassing cultural functions and social occasions, expressing opinions on international issues affecting India and on issues related to the US–Indian bilateral ties. This section provides an overview in terms of the major issue areas that have attracted the interest of the India Caucus. The discussion of these issue areas and the political salience of the India Caucus will allow subsequent evaluation of the effectiveness of the India Caucus later in this chapter.

The Burton Amendments

The first successful lobbying endeavor by the India Caucus can be best seen in how Dan Burton's annual legislation threatening to cut aid to India was handled over the 1990s. Burton, the conservative Republican, for many years has been India's fiercest critic on the Hill, and annually proposed an amendment to the foreign aid bill to reduce or eliminate US assistance to India for its alleged human rights violations in Kashmir. These amendments not only tapped into anti-India and/or pro-Pakistani sentiment that characterized Congressional attitudes up until the 1990s, but also appealed to the widespread distaste for foreign assistance in Congress. Because Burton usually justified these measures as a way of compelling New Delhi to improve human rights behavior, the amendments over the years garnered support across the political spectrum. Burton has never succeeded in having one of his anti-India measures signed into law, but in 1992, the House did adopt a Burton Amendment to eliminate development assistance to India (Hathaway, 2001, pp. 21–34).

By mid-1990s, however, the shift in Congressional attitudes toward India had made Burton's task infinitely more difficult. The turning point occurred in 1996, when the Burton Amendment lost by a resounding 169 votes. A year later, an overwhelming 342 legislators voted against the Burton Amendment and 82 voted in favor of the amendment, leading to its defeat by a margin of 260 votes—a record that would impress even the most cynical lobbyist. Some two-dozen lawmakers made speeches praising India's democratic setup and its efforts to improve its human rights record while reflecting on the business opportunities India represented to the US economy.[4] By

---

[4] Rajghatta (1997). Significantly, almost every Congressman who spoke for India said, "New Delhi did have human rights problems and was admitting as such. But it also had redressal forums in the form of an active judiciary, a dynamic press and an alert NGO community."

the early 2000s Dan Burton's legislation was seldom taken up with any interest. Although he drafted amendments in each of the 1990s, he chose not to offer them, thereby sparing himself the ignominy of further smashing defeats.

Gilman–Ackerman Kargil Resolution

In June 1998, India Caucus members' offices were flooded with the e-mails from Indian Americans demanding a resolution condemning Pakistan's incursion in the Kargil hills of the Kashmir valley. Lawmakers complied with this demand. A few days later President Bill Clinton cited Congressional pressure in urging Pakistani Prime Minister Nawaz Sharif to withdraw his forces from the Indian side of the LOC (Lancaster, 1999). Prior to a July 4, 1999 meeting between President Clinton and the Prime Minister of Pakistan, when the latter pledged he would take concrete steps to restore the LOC in Kashmir, the HIRC approved a resolution (Gilman–Ackerman Kargil Resolution) calling on the Clinton administration to oppose Pakistan's support for the incursion into Kashmir and to block loans from international financial institutions until Islamabad withdrew its forces from the Kargil-Drass-Batalik areas. Though resolution did not come to the full House for voting the Resolution was passed by 22 votes in favor, 5 opposed, and 1 abstaining in the HIRC.[5]

The Goodling Amendment

Offered by a hawkish Republican Congressman, William F. Goodling, this amendment proposed withholding American assistance to countries that voted less than 25 percent of the time with the United States at the United Nation. It suffered a resounding defeat in the House of Representatives on July 21, 1999 by a margin of 256 votes to 169 votes (Chandran, 1999). The Goodling Amendment clubbed India in with countries like North Korea, Libya, Cuba, and Syria, and was proposed in the context of a rousing debate over amendments

---

[5] http://www.usindiafriendship.net/congress/votingrecord/kargil.html, accessed on 22 October 2004.

considered in the House to the State Department authorization bill. Among those who led the spirited defence on India's behalf included Gary Ackerman, James C. Greenwood, Benjamin Gilman, Sam Gejdenson, Frank Pallone, and Cynthia McKinney (ibid.).

In a "dear colleague" letter sent to all 435 lawmakers in the House prior to the voting, Gary Ackerman (D-NY) and James C. Greenwood (R-PA), Co-Chairmen of the India Caucus, said

We do not believe that a nation's voting record on recorded votes in the UN is a fair way to assess whether a country shares our values or our positions in the General Assembly. In the General Assembly, 78% of resolutions were adopted by consensus and when those votes are taken into consideration, India supports the US position 84.2% of the time; on votes designated as important by the State Department, India's voting coincides with the US, including consensus, is 75%. Unlike Libya, Laos, Viet Nam, Syria, Cuba and North Korea, countries similarly affected by the Amendment, and that have consistently demonstrated their hostility toward US interests, India has sought to expand relations with the US on a broad range of economic, security and cultural issues and this amendment would undermine Indo-US relations at a time when the post-Kargil prospects held promise proved to be timely. (Usindifriendship.net, 2004c)

Permanent Membership in United Nations Security Council

The permanent UNSC membership for India has been on the lobbying agenda of India Caucus members since the Caucus' inception. Members like Gary Ackerman, Joe Wilson, Sherrod Brown, Ed Royce, Frank Pallone, and so on have been pushing India's case for permanent membership in the UNSC. The founder of India Caucus, Frank Pallone, introduced a resolution in the House of Representatives, on February 26, 2003, "Expressing the sense of the House of Representatives that India should be a permanent member of the United Nations Security Council." Stressing that it is morally wrong to ignore the voice of over one billion Indian people, Pallone said, "It is time for the Congress and the Bush administration to recognize the importance India plays in the region and the world and support its bid for a permanent seat at the UN Security Council" (*Indian Express*, 2003). Pallone justified India's case by stressing its location, its large population, its history of participation in UN peacekeeping operations, and its leadership in the Non-Aligned Movement (NAM). In his address, Pallone also pointed out that India is committed to wiping out terrorism not only within its own territory but also in other parts of the world. Pallone asserted that India would be a stabilizing force in the South Asia region, and would help peace efforts in Central Asia and all parts of an increasingly connected world (ibid.).

In 2004 Pallone again urged President Bush to support India's bid for permanent seat in the UNSC and praised India for its democratic values, human rights record, and its economic progress.[6] The United States has subsequently, albeit indirectly, endorsed India's case on the same grounds expressed by Pallone in December 2004. India Caucus continued their advocacy for India's inclusion in the UNSC as a permanent member. The final culmination point of this constant lobbying effort can be seen during President Barack Obama's visit to India in 2010 when he declared that the United States would support India's bid for the permanent membership in the UNSC in his address to the Indian Parliament. During his meetings with PM Modi, President Obama has reiterated the US support to India's bid for permanent seat in the UNSC.

Applauding Indian Democracy and Indian Independence Celebrations[7]

India Caucus members have advocated for aid for India's natural disasters such as Gujarat earthquake victims[8] and in its effort to

---

[6] "Pallone urges U.S. to Support Permanent Seat for India on U.N. Security Council," *Press Release,* 16 December 2004.

[7] Interview with former Indian Ambassador to US Lalit Mansingh, 24 May 2005, New Delhi.

[8] The caucus members have showed concern for the natural calamities in India and lobbied in Congress for the Gujarat earthquake relief grant introducing legislation. The initiatives were taken by Rep. Jim McDermott and Rep. Gary L. Ackerman, and the resolution was passed by an overwhelming 406–1 vote. On February 8, 2001, the same resolution was unanimously passed in the Senate

change the perceptions of US policy makers in both the executive and legislative branch, have lobbied continuously for highlighting a positive image of India by reference to its commitment to democratic values and principles and praising India on the occasions of Indian Independence Day and Republic Day.

India Caucus members have applauded Indian democracy, its election process, and its continued adherence to parliamentary and representative government and institutions. They have pointed out that, unlike its neighbors, India is governed by a democratic government that is elected through free and fair elections.

In a press release dated October 7, 1999, Gary L. Ackerman (D-NY), then Co-Chairman of the Congressional Caucus on India and Indian Americans, congratulated the people of India for yet again demonstrating their abiding faith and passion for the democratic process and rule of law by freely, fairly, and openly electing a new national government of their choice. He went on to say

> I salute the people of India for yet again being the beacon of democracy in an area of the world where totalitarianism, military rule and fundamentalism have far too often been the rule rather the exception. India serves as a shining example for the entire world to see that it is possible to be an emerging economy and have a democratic government founded on rule of law.[9]

On November 16, the House of Representatives passed by an overwhelming vote of 396 to 4 a resolution affirming strong support for Indian democracy.[10] The resolution stressed that India and the US "share a special relationship," lauded India as "a shining example of democracy for all of Asia to follow" and urged the President Clinton to visit India and "broaden [the] special relationship with India into

---

as concurrent resolution (S. Con. Res. 6) which was co-sponsored by Mr Biden and Mr Nickels. "Rep. Ackerman to Explore Reconstruction Assistance for Earthquake-Stricken Gujarat," *Press Release*, 31 January 2001.

[9] "Rep. Ackerman Applauds Indian Democracy," *Press Release*, 7 October 1999.

[10] The resolution was introduced by Rep. Gary Ackerman (D-NY), and cosponsored by Rep. Sam Gejdenson (D-CT), Rep. Tom Lantos (D-CA), Rep. Sherrod Brown (D-OH), and Rep. Alcee Hastings (D-FL).

a strategic partnership." Rep. Sherrod Brown (D-OH) commented that

> it is pretty clear that if this country of one billion people can overcome its problems and elect a government that serves the people's needs, then our State Department, our U.S. Trade Representative's Office and the Republicans in this Congress should quit lavishing all their attention on the People's Republic of China and start working with our sister democracy in India to bring stability to South and to East Asia (H. Con. Res. 211, 1999).

This statement in the 1999 can be considered as much of significance given the resent status of the US–India relationship which is defined in the terms of a comprehensive strategic partnership, in which the common democratic values and the shared security interests in the South to East Asia are focused.

On January 24, 2000, in a press release, Rep. Frank Pallone, on the occasion of Republic Day, said,

> Exactly one half-century ago, on January 26, 1950, India became a Republic, devoted to the principles of democracy and secularism. Since then, despite the challenges of sustaining economic development and promoting tolerance and coopera-tion amongst its many ethnic, religious and linguistic commu-nities, India has stuck to the path of free and fair elections, a multiparty political system and the orderly transfer of power from one government to its successor. And, despite external threats to its own security, India still remains committed to playing its rightful role as a major force for peace, stability and cooperation in Asia.[11]

In the House, Pallone also highlighted the rich tradition of shared values between the United States and India, the key aspects of Indian Constitution, particularly its section of Fundamental Rights, which is derived from American Constitution's Bill of Rights, and the

---

[11] "Pallone Salutes Indian Republic Day", *Press Release*, 24 January 2000.

moral support that the Indian Independence movement under the leadership of Mahatma Gandhi got from American intellectuals, political leaders, and journalists.[12]

On January 25, 2001, in honor of India's Republic Day, Rep. Jim McDermott in the House of Representatives while acknowledging India's linguistic and religious diversity and its strong federal republic that has withstood massive pressures from within and without to remain one of the most stable democratic republics in the world, said that the United States and India have had a wary relationship for much of mutual history and their common commitment to peace, democracy, and multiculturalism will soon bind the two nations together as strong allies.[13]

On August 3, 2001, Rep. Crowley and Rep. Frank Pallone made statements in House of Representatives on 54th anniversary of India's Independence. Crowley praising India as the world's largest democracy stressed that the United States need to recognize India's importance as a great democracy and as a force for stability in South Asia. Being the only democracy and one of three nuclear powers in the region India has the potential to be a force for economic development and political stability. On July 23, 2003, Rep. Joe Wilson, praised India on its Independence Day and its people for faithfully adhering to the democratic principles (Usindiafriendship.net, 2004a, 2004b). On March 11, 2004, Rep. Joseph Crowley made a statement before House of Representatives honoring India's Republic Day. He praised India for representing the ideals of freedom and liberty and Indians for their academic success, business prowess, and social acceptance specifically in the United States.[14]

These statements and resolutions by the India Caucus members were of great importance in facilitating the Vajpayee and Bush administrations' initiatives for giving a shape to the India–US strategic partnership. India's democratic credentials and each parliamentary election since the formation of India Caucus have been applauded in the US Congress which was not the case prior to the

---

[12] Ibid.

[13] Ibid.

[14] *House Concurrent Resolution 15*—"Commending India on its Celebration of Republic Day."

existence of the India Caucus. It was strange that despite its commitment toward democratic principles and institutions the US Congress had no good words for India, the world's largest democracy with a vast multilingual, multicultural, multireligious society, and also arguably, the first non-Western and nondeveloped country to be a full-fledged democratic country. India Caucus members played a significant role in highlighting India's credentials as a successful democracy and the need for the United States to engage India in the region which is full of the undemocratic regimes, including China and Pakistan.

TERRORISM: INDIA AND PAKISTAN

India has been a frequent victim of terrorism. This non-state asymmetrical warfare remains one of the biggest threats to India. Even before 9/11, the India Caucus had raised issues with terrorism committed against India and other nations. Rep. Frank Pallone, is on record as having repeatedly condemned the ongoing campaign of terror and violence in Kashmir. Pallone repeatedly cited Pakistan's active role in supporting the militants who have been waging a campaign of terror in Jammu and Kashmir. In 2000, Pallone also stressed reliable reports from Western media organizations citing Pakistan as a base and training ground for terrorist groups. He continued, that, given the shared threat that the United States and other countries faced from international terrorist organizations, the State Department should explore ways to step up US cooperation with those countries in the struggle against terrorism.[15] Pallone welcomed the fact that a clear link between Pakistan and official support for terrorism has been established in the US State Department's Patterns of Global Terrorism, 1999 Report, and stressed that the administration must be prepared to follow through with the threat of declaring Islamabad a state sponsor of terrorism. "One of the most dramatic findings of the report is that Pakistan, traditionally an ally of the United States, is guilty of providing safe haven and

---

[15] "Pallone Resolution on Terrorism," 106th Congress, 1st Session, 27 January 2000.

support to international terrorist groups," Pallone said, "The State Department stopped short, however, of adding Pakistan to the list of seven nations that are described as state sponsors of terrorism."[16]

In the year 2000 Islamic terrorist group Harkat-ul-Mujahudeen group hijacked an Indian Airlines plane full of passengers, forcing the Indian Government to free some other terrorists for the safe return of passengers. Frank Pallone raising the issue said that the Indian Airlines hijacking crisis was only the latest in a long series of incidents that pointed to Pakistan's role in promoting violence and instability in the region. Pallone (2000) also pointed that the hijackers of the Indian Airlines plane were part of the Harakat-ul-Mujahudeen, which the US State Department has described as an "Islamic militant group based in Pakistan." Pallone then introduced a Resolution in the House of Representatives calling on the US Secretary of State to designate Pakistan as a state sponsor of terrorism. The legislation (House Resolution 406), introduced on Thursday, January 27, 2000, with Rep. Bill McCollum (R-FL) as a co-sponsor, was later referred to the House Committee on International Relations.

The resolution stated that

1. the Secretary of State, pursuant to the Export Administration Act should designate the Islamic Republic of Pakistan as a country, the government of which has repeatedly provided support for international terrorism; and
2. in addition to terrorist organizations themselves, those countries that harbor terrorist organizations or provide them with technical, financial, political, or other support should also be held accountable; and
3. given the shared threat that the United States and other countries face from international terrorist organizations, the State Department is urged to explore ways to step up US cooperation with those countries in the struggle against terrorism.[17]

---

[16] Pallone, State Department Report on Pakistani Link to Terrorist Groups Demands Increased Action and Vigilance, *Press Release,* 3 May 2000.
[17] Pallone Introduces Resolution Calling for Pakistan's Designation as State Sponsor of Terrorism, *Press Release,* 28 January 2000.

Congressman Robert Wexler (D-FL) also submitted a strongly worded statement to Secretary of State Madeleine Albright, who testified, before the HIRC condemning Pakistan's support for and links to terrorist organizations in the wake of evidence that linked Pakistani terrorist organizations to the hijacking of the Indian Airliner. Concerns were also raised over the military coup in Pakistan which toppled the nation's democratically elected government at the time.[18]

Terrorism is one of the issues which brought the Bush Government closer to India. Since the September 11 attack, the fight against terrorism became the main thrust of the US policy making. As a result, India's fight against terrorism also became more prominent in US Congressmen's statements and resolutions. Caucus members Gary Ackerman and Gilman expressed their condolences following terrorist attack in Srinagar in October 2001. Expressing solidarity with India the US lawmakers, along with many other India Caucus members like Frank Pallone, Ackerman, and Gilman also condemned the terrorist attack on Indian Parliament in December 2001. They released press statements condemning the attack and called for punishing the terrorists.[19] Representative Frank Pallone defended India's Terrorist Ordinance against criticism from Dan Burton, and criticized the continued link between Pakistan and Taliban forces.[20]

In 2002, the same India Caucus members expressed their concern over growing incidences of terrorism in India. They again condemned Pakistan for supporting terrorists in Kashmir and also demanded that Pakistan be declared a terrorist state. Representative Gilman compared India's fight against terrorism to America's war on Al-Qaeda and urged the Bush Administration to put pressure on Pakistan.[21] Rep. Ed Royce condemned the attack on the Swaminarayan Temple in Gujarat in the House of Representatives.[22] Congressman Joe Wilson, then Co-Chairman of India Caucus, condemned the terrorist attack

---

[18] Statement Submitted to Madeleine Albright by Congressman Wexler, 16 February 2000.
[19] Press Release, 13 December 2001; "Letter to Indian Prime Minister Vajpayee," 19 December 2001.
[20] Press Release, 5 December 2001; Press Release, 12 December 2001.
[21] Press Release, 3 January 2002.
[22] Congressional Record, 5 September 2002.

on Kashmiri civilians in a statement in the House.[23] Representatives Frank Pallone and Gilman in letters and press statements demanded that Pakistani President General Pervez Musharraf stop cross-border terrorism and put an end to incursions into India when he came to America.[24] The then India Caucus Co-Chairman Joe Wilson condemned the terrorist attack in Kashmir in the year 2003 and blamed Pakistan for the terrorist attack.[25]

India has been the one of the worst affected countries by terrorism; according to the data from the National Bomb Data Center, between 2004 and 2013, India witnessed an average of 298 IED blasts and 1,337 resulting casualties (*The Times of India*, 2014a). Similarly, the third edition of the Global Terrorism Index 2015 places India sixth out of 162 nations most affected by terrorism in 2014. India has figured 14 times in the top 10 terrorists affected countries during 2000–2014. Most of the Islamic terrorist attacks have been masterminded and carried out by the Pakistan-based terrorist groups, namely Lashkar-a-Taeba, Hizbul Mujahideen, and Jash-e-Muhammad, and their affiliates in India (Global Terror Index, 2015). These Pakistan-based terror outfits have masterminded some of the most horrendous terrorist attacks in the Indian cities, including the Mumbai terror attack in November 2008, carried out by Lashkar-e-Taeba.

The India Caucus leadership has been vocal on exposing the Pakistan passivity and support to Pakistani terror outfits engaged in terrorism in India. In the wake of serial bomb blast in Mumbai in 2006, Frank Pallone came down heavily on Pakistan' failure to live up to its promise to reign in terror outfits and said, "Pakistan still lacked appropriate laws to deter terrorist cells from looming and growing within their borders" (*Outlook*, 2006). Similarly in the wake of 2008 Mumbai terror attack the India Caucus have criticized Pakistan's failure to stop cross-border terrorism. Recently, echoing India's stand to prosecute the culprits behind the Mumbai attacks in 2008, US Congressman and House Foreign Affairs Committee

---

[23] *Statement in House,* 17 July 2002.
[24] Press Release, 29 May 2002; *Statement in House,* 16 May 2002; "Letter to Pakistan President," 28 May 2002.
[25] Wilson Condemns Recent Terrorist Attack in Kashmir, Press Release, 26 March 2003.

Chairman Ed Royce, during his visit to Indian in March 2015 blamed Pakistan Inter-Service Intelligence (ISI) for supporting them and called on Pakistan to hand over those responsible either to India or present them before the international court in Hague to be tried for crimes against humanity (*Deccan Chronicle*, 2015).

Caucus Lobbying Against Military Coup in Pakistan

Caucus members also became active when a military regime took over Pakistan. Frank Pallone, urged the Speaker of the House of Representatives to expedite consideration of House Concurrent Resolution 200 that expressed the strong opposition of Congress to the military coup in Pakistan and called for a civilian, democratically elected government to be returned to power in Pakistan.[26] Wexler demonstrated concern about Pakistan's links to terrorism and requested President Clinton to seek concrete commitments from Pakistan during his visit for restoration of democracy, ending support for terrorism, and signing agreements on nonproliferation.[27] Rep. Jim McDermott made a statement in the House of Representatives on March 14, 2000 bringing attention to the situation in the state of Pakistan; he said that by including Pakistan in his visit, Clinton had rewarded a military government.[28]

Lobbying became quite visible after military coup in Pakistan and after the Kargil conflict. The Caucus members lobbied inside

---

[26] Pallone calls for House action on resolution condemning Pakistani coup, Press Release, 10 March 2000.

[27] Wexler concerned about Pakistan's links to terrorism Letter to President Clinton, 12 March 2000.

[28] "Of Presidents and Pakistan," Rep. Jim McDermott Statement in the House of Representatives, March 14, 2000. "Mr. Clinton should put aside the gentle language of diplomacy and use this opportunity to demand that Pakistan move without pause towards full and fair elections. Pakistan is a sick state. Democratic elections will not cure what ails Pakistan; however, the healing process cannot begin without them"; Pallone, "Pakistani Commitment to Return to Democracy 'Not Serious'," Press Release, 30 May 2000. In a press release on May 30, 2000, Rep. Frank Pallone said that General Pervez Musharraf's statement of support for the May 12th ruling by Pakistan's Supreme Court calling for a return to democracy in three years should not be considered by the United States and the international community as an acceptable commitment to restore democratic rule.

and outside Congress against the Musharraf regime and demanded sanctions to be imposed on Pakistan. The Caucus members strongly criticized provisions of the Fiscal year 2000 Defence Appropriations Conference Report that gave the President power to waive the sanctions imposed under the Pressler Amendment by giving logical arguments against the waiver authority. The 1985 Pressler Amendment provided that no assistance shall be furnished to Pakistan and no military equipment or technology shall be sold or transferred to Pakistan and it require yearly Presidential certification that Pakistan does not possess nuclear weapons.

On October 6, 1999, Rep. Frank Pallone, expressed concern that the current strategy of giving discretionary waiver authority to the administration did not guarantee that the US–India economic relationship would be put on track, and pointed out Pakistan's nuclear hobnobbing, its unstable regime, its Kargil misadventure and allowed CIA's to report that Pakistan had obtained nuclear capability M-11 short-range missiles from China and medium-range missiles from North Korea. He emphasized that "It was this type of nuclear instability that the Pressler Amendment was intended to address. Pakistan's failure to act in good faith should not be rewarded in this way."[29] About a week later, Pallone made another statement in the House of Representatives expressing concern about some provisions on the Rule Fiscal Year 2000 Defence Appropriations Conference Report that would give the President authority to waive certain sanctions against India and Pakistan. He said

> Pakistan's army has ruled the country for 25 of its 52-year history, so Army takeovers have been a relatively common occurrence. But this time, the subversion of civilian government means that Pakistan's nuclear arsenal is under direct control of the military leaders—the same hard-line forces who precipitated Pakistan's incursion onto India's side of the Line of Control in Kashmir earlier this year, greatly heightening tensions in the region.[30]

---

[29] Pallone Decries Waiver of Pressler, *Press Release*, 6 October 1999.
[30] Pallone's *Statement in House of Representatives*, 12 October 1999.

He welcomed the provision of the Conference Report, which provided for extended waiver authority of the Glenn Amendment economic sanctions and said that he lobbied for a suspension—if not an outright repeal—of the Glenn Amendment.[31]

On the same day, Rep. Benjamin A. Gilman (R-NY), then Chairman of the HIRC and India caucus member, objecting the language of conference report on the Fiscal Year 2000 Department of Defence Appropriations Bill said,

> In light of the recent developments in Pakistan, I strongly urge the conferees to modify the language contained in the conference report which allows the President to waive U.S. sanctions that prohibit the transfer of defense items, articles, or equipment to Pakistan. I am concerned that the resumption of U.S. defense sales to Pakistan would only serve to assist those who are supportive of today's possible military coup.[32]

Raising his concern for the possible resumption of US military supply to Pakistan, McCollum remarked

> The Department of Defense Appropriations conference report allows the President to waive certain sanctions against India and Pakistan under the Glenn and Pressler amendments. While I am pleased that the economic and technological restrictions have been lifted, I am gravely concerned about the prospect of military exchanges with an unstable Pakistan.[33]

Criticizing the Pakistani military incursion into Kargil and ISI sponsored terrorism in the Kashmir; he appealed the Congressmen to carefully consider the ramifications of repealing this provision.

Rep. Holt (D-NJ) urged President Clinton not to resume arms sales to Pakistan. "For the fourth time in Pakistan's 52-year history,

---

[31] Ibid.

[32] Gilman, "Continue Pakistan Military Assistance Sanctions," *Press Release*, 12 October 1999.

[33] McCollum, "Stop Resumption of Military Ties to Pakistan", Extension of Remarks in the House of Representatives, 13 October 1999.

the Pakistani military has decided not to respect the rule of law and abide by a democratic constitution," and that "If Pakistan's military leaders cannot respect their nation's constitution, there is no reason to presume they will respect its international obligations. It would be foolish to reward their reckless behavior by lifting sanctions now."[34]

Commenting on the same conference report, passed by the House, Greenwood said,

> The decision of the Pakistani military to undertake a coup-d'etat against the legitimately elected democratic government in Pakistan is unacceptable. Considering the well-documented role the Pakistani military leadership played in the recent conflict in the Kashmir, this coup also signals potentially increased friction in that troubled area as well. It is for these reasons that I oppose any resumption of arms sales at this time. It is my further hope that this new military junta will quickly turn the reins of government back to those rightfully elected to govern Pakistan. By following the example of their Indian neighbors, who have just completed democratic elections, and embracing the rule of law, stability can be restored in Pakistan and maintained in South Asia.[35]

Congressman Robert Wexler (D-FL), on the other hand, strongly urged President Clinton not to exercise the waiver authority and pointed out, "The illegal removal of the Sharif government threatens the stability of the entire South Asia region."[36]

Howard Berman argued on similar lines and said,

> It would be a mistake for the Clinton administration to waive existing sanctions that prohibit arms transfers and military training. In addition, the administration should immediately take steps to invoke section 508 of the Foreign Operations

---

[34] Holt Urges Military Sanctions Against Pakistan, *Press Release*, 13 October 1999.

[35] Greenwood Statement on fiscal year 2000 Department of Defense Appropriations conference report, *Press Release*, 13 October 1999.

[36] Congressman Wexler Calls on President Clinton to Withhold Military Assistance to Pakistan, *Press Release*, 14 October 1999.

Appropriations Act, which prohibits certain foreign assistance to any country whose duly elected head of government has been deposed in a military coup.[37]

Frank Pallone went to the extent of drafting a legislation to prevent the administration from waiving the Pressler Amendment prohibition on US military assistance to Pakistan. "The intent of my legislation is essentially to return to the status quo on the Pressler Amendment," Pallone said and believed that "Congress made a mistake in granting the President waiver authority over Pressler, particularly in light of military coup in Pakistan, it is unacceptable to consider arms transfers to Pakistan."[38]

In the House of Representatives, October 18, 1999, Pallone introduced the bill to remove the waiver authority for the prohibition on military assistance to Pakistan, which was referred to the Committee on International Relations be it enacted by the Senate and House of Representatives of the United States of America in Congress assembled. Section 9001(a) of the Department of Defence Appropriations Act, 2000 was amended:

1. by inserting *"or"* before *"section 2(b)(4)"*;
2. by striking *"or section 620E(e) of the Foreign Assistance Act of 1961, as amended, (22 U.S.C. 2375(e))."* H.L.C.[39]

Similar arguments were made by Congressmen Barney Frank in his letter to the President Clinton[40] and by Jim Saxton, a senior

---

[37] Remarks of Howard Berman in the House of Representatives, 14 October 1999.

[38] Pallone to Introduce Legislation to Block Waiver of Pressler, *Press Release*, 14 October 1999.

[39] *HR 3095 IH*, 106th Congress, 18 October 1999.

[40] Barney Frank in a letter to President Clinton wrote that the recent coup in Pakistan was a repudiation of democracy—and even an imperfect democracy is preferable to a military coup and military rule and then urged him to continue to maintain the sanctions against Pakistan until legitimate democratic civilian rule is re-established, and the government gives full assurances that it will not undertake any military ventures in Kashmir. Letter to President Clinton by Barney Frank, 15 October 1999.

member of the House Armed Services Committee, in his letter to the President said that his administration had expressed strong disapproval of this military coup, yet no specific action had been taken. He continued, "In light of Pakistan's nuclear weapons and missile proliferation, its acrimonious relationship with our important ally India in the Kashmir region and alarming cross-border terrorist activities, our diplomatic ties with Pakistan should be seriously re-examined with renewed fervor."[41]

Pallone urged his colleagues to join in his initiative to prevent the administration from waiving the Pressler Amendment and stressing the relevance of Pressler Amendment. On the dangers of reopening the American arms pipeline to Pakistan, Pallone said, "The United States obviously can't bring about democracy in Pakistan, or change Pakistan's international behavior, overnight. But we can avoid the policies that encourage Pakistan's military leaders to seize power, to foment instability in South Asia...."[42]

Representative Sam Gejdenson (D-CT) urged the President Clinton to refrain from using the new waiver authority it has been granted on the Glenn and Pressler amendments, and said, "By declaring Martial Law, General Musharraf has instead declared to the world his disregard for the rule of law."[43] Rising in strong support the House resolution-condemning coup in Pakistan, Rep. Brown stated in the House, "if a nation of one billion people with more Muslims than all of the people that live in Pakistan can hold an election, then we ought to be using India as an example of how the rest of the world should behave."[44]

Frank Pallone criticized the Republican leadership's failure to bring a resolution condemning the coup in Pakistan to a vote in the House of Representatives and strongly supported a resolution praising India's recent Parliamentary elections. That resolution,

---

[41] Letter to President Clinton by Jim Saxton, 18 October 1999.
[42] The Coup in Pakistan and the Importance of Maintaining the Pressler Amendment, Rep. Pallone Morning Hour, *Statement in the House of Representatives*, 19 October 1999.
[43] Gejdenson Urges Clinton Against Use of Recently Won Waiver Authority on Pakistan, *Press Statement*, 14 October 1999.
[44] Rep. Brown supports House Resolution Condemning Coup in Pakistan, *Statement in House*, 27 October 1999.

sponsored by Rep. Gary Ackerman (D-NY) passed the House overwhelmingly.[45]

Rep. Ileana Ros-Lehtinen (R-FL) and Rep. Gary Ackerman (D-NY) succeeded Republican Rep. Joe Wilson (R-SC) and Rep. Joe Crowley (D-NY) in January 2005, as Co-Chair of the Congressional Caucus on India and Indian Americans. This was Ackerman's second stint at the Caucus where he served earlier between 1998 and 2000, leaving an unbeaten legacy. In 2005 again he introduced legislation requiring the CIA director to report to Congress on Pakistani proliferation activities. The measure was adopted by the full House as an amendment to the Intelligence Authorization Act. Ackerman also raised doubts regarding Musharraf and urged the Bush administration not to rely on him. He further argued that Musharraf would only battle extremists and terrorists in a limited way, and that he had in reality strengthened the military's role in Pakistani governance rather than bring democracy, and has done little to cut the ties that his military and intelligence services have to extremists and terrorists in Pakistan.[46] Ackerman has also been critical of Pakistan on nuclear issues.[47]

An increasingly prominent spokesperson for the Caucus has been Rep. Ileana Ros-Lehtinen (R-FL). During President Bush's first term in the White House, Ros-Lehtinen made many pro-India statements and was courted by some Indian–American organizations and leading Republican Indian Americans, who held fund-raisers for her re-election campaign. At one event in 2003, she said India had stood shoulder to shoulder with the United States in the trying times

---

[45] Pallone criticizes delay in House resolution on Pakistani coup; Praises India's Commitment to Democracy, *News Release*, 17 November 1999.

[46] Public Statement by Ackerman. Retrieved 2 July 2012, from http://www. votesmart.org/speech_detail.php?speech_id=55211&keyword=indian&phrase=&contain=

[47] Ibid. "I continue to believe that our administration is ignoring the law by failing to make a determination on the application of sanctions against Pakistan for the transfer of nuclear weapons designs and related technologies to terrorist states. Until someone in the administration provides me with a detailed explanation of why Pakistan should not be sanctioned under either Glenn or Symington's amendments, I will continue in this belief and will continue to raise it at every appropriate opportunity."

after 9/11 and that India could be an important defence and trade ally.[48] Ros-Lehtinen joined Ackerman and others in a letter sent to President George W. Bush urging him not to sell F-16 fighter aircraft to Pakistan, she recalled. The Caucus, she emphasized, would work with the White House. "With all the nations that are getting into the nuclear club and this global war on terror, more and more we depend on allies like India to help us in that troubled area," Ros-Lehtinen said.[49]

Missile Technology Transfers to Pakistan from China

The Missile Technology Regime, created during the waning days of the Cold War period in 1987, aimed primarily at curtailing the proliferation of missiles capable of delivering nuclear weapons. However, in the early to mid-1990s the concerns were raised over the proliferation of missile technology especially to the countries such as North Korea, Pakistan, Iraq, Libya, Syria, and other rogue states. India's concerns were mainly because of the Chinese transfer of missile technology to Pakistan, which ultimately forced India to venture into its own missile defence program (for more details, see Ganguly, 2014; Sharma, 2009). India's security concerns over the China–Pakistan missile technology nexus was raised by the India Caucus members.

On May 22, 2002, Pallone expressed his concerns regarding the continued transfer of missile technology from China to Pakistan in the House and urged President Bush to use his authority to stop Chinese transfer of missile technology to Pakistan, where such facilities are not safeguarded. However, Chinese authorities did not effectively ban technology transfers, despite their pledge in May 1996. In November 2000, China entered into an agreement with the Clinton administration that prohibited China from transferring missiles or missile technology specifically to Pakistan. Apparently, missile technology transfers continued even after this specific prohibition.

---

[48] *IACPA News*. Retrieved 22 May 2004, from http://www.iacfpa.org/p_news/ nit/iacpa-archieve/2004/11/26/cap-latenews1-26112004.html

[49] http://www.votesmart.org/speech_detail.php?speech_id=55211&keyword=in dian&phrase=&contain=, accessed on 2 May 2004.

Pallone strongly emphasized the importance of termination of missile technology transfers from China to Pakistan given an unstable military regime in Pakistan and the escalating conflict in Kashmir.[50]

US Military Sales to Pakistan

A particular consequential area where the India Caucus has made their mark relates to US military sales and military assistance to other countries. In particular, the Caucus has been very vocal against the military sales and assistance to Pakistan. They raised the issue on the ground the unreliability of Pakistan's assistance in the US War on terror, unstable regime, and the growing nuclear and defence nexus between Pakistan and China.

For example, in a press release, on February 12, 2002, Rep. Frank Pallone, Jr. (D-NJ) reiterated to President Bush his strong opposition to lifting the ban on military assistance to Pakistan (which was placed in the wake of Pakistan's nuclear test and Kargil intrusion) to the president's proposal in his Fiscal Year 2003 budget to provide Pakistan $50 million in military assistance. Pallone, voicing his concern in a letter sent to President Bush, argued:

In your FY 2003 budget proposal you have requested $50 million in military assistance to Pakistan... Frankly, I don't see that the situation has changed in Pakistan to justify such a turnaround. It is alarming that you are proposing military assistance to a country that verbally condemns terrorism on a global level, but that actively supports terrorist activities in its own backyard

He further continued

Historically, US military assistance to Pakistan has been used to arm cross-border terrorists in their attacks on Indian civilians in Kashmir and throughout the nation, South Asia is a very volatile, unstable region and given the current military

---

[50] Transfer of Chinese Missile Technology to Pakistan, Pallone's *Statement in House of Representatives*, 22 May 2002.

standoff between Pakistan and India, $50 million worth of U.S. weapons will only aid future conflict in that region.[51]

Rep. Crowley also demonstrated concern over the proposed sale of F-16 to Pakistan, and argued that Pakistan has not moved forward with promises of democracy, fighting its internal extremists, enforcing human rights, or respecting minorities and has not let US interrogators question Abdul Qadeer Khan, the Pakistani former head of an international nuclear black market (*Congressional Statement*, 2006).

When Obama administration sought to increase the military aid and economic assistance to Pakistan India Caucus members mainly Rep. Frank Pallone, Gary Ackerman, and Robert Menendez questioned the intentions of Pakistan. They argued that Pakistan was, despite superficial appearances, in fact a failed state and it will use military aid for war against India (*Dawn*, 2012). Indeed the India Caucus members have echoed the dangers and security concerns of India arising out the US military aid to Pakistan.

INDIA CAUCUS AND MILITARY ASSISTANCE TO INDIA

While US military assistance to Pakistan has been criticized and restrained by the India Caucus, the Caucus members have promoted the need for the United States to pay more attention to Indian defence needs arising out of its security challenges emanating from dual threat of China–Pakistan defence and nuclear nexus in a tense militarized region. India's inability to meet its defence needs from its indigenous defence industry, its heavy reliance on import of defence products, its need of modernization of its defence industry base further necessitated India to look toward the United States and other nations with modern defence industry base. India has been heavily relied on Russian defence industry which constitutes more than 75 percent of India's armory. India also needed to diversify its source of acquisition of arms as Russian products were becoming obsolete.

---

[51] Pallone asks Bush to reconsider budget proposal providing Pakistan $50 million in military assistance, *Press Release*, 12 February 2002.

The India Caucus members have justified military sales to India and its members have from time to time advocated for the sale and transfer of a missile defence system to India. As noted above, they have also urged the United States to intervene in Chinese missile technology transfers to Pakistan.

Sale of Military Radar from Israel to India

Since there was an embargo on sale of high-tech arms to India because of its non-signatory status of the Nuclear Non-Proliferation Treaty (NNPT), India was not allowed to acquire any arms which involved the American collaboration. India needed to buy military radar system for its missile defence system program, but it needed the US Presidential waiver as the Israeli radar system involved the American technology and collaboration too.

On May 28, 2003, Rep. Frank Pallone commending the Bush administration's decision to approve the sale of a military radar system from Israel to India, urged the administration to go further by lifting restrictions on the sale of a missile defence system. The New Jersey Congressman urged the President Bush to take the next step and allow the sale of a defence shield that protects land from short- and long-range ballistic missiles, as proof the United States is serious about its relationship with India and about its support for democracy. "Given the importance of these ties, I urge you to lift existing restrictions on the sale of a missile defense system from Israel to India," Pallone wrote in his letter.[52]

Several days before US Secretary of State Colin Powell was scheduled to leave for India, Frank Pallone, Jr. (D-NJ), requested him to voice his support for the sale of an Israeli Arrow Weapon System to India. He argued that a defence shield that protects land from short- and long-range ballistic missiles would be a positive step for the US–India relations as well. Pallone said, "India's interest in the Arrow Weapon System is to improve missile defense, not offense, which is a key factor regarding this sale that needs to be considered."[53]

---

[52] Pallone Lauds Bush Administration Approval of Sale of Military Radar from Israel to India, *Press Release*, 28 May 2003.
[53] Pallone urges Secretary Powell to support sale of Israeli missile defense system to India, *Press Release*, 23 July 2002.

In his massage to Powell, Pallone further said, "For the past several months, the US and India have participated in numerous joint military exercises which have fostered a strong defence relationship between the two countries, which share democratic interests and have been working well against global terrorism."[54]

The Caucus members lobbied for the enhancement of the US–India defence partnership. In fact their continuous lobbying effort has yielded a deepening defence and military relationship between the US and India, marked by frequent joint military exercises, defence pacts, and agreements which involves joint research, development, production, and defence commerce underpinning the US–India defence relationship.

Since the year 2004, the US and India have been pursuing a strategic partnership. A 10-year defence agreement was signed between the US and India in June 2005 which has been renewed in June 2015 for another 10 years (Garamone, 2015; Sharma, 2015b). Since the signing of the defence agreement there has been significant progress in the US defence relations, both in terms of the volume of defence trade and the frequency of joint military exercises. The US is now India's second largest arms supplier—though accounting for just 7 percent of its purchases. But in the last three years, American defence giants such as Lockheed Martin and Boeing have made significant inroads into the Indian defence market and now top India's arms supplier list, India has bought US defence products worth more than $10 billion in the last 10 years.

India Caucus on Clinton's Visit to South Asia

During President Bill Clinton's visit to South Asia in 2000, the India Caucus urged the Clinton administration not to visit Pakistan. Their argument was that Clinton's visit would be tantamount to acknowledging Pakistan's military regime by undermining the democratic principles for which both India and the US were concerned. Congressmen Gary L. Ackerman, Frank Pallone, Robert Menendez, and Sam Gejdenson, a Ranking Member of the HIRC, commended

---

[54] Let Israel Sell Arrow Missile Defense System to India, Pallone tells Powell in *India Abroad*, 32(48), (2002).

the administration on President Clinton's scheduled visit to India. While expressing concern about a possible stop in Pakistan and urged President Clinton not to include Pakistan in the itinerary of his proposed visit to the Indian Sub-Continent in March 2000 and said that it would be a wrong signal the United States would be giving to world as Pakistan was involved in terror activities worldwide.[55–57] "Pallone and Ackerman urged Clinton to press President Musharraf on democracy, proliferation and terrorism,"[58,59]Dismayed at Clinton's decision to visit Pakistan representative Jim McDermott said,

> I hope that President Clinton will use this opportunity to press General Musharraf on his languishing plans to restore democracy to Pakistan.... I also hope that since President Clinton is going to Pakistan, he will not leave until he has a full explanation as to why Pakistan allows a multitude of terrorist groups to attack India from its lands.[60]

Condemning the Taliban's Move against Minorities in Afghanistan

Furthermore, the India Caucus has been critical of the repression of Indians and Hindus living abroad. For example, in May 25, 2001, the HIRC unanimously condemned Taliban Government's move in Afghanistan to require Hindus to wear symbols identifying their religious identity.[61] India Caucus member Rep. Gilman stated that the

---

[55] Rep. Ackerman Urges President Clinton Not to Visit Pakistan if Military Regime Doesn't Heed Washington's Urgings on Terrorism & Democracy, *Press Release*, 26 January 2000.

[56] Clinton Visit to Pakistan Would Send the Wrong Signal, *Statement to Madeleine Albright by Congressman Gejdenson*, 16 February 2000.

[57] Letter to House Members by Congressman Robert Menendez, 24 February 2000.

[58] Pallone Calls on Clinton to Press Musharraf on Democracy, Proliferation and Terrorism, *Press Release*, 7 March 2000.

[59] Rep. Ackerman Urges President Clinton to Seek Guarantees on Democracy's Return to Pakistan, *Press Release*, 7 March 2000.

[60] Congressman McDermott dismayed at Clinton's decision to visit Pakistan, *Press Release*, 7 March 2000.

[61] Usindiafriendship.net (2004c). On June 13, the House passed the Resolution, which was cosponsored by over 80 lawmakers, by a vote of 420 to 0.

world has not seen "anything like this since Nazi Germany required the Jews to wear yellow badges." Gilman also said in many different ways Pakistan had provided support for the Taliban and, therefore, it was appropriate that this resolution called on Pakistan to use their influence with the Taliban to get them to revoke the edict. Rep. Engel stated, "Pakistan is one of three countries that recognize the Taliban regime and the only country with military ties to Taliban. This resolution calls on Pakistan to use its influence to get the Taliban to revoke the edict."[62]

LOBBYING BY THE INDIA CAUCUS FOR INDIAN AMERICANS

In addition to lobbying for a deeper US–India engagement, raising India's security concerns and highlighting India's credential as a successful democracy, the India Caucus has also been actively lobbying to promote and protect the Indian–American community's cause and has taken up domestic issues, such as racial violence and hate crimes, education, small and minority businesses, immigration and family reunion, political empowerment (of the Indian–American community), the glass ceiling, health, and human service-related issues. Although their lobbying effort on this front has been less vocal than on issues related to the US–India bilateral ties, Caucus members have demonstrated their willingness to fight for the cause championed by Indian Americans and have therefore added their voices and influence to activities undertaken by domestic interest groups run by Indian Americans. Three examples are provided below.

Resolution against Attacks on Sikhs in the United States

The Sikh–American community, over 500,000 in numbers in America, are easily identified by their turbans and beards, which are required articles of their religion, became the victim of both verbal and physical assaults because of misguided anger toward Arab Americans and Muslim Americans after 9/11 terror attacks in 2001.

---

[62] Discussion Note, 107th Congress, 1st Session, 25 May 2001.

On October 2, 2001 condemning bigotry and violence against Sikh Americans in the wake of terrorist attacks in New York City and Washington, DC on September 11, Senator Durbin submitted a concurrent resolution; which was referred to the Committee on the Judiciary Senate Concurrent Resolution 74.

Durbin said that all Americans were united in condemning, in the strongest possible terms, the terrorist attacks against the United States on September 11, 2001. But it was also resolved by the Senate (the House of Representatives concurring), that, the civil rights and civil liberties of all Americans, including Sikh Americans, should be protected. Condemning bigotry and any acts of violence or discrimination against any Americans, including Sikh Americans, it called upon local and Federal law enforcement authorities to work to prevent hate crimes against all Americans, including Sikh Americans (S. Con. Res. 74, 2001).

Resolution: Honoring the Indian–American Friendship Council

On July 26, 2002, Rep. Frank Pallone and Rep. Sherrod Brown submitted the resolution in House of Representatives (H.RES.512) honoring the Indian–American Friendship Council, which was referred to the Committee on International Relations.

It acknowledged that Indian–American Friendship Council which was founded in January 1990 with a commitment to promoting relations between the United States and India, and it had been successful in carrying out its mission of improving US–India relations, promoting global democracy, protecting and representing the interests of the Indian–American community, educating members of Congress, as well as fostering relationships between members of Congress and Indian Americans nationwide. The Council was also praised for being instrumental in moving forward on efforts ranging from rebuilding Gujarat following the disastrous earthquake, to supporting the fight against terrorism following the September 11, 2001 attacks against the United States and the 13 December 2001 attack on the Indian Parliament.[63]

---

[63] House Resolution 512-Honoring the Indian American Friendship Council.

Hindu Priest as Guest Chaplain in House

On May 15, 2000, in a press release, India Caucus member Sherrod Brown (D-OH) requested the House Chaplain to set aside a day for a Hindu priest to deliver the invocation opening a daily session of Congress. "There are hundreds of thousands of practicing Hindus in this country. We should fulfil our responsibility to represent the religious diversity of this country by including a Hindu priest as a guest chaplain," Brown said.[64]

Finally, on September 14, 2000, his efforts made Venkatachalpathi Samuldrala, from the Shiva Vishnu Hindu Temple in Parma, Ohio, the first-ever Hindu guest priest to deliver the opening prayer in the House of Representatives. It was delivered before Prime Minister Atal Bihari Vajpayee's address to a joint session of Congress. Brown was also the first lawmaker to request House Speaker Dennis Hastert, Illinois Republican, to invite Vajpayee to address a joint session of Congress, "Today is a great day for Indian-American relations. For the first time, a Hindu priest has conducted the opening prayer at a session of Congress. For the first time, Indian Prime Minister Vajpayee will address a joint session of Congress" (Haniffa, 2004a).

Brown later commented that, "Nothing could be more important than listening to the leader of the world's largest democracy. His presence in Congress is a great step in US–India relations."[65]

THE EXPANSION AND EVOLUTION OF THE INDIA CAUCUS OVER TIME

From its original eight person membership, the India Caucus reached 50 by 1994 and within a decade more than 180 representatives were listed on the India Caucus membership list. In 1998 a vision for the future of the Caucus can be found in a press release from Co-Chairman Gary Ackerman.

---

[64] Brown requests Hindu priest be chosen as guest chaplain in House, *Press Release*, 15 May 2000.
[65] "Brown Welcomes Northeast Ohio Hindu Priest as Guest Chaplain in House," http://www.house.gov/sherrodbrown/india914.html, accessed on 22 May 2004.

Ackerman said that he wanted to establish a series of task forces to allow the active members of the Indian–American community to assume visible leadership roles. He added, "I envision we will have task forces devoted to immigration, international trade, US economic sanctions on India, international terrorism and other issues of concern to the Indian-American community and of importance to India–US relations."[66]

During the 107th Congress the Co-Chairman Jim McDermott and Ed Royce wrote letters to fellow members of the House and tried to convince them that to reach out to the Indian–American community, stating that as a community that has taken full advantage of opportunities in America it was important to join the Caucus. They clearly stated that Indian Americans had distinguished themselves in many fields, including medicine, science, business, and the arts.[67]

In 2004 the India Caucus membership reached to around 185 and many were likely to join the Caucus. On this, Joe Wilson, the Republican Co-Chairman, believed that expanding the membership of the Caucus is no longer a hard task. This is because the Indian–American population in the United States had made such a positive impact that it did not take long to explain to people importance of the community.[68]

Congressman Benjamin Gilman (R-NY) attributed the growing number of Caucus members to a growing US–India relationship, which is based on the solid foundation of a shared commitment to democracy, individual rights, freedom of expression, and India's economic reforms. India came to offer enormous opportunities for trade and investment for the US companies. At the same time the United States and India had to confront many of the same international threats including terrorism.[69] The former Prime Minister Atal Bihari Vajpayee had aired similar views on the growing membership of India Caucus, which according to him reflected both the growing

---

[66] http://www.usindiafriendship.net/Congress/Caucus/Caucus.htm#, accessed on 14 October 2004.
[67] Congressional Caucus on India and Indian Americans. Retrieved 14 October 2004, from http://www.indiaus-sc.org/ccia.htm
[68] Ibid.
[69] Ibid.

confidence of Indian–American community and the increasingly close relationship between India and the United States on wide ranging issues. Vajpayee perceived the India Caucus as a bridge between the strong Indian–American community and their elected representatives (Embassy of India in the US, 2000).

The Congressional Caucus on India and Indian Americans in the 108th Congress (2004) took on a more ambitious agenda. In its "mission statement" the Caucus saw itself as a forum in which members of Congress would address concerns vital to India. By promoting dialogue on issues of interest to India and the Indian–American community, the Caucus would strive to strengthen bilateral relations between the United States and India, promote trade with India, enhance economic development in India, and improve the overall standard of living for Indians and Indian Americans.[70] The Caucus would primarily focus on the issue areas of

- *US–Indian relations*, to include trade, security cooperation, global terrorism, the Kashmir issue, and economic and humanitarian assistance;
- *Developments in India and on the Indian Sub-Continent*, to include economic development, health care, inter-communal relations, the status of religious and other minorities, corruption, and the Tibetan exile community; and
- *Issues of Interest to the Indian–American Community*, including the facilitation of trade and commerce with India, small business, visas, education, health care, and the promotion of Indian culture in the United States.

The Caucus would pursue its work with the assistance of Task Forces and to facilitate dialogue on these critical issues, the Caucus would solicit briefings from the State Department, the US Agency for International Development, non-governmental organizations, international organizations, officials from India and elsewhere in the Sub-Continent, and other organizations involved in Indian or

---

[70] India Caucus Mission Statement and By-Laws 108th Congress. Retrieved 14 October 2004, from http://www.zazona.com/ShameH1B/Library/Archives/IndiaCaucus-

Indian–American affairs.[71] The Caucus from the 108th Congress also proposed to create a "Brain Trust" of the past Chairman of the India Caucus to utilize their skills and knowledge of Indian issues by offering draft op-ed columns, speeches, or other outreach materials on issues of interest to members. It would also arrange a conference for Indian–American business leaders to discuss trade and economic development on the sub-continent with members of the Caucus.

Frank Pallone is credited with successful expansion of membership of India Caucus. However, it was Stephen Solarz, who used to be the lone speaker for India in the US Congress during the Cold War period. Professor Robert Hathaway, director, Asia Program, Woodrow Wilson International Center for Scholars, who in his previous incarnation served as a senior Congressional Staffer for over 12 years on the House Foreign Affairs and later HIRC and has monitored the Caucus since its inception, in offering a historical perspective, acknowledges that the Caucus has indeed come a long way since the days before its creation—"before India had any friends on the hill."

Hathaway opines, "Actually, the person who brought me to the Hill was [former Democratic Congressman] Stephen Solarz [of New York], Chairman of the Asia Subcommittee for twelve years in the

---

[71] The Caucus would also work to provide its members with information on developments in India, including ongoing summaries of political and economic developments, relevant legislation, media reports, and press releases and other materials that members could use to communicate their activities to constituents. From time to time, the Caucus would sponsor events to commemorate or celebrate Indian holidays, festivals, and other special occasions as well. http://www.zazona.com/ShameH1B/Library/Archives/IndiaCaucus-, accessed on 15 October 2004.

The India Caucus of 108th Congress also came up with a set of proposed activities. The Caucus would serve primarily as a forum for information sharing on issues affecting India and the IndianAmerican community. The Caucus would arrange regular briefings on legislative and policy initiatives and other issues of interest to Caucus members by U.S. officials, visiting officials from India and the sub-continent, leaders of the Indian–American community, and other experts on subjects of interest to the Caucus; one topic in particular would be the mutual problem of global terrorism that the United States and India face. It would provide regular summaries of ongoing developments in India, the sub-continent, and the Indian–American community.

1980's and early 1990's, and was known as India's only friend in the Congress" (Haniffa, 2005a). He recalled,

> Every year, India's adversary on Capitol Hill, Republican Congressman Dan Burton of Indiana, used to go to the floor and offer legislation to either slash US assistance to India or cut it altogether and Solarz would dutifully trudge over to the floor of the House and I would dutifully follow him and as we walked onto the floor, it was like we had leprosy or something – everybody else would sort of shy away from us and Solarz was literally the only person who was prepared to stand up and argue that India is a democracy, that India deserves our support, and we should be fighting for close US–India ties (ibid.).

Hathaway further observed that when an issue concerning India was being discussed on the floor, members of the House literally elbowed one another out of the way, jostling one another, trying to get a place at the microphone to speak on behalf of India and warm US–India relations (ibid.).

The expansion of India Caucus from eight members to around 185 members reflects the changing perceptions about India in the US Congress, in which the expanded Caucus has played a significant role by highlighting the strategic and economic significance of India in the changed international scenario and India's commitment toward democratic institutions, values, and principles.

However, the questions have been raised on the declining number of members of the India Caucus in the House. From the eight membership for the Congressional Caucus on India and Indian Americans that began in 1993 touched a record number of 186 in the US House of Representatives. But over the past few years, especially after the conclusion of the US–India civilian nuclear deal, the number of India Caucus membership has been on decline. In the 112th Congress, there were 135 members. According to the latest figures, the number has dropped to a 110 Congressmen, partly because there has been no fresh drive from the Indian–American community (*The Times of India*, 2013).

However, this decline in number of Caucus membership has been due to lack of interest on the part of lawmakers, it attributed to a number of factors. Ashok Mago, a Dallas-based business leader, and the Chairman of USINDIA Forum and Sampat Shivangi, president of the bi-partisan IAFPE, attribute this because of lack of major issue which can galvanize the Indian–American community. After the nuclear deal, which saw not only the rise in numbers of India Caucus members but also activated all the modules of Indian lobbying, there has not been any major issue which could encourage the Indian–American community to press their representatives to be on India-related issues and join the India Caucus. Also, this drop in the number of India Caucus has been either due to retirement or the defeat of previous members in the recent elections.

It is widely believed among the Indian–American community leaders that to increase the India Caucus numbers the Indian Americans from across the nation will need to come out and support it and ask their representatives to join the caucus. For this now the platform has been created and the rejuvenation of the US–India relations under PM Modi has brought many issues on the forefront which is likely to re-energize the Indian–American community, which augurs well for the numerical strength of the India Caucus too.

FRIENDS OF INDIA IN THE US SENATE

Though the India Caucus increased in number and strength in the Lower House, the need for the formation of India Caucus in the US Senate also arose. Since the Senate is a very powerful wing of the US legislative system and the most powerful second chamber in the world. It is the Senate and, not the House, which ratifies all the important appointments made by the President, and all treaties must pass through the Senate to be officially adopted as binding on the United States.

While the India Caucus reached 185 members in the House, it was not as effective as it could be, since there were no strong supporters of Indian Americans or India in the US Senate. Lalit Mansingh, as chief of the mission of India in the US needs to be credited with foresight and initiative to shape events that ultimately culminated in the creation of an India Caucus in the US Senate. The idea for the formation of India Caucus in the Senate faced several hurdles, since Senators are busy and many more varied demands and responsibilities imposed upon them given their more diverse constituencies. There had also been no Caucus dedicated to a single country ever formed in the US Senate.[72]

Lalit Mansingh spoke to the Republican Senator Bob Dole, who once a Presidential candidate, Senators from Democratic Party and to the Indian–American community leaders who were very much interested in the formation of the Caucus in the US Senate. The efforts bore initial fruit when a promise for creation of an India Caucus in the Senate was made by John Cornyn on September 17, 2002, at the annual awards banquet of the Greater Dallas Indo-American Chamber of Commerce Texas.[73]

According to Mansingh it took time to form the India Caucus in the Senators because the Senators were expected to give their approval in writing and not just in words. It was also decided to make it would be better to wait for a larger group to be formed initially by enlisting as many Senators as possible before launch.[74]

"Friends of India," a bipartisan organization, formed in the US Senate, is similar to the India Caucus in the United States, House of Representatives. This was the first time in the history of the US Senate that a country-focused Caucus was constituted. Senator Cornyn, a Republican from the Texas,[75] announced that the Co-Chairperson of "Friends of India" in the US Senate would be Democratic Senator Hillary Rodham Clinton of New York (Haniffa, 2004b). Cornyn undertook the job of creating an India Caucus in the US Senate, because of the incredible experience he had in India and because of the importance of the US–India relations. Cornyn acknowledged that it was unfortunate that despite both the United

---

[72] Interview with former Indian Ambassador to the US, Lalit Mansingh on 24 May 2005.

[73] John Cornyn, Senator Who Made the Difference, *Press Release*, 23 April 2004. Retrieved 22 May 2004, from http://www.usindiafriendship.net/congress/friends/friends.htm

[74] Lalit Mansingh earlier had a success on this front as during his tenure in the UK, along with the Indian chief of the mission in UK had formed "Labour Friends of India" in the Britain joined by 110 Members of Parliament.

[75] Senator Cornyn was the keynote speaker at the Second Annual Capitol Hill Gala Dinner of the American Association of Physicians of Indian Origin on the night following AAPI's two-day legislative conference.

States and India being democracies with so much in common, the two countries "did not have good relations." Cornyn described it the logjam during the "as an accident of history," which had to be put right.[76] The formation of the Caucus with more than 25 percent of the Senate members owe to the recognition of the contribution by the Indian–American community to American society, the positive perceptions about India in the US Congress which was very much the combined efforts of the India lobbying represented by the India Caucus amidst the growing strategic and economic importance of India in the United States in the changed international scenario in the post-Cold War era, particularly in the wake of 9/11 and the military rise of China.

Subsequently, the name of some of the most powerful and influential lawmakers were listed on the "Friends of India" Caucus list. Republican Senators include Senator Orrin Hatch, Chairman of the Senate Judiciary Committee, Charles Grassley, head of the Finance Committee, Thad Cochran, Chairman of the Appropriations Committee, Senate Majority Leader Bill Frist, Tennessee Republican, and Minority Leader Tom Dachle. The leading Democrat members included Senators Paul Sarbanes, Joe Lieberman, and Edward M Kennedy. Today, the Senate India Caucus comprises 34 bipartisan members with the stated goal of building upon the common tradition of democracy by supporting regional and global security and prosperity for the United States and India.[77]

The role of Senate India Caucus, under the leadership of its founder Co-Chairmen Senator John Cornyn and Senator Hillary Clinton, in helping to reshape and facilitate America's policy toward Indian has been significant. The Senate India Caucus has given much needed support to the Indian lobby in strengthening the US–India strategic partnership. The landmark US–India civilian nuclear deal bill would not have seen its day without approval from the US Senate. The role that the Senate India Caucus played in the passage of the civilian bill in the upper chamber with more than two-third majority approval is commendable. (The role of Indian lobbying in

---

[76] Ibid.
[77] Senate India Caucus, Retrieved 12 December 2015, from http://www.cornyn.senate.gov/public/index.cfm?p=senate-india-caucus

the passage of US–India civilian nuclear deal bill is discussed in more detail in Chapter 6.)

Prior to the formation of the Senate India Caucus, the effectiveness of India Caucus in the House was questioned on the basis of its limitation on real impact on US foreign policy-making process toward India. It was being questioned on the ground that the inner group is confined to the House of Representatives only where not much of the actual foreign policy decisions are taken. The members of the Senate, with larger and more diversified constituencies, had resisted the temptation to align themselves so decidedly with what is still a numerically modest US ethnic group. However, the formation of India Caucus in the US Senate in April 2004 addressed this concern, and proved their effectiveness during the significant role in the passage of the US–India Civilian nuclear deal in the US Congress.

EVALUATION OF INDIA CAUCUS

The lobbying activities of India Caucus have been closely watched by critics and it has its share of criticism too. Despite being one of the largest of its kind, only a fraction of its members are concerned for helping the Indian–American community or making a tangible contribution to improving the US–India relations. The majority only pay lip service to stated Caucus goals. Its performance has been questioned on the ground that it is content to just bandy its growing numbers and send out press releases about what it is doing to promote the US–India relations, simultaneously hardly doing anything substantive or tangible to promote the US–India relations, and more importantly to help address the Indian–American community's issues and concerns. It has been alleged that the Caucus has been taking the community for granted.

McDermott, the former Co-Chair of the India Caucus, himself is a critic who is of the opinion that Indian–American community is being taken for granted by many lawmakers, particularly those who claim to be members of the Caucus. McDermott cites the example of the number of times he and another founder-member, Robert Menendez, tried to win Congressional support for appropriation of $120 million for 2001 earthquake victims in Gujarat. He pointed out that even an amendment seeking $20 million could not win the required support in the House. Influential Republicans like Benjamin Gilman of New York and Ed Royce of California—both prominent members of the India Caucus—refused to co-sponsor it, since the administration convinced them that seeking such an appropriation would complicate President George W. Bush's tax bill (Maitra, 2003). Another example is failure to garner support of 100 Congressmen to enact a resolution on honoring Dalip Singh Saund, the first Indian origin Congressman, in 2003. This could have been easily done given the 163 members listed on India Caucus in 2003, but only 33 signed in favor of the resolution.

Although India Caucus claimed a membership of around 185, only 25 percent of these members take an active interest in the affairs of the Indian–American community and very few really care about India.[78] Though most of the Caucus members cast pro-India votes, their activities on behalf of the community do not extend much beyond that. Not only that, some legislators seem not even to know that their secretaries have signed them up India Caucus membership.

Also, sometimes personal rivalries also seem to have dented the organization's efficacy, although by its very nature this development is not easy to document. In early 1999, Pallone was forced out as Co-Chair of the India Caucus and was replaced by Ackerman. James Greenwood (R-Pa) was selected Co-Chair at the same time but left active management to Ackerman. A number of Caucus members felt that Pallone had used the organization too much for his personal ambitions and hoped to garner for them some of the recognition Pallone had gained through his activity. A less contentious succession saw the Ackerman–Greenwood team replaced by Jim McDermott (D-Wash) and Ed Royce (R-Calif).

Questions were raised on India Caucus's effectiveness as its influence was limited primarily in the House of Representatives. Whereas much of the real work of the Congress is completed long before a bill gets to this point. In the case of India-related issues, the appropriations committees of the two houses have usually been the key battleground. Members on these committees, for instance, made the controversial 1999 decision to ease nuclear-related restrictions

---

[78] Interview with Stephen Cohen, Senior Fellow at Brooking Institution, at Observer Research Foundation, New Delhi, October 2004.

against Pakistan by giving President Clinton the authority to waive the restrictions imposed under the Pressler Amendment. This happened despite the lobbying effort by the prominent members of India Caucus. In fact, they had openly criticized this move on all the platforms and had warned the House as well as Clinton administration about prevailing undemocratic regime in Pakistan and had urged not to reward Pakistan with this kind of relief. But in the crucial appropriations area, the Caucus had yet to demonstrate any particular clout to prove its impact on policymakers.

For most of the members of Congress, sub-continent was something of an abstraction, and primarily a domestic political chit. For instance, it appeared that House Speaker Dennis Hastert (R-Ill) extended the invitation to Prime Minister Vajpayee to address a joint session to be held in September 2000 only after having been persuaded that such a gesture was necessary to keep Clinton and the Democrats from garnering all the political credit in the Indian–American community for improvement in the US–India ties. The speaker was reportedly influenced by the argument of Representative Rick Lazio (R-NY), who was in a tight race with first lady Hillary Clinton for a New York Senate seat. He told the speaker about his fear that snubbing the Indian Prime Minister could cost him votes in New York's large Indian–American community. Some Indian–American leaders are concerned that the community is being manipulated by politicians for raising campaign funds than in promoting the interests of Indian Americans.

In those days, the Indian–American community lacked political maturity to distinguish between community's genuine advocates and other lawmakers whose commitment is directly proportional to the size of the political donation they receive. The community needed to be more proactive and ask their Congressman of their constituency to address their issues, by naming an issue and then asking their representatives what actions they are going to take on the issue. India Caucus found it difficult to ensure a bi-partisan support on domestic issues concerning the Indian–American community, given the divide between the two major parties. Also as a population, the Indian–American community did not constitute a significant voting bloc. However, by 2004, on major foreign policy issues toward India the Caucus had made its presence felt.

The very presence of India Caucus in the House reinforced the administration's preference for dealing with the Senate, which can pass amendments that are not germane to legislation under consideration. Senator Brownback, in particular, has used his Chairmanship of the *Senate Foreign Relations Subcommittee* on Near Eastern and South Asian Affairs as a platform to advance a wider agenda at a time when the comparable House Committees are involved in jurisdictional and personal disputes that make them ineffective. The Clinton administration was forced to react to Brownback's promise to introduce legislation removing all remaining nonmilitary sanctions toward India (Rubinoff, 2001).

Dan Burton's annual amendments to slash assistance to India have found little support in recent years. It seems that he has been successfully marginalized and discredited by the India Caucus (The Hill, 1997). Although Burton prepares an anti-India bill almost every year, due to fear of defeat in the house he stopped to introduce it. It is noteworthy that the India Caucus along with USINPAC lobbied successfully to defeat the candidacy of Rep. Dan Burton for the Chairmanship of the House Subcommittee on South Asia. Burton's office expressed its acknowledgement of "some tension" with Indian Americans. Burton finally took the Chairmanship of Government Reform's Human Rights and Wellness Subcommittee (*Washington Times*, 2003).

By 2004 India Bashers in Congress, who continually attempted to drag the Kashmir issue at every available opportunity, were reduced to a minority group of about 46 members in the House. With the retirement of such stalwarts as Gerald Solomon (R-NY), Chairman of the Rules Committee, and Robert Livingston (R-La.), Chairman of the Appropriations Committee, most of Pakistan's supporters in the House, outside the Black Caucus and the Armed Services Committee, were marginalized and discredited too. Other legislators, such as Tom Harkin and Dana Rohrabacher, have been silent since the coup in Islamabad. And another setback to this India bashers group was Senators coming together and forming India Caucus in US Senate on April 29, 2004. Significantly, India's critics like Minority leader Tom Daschle and Dana Rohrabacher also joined the Caucus.[79]

---

[79] Cornyn, Clinton announces Senate India Caucus. Retrieved 22 November 2004, from http://www.cornyn.senate.gov/ news/record.cfm?id=220896

The first ever conference on "Measuring the India Caucus" was organized by Bridging Nationals, a nonprofit policy-oriented organization founded by Prakash Ambegaonkar to assess the effectiveness of India Caucus. It elicited a "no-holds barred" scathing criticism and a stout defence of the more than 180-member body in a standing-room only interactive session on Capitol Hill.

Robert Hathaway, who has monitored the Caucus since its inception, in offering a historical perspective, acknowledged that the Caucus has indeed come a long way since its inception when India hardly had "any friends on the Hill." He conceded that the India Caucus "is to an important extent—certainly not exclusively—but to an important extent, responsible for that sea-change and it genuinely is a sea-change in the attitude of members of Congress about India and about the importance of the US–India relationship" (Haniffa, 2005, p. A6).

He lauded Congressman Frank Pallone for the creation of the India Caucus and stretching it from eight members to more than 180 members in a relatively short period of time. But at the same time he was concerned about Caucus not fulfilling its full potential and for many members of the Caucus, it is more of a booster club, a cheerleading organization and as a cash cow than a serious policy-oriented adjunct to Congressional work (ibid.).

He also suggested some points to make the Caucus more effective in the years ahead. To make it a more effective organization, he suggested, it has got to become more genuinely bipartisan. Hathaway argued that so long as the Congress remains under the control of the Republicans, it is really going to be much more effective more Republican members join it.

Hathaway does not consider the India Caucus as the largest country Caucus in the Congress as something big achievement. According to him, it is actually irrelevant and size is not everything. He points out that

> maybe 20 members are active. If you want the Caucus to be effective, push those other members to be serious, not simply to add their names on a roll. It has been established in a couple of instances, that they don't even know they are members.

He argued that "being pro-India in my judgment does not mean you need to be anti-Pakistan. Don't make this a zero-sum game.

Find ways to work with the Pakistan-American community, with those members of Congress who are sympathetic to Pakistan—you have got interests in common" (ibid.).

The assessments by Jonah Blank, Chief Policy Advisor for South Asia to the powerful SFRC, and Varun Nikore the founder and President of Indian–American Leadership Initiative, measured the performance, in terms of goals India Caucus has set for itself. Their assessment is that the India Caucus focused more on foreign policy issues than the issues concerning India Americans at local level. In fact, it has been hijacked by foreign policy issues and has ignored domestic Indian–American issues. The kind of legislations, and press releases and statements that Caucus members address in the House reflect that India Caucus has been focusing more on improving the US–India relations and issues related to bilateral ties.

When India Caucus was formed in the US Senate, analysts were not able to make a comparison on the performance between the Caucus in House and the Senate. But, now one can say that the both Caucuses have been actively vocal on the issues related to the US–India relations, which was very much demonstrated during the civilian nuclear deal bill and debates surrounding the sale and transfer of defence and sensitive technology to India.

Hathaway, pointing toward the changed perception and situation concerning India among the Congressman, notes that Dan Burton indeed, no longer offers the infamous Burton Amendment. He got clobbered so badly a couple of years in a row in the late 1990s that he simply gave up the effort.

The criticism on the performance of India Caucus and Caucus as a "cash cow" was contested by Frank Pallone. He clarified that sometimes the expectation is too much and one needs to look into the goal that it envisioned when the Caucus was created in 1990s. He is of the view that the purpose of the Caucus from the very beginning was to try to bring members together to talk about the US–India relations and issues that also might impact the Indian–American community and to basically create a positive consensus-based support for improved relations between the United States and India in the US Congress. Acknowledging the support provided by the Indian–American community organizations, Frank Pallone echoes that it was an effort to try to get members of US Congress to be more supportive and more knowledgeable and educated about Indian–American issues, and stop those who were anti-Indian making progress in turning the US Congress against the improved US–India relations (Haniffa, 2005c).

Summing up, though the India Caucus has to be more effective in its stated goal, the role played by the Caucus members is significant in creating a favorable perception about India among the US policy makers. The very presence of India Caucus in both the Houses of Congress has given India and Indian Americans a strong platform and institutional base in the US policy-making system. The debates and resolutions by the India Caucus members show the changed perceptions and attitudes in the US Congress and highlights the role that lobbying by India Caucus has played in shaping the foreign policy of the United States toward India. The presence of India Caucus in both the houses has ensured the ongoing deepening strategic partnership between the United States and India. The lobbying influence in recent years has been demonstrated during the passage of historic and exceptional US–India civilian nuclear deal in the Congress. This will be dealt in the following chapters which deal with changing perceptions about India in the US Congress and the overall impact of Indian lobbying on the US–India relations.

5

The American Perception about India: The US–India Relations and Indian Lobbying during the Cold War Period

Throughout the Cold War, the US–India relations were marked by missed opportunities despite many shared interests and political values. Even though both are continental-sized democratic nations with a natural interpersonal affinity, their international and bilateral issues were seen in often divergent, conflicting, and incongruous ways. The United States and India found themselves in opposing camps during the Cold War years, and each was unable to understand the logic of other's alliances. As a result, both nations did not come together during the Cold War years to forge a sound bilateral relation despite opportunities in the field of economics, politics, or defence. The common values that both nations shared in the form of liberal democracy did prevent both nations from becoming real antagonists.

A very significant role was played by the US legislative and executive branch in regard to shaping perceptions about India. Perceptions about India were very negative and it was often seen in an unflattering way which was damaging for India. This chapter looks at the negative perception about India that had been dominant among the US Congressmen and executive officials during the Cold War period and how it created hurdles for the development of a favorable environment or a positive platform on which they could come together and form a sound bilateral relationship. In particular, it will focus on US Congressional debate regarding foreign aid and nuclear issues, and how this debate often harmed foreign aid prospects and the possibility of help in the field of nuclear technology to India. It also looks at how the lack of Indian lobbying allowed these negative perceptions to persist in the United States. This chapter then provides insights into the initial phase of Indian lobbying efforts, which began to register itself at Hill during the waning days of the Cold War and early years of the post-Cold War period.

A HISTORICAL PERSPECTIVE OF THE US-INDIA RELATION: A CONFLICT—RIDDEN PAST

India has long been a nation of immense potential. Its status as the world's second largest population market, its democratic parliamentary system of government, and its Anglo-judicial system have all been in place since the country's inception in 1947 (Gupta, 1995, p. 58). However, the United States and India have not had close relations despite India being the world's largest democracy, and the United States the world's pioneering and most vocal democracy. Various analysts have attempted to understand why the India–US relations during the Cold War period, and even as late as almost the mid-way point of Bill Clinton's second term in the post-Cold War, could not forge a sound partnership despite having many similar political and economic interests and common values.

Moral indignation and mutual incomprehension, even at times a sense of betrayal, were the defining characteristics of relations between India and the United States over the second half of the twentieth century. Although seemingly linked by common values and a shared commitment to democratic pluralism, the two countries frequently found more reasons to quarrel than to collaborate. Even on those relatively rare occasions when the two worked in tandem, bruised sensibilities, and bitter recriminations soon undermined the relationship (Hathaway, 2003, p. 7).

This can be attributed to many factors, most of all, Cold War dynamics. India's ties with USSR despite its policy of Non-Alignment, as well as the complex relationship between the various actors in East and South Asia meant that India had to balance its interests between the United States, the USSR, China, and Pakistan. India and the United States distanced themselves from a tranquil closeness due to their conflicting interpretations of and strategic approaches to the Cold War. Each nation pursued different goals: India, to protect its independence by respecting national independence via noninterference, and the United States, to protect its national interests, and project military power to contain communism and maintain its super power status (for a detail insight, see Kux, 1992). The importance of territorial and geopolitical strategies in foreign policy during the Cold War was very important. Some prominent historians, such as Dennis Kux, Andrew J. Rotter, and H.K. Brands, explored this troubled relationship and characterized the US–India relationship during the Cold War period as one of the two nations being "estranged democracies," "comrades at odds," or being in a state of "cold peace," respectively (for a detail insight, see Brands, 1990; Kux, 1992; Rotter, 2000). The NNPT, differing economic policies, Kashmir complications, and more significantly, America's economic and military build-up of Pakistan as a global bulwark against Soviet communism further created hurdles for a warm India–US relation.

India after having won independence in 1947 from British colonial rule was faced with the problems of nation building. The leadership of India after the partition (the creation of Pakistan for Muslims in India under the British rule) realized that India needed to utilize its resources to develop its young economy. With this as its primary goal, India chose not to enter the escalating Cold War by starting the NAM, a strategy intended to safeguard India's Independence by advocating that each nation choose its own system of governance, and intended to provide backing to new nations that were emerging from colonialism so that they would not have to rely on the two superpowers for support. Non-Alignment promulgated by Jawaharlal Nehru, India's first Prime Minister—meant that India would not align with any of the two military blocks and rely on any of the superpowers for protection, but would need to build up its own defence system to be ready for any intrusion (Singh, 1984, p. 181).

However, although Non-Aligned nations in principle were not supposed to side with either the United States or USSR, they began to do so anyway (ibid., p. 181). The USSR and the Eastern bloc supported the Non-Alignment rhetoric that no nation should impose its system of government onto another (nation). The Non-Aligned nations (some 120 countries) made many joint stands against the United States and the Western European interference in the world. Calls for a unified Vietnam, the Palestinian liberation movement, the condemnation of the US sponsored and backed dictatorial Pinochet Government in Chile, and against the return of the US naval base at Diego Garcia to Mauritius, are examples of stands taken by Non-Aligned states against the United States and its European allies during the Cold War (Gupta, 1983, p. 8–23).

India, under the leadership of Indira Gandhi, also took vocal positions against American economic support of South Africa (the United States was South Africa's largest trading partner at the height of Apartheid), and against interference in Afghanistan. This was articulated without direct condemnation of the USSR (ibid., pp. 38–47). India's leadership role in the NAM, and its stance on independence for all nations, caused a rift between itself and the US. John Dulles, US Secretary of State, labeled the Non-Alignment as "immoral" as it did not take a stance between what the United States considered right and wrong (Perish, 1996, p. 229). India's argument that Non-Alignment was an assertion of "peaceful coexistence" was not enough to persuade Washington, and Nehru was branded as crypto-communist (ibid., p. 239).

It is important to understand why India spurned relations with the world's most prosperous democracy during this time. Andrew J. Rotter observes that a part of India's colonial past comprised its inactiveness in the Great Game of the 1850s when Britain and Russia were competing against each other to gain control of strategic locations in South Asia, grabbing land and setting borders almost at whim. Non-Alignment was an understandable post-colonial move away from Britain that marked a sharp delineation between the colonial era and independent India. Indian leaders also perceived the Cold War as a new version of the same pre-occupations of the great powers that had powered the Great Game and colonialism, though now the contest was between Soviet Union and the United States. This time, however, rather than being a passive victim of great power politics, sovereign India envisioned that Non-Alignment and neutrality would constrain the ability of the great powers to treat South Asia as simply "a contest of economic and military aid, of alliance building, and of rhetoric and propaganda" even if there was not going to be a shooting war between the United States and the Soviet Union (Rotter, 2000, p. 38).

Non-Alignment was also seen to be a cost-effective way to keep all external powers out of Asia due to the concern about the impact of great power imperialism (Thakar, 1999). It has been also interpreted in the context of India's focus on developmental goals. India wanted to maintain friendly relations with all nations and especially the two power blocs led by the United States and the USSR in order to gain access to capital and technology to power its independent development. Past colonial experience figured equally in this foreign policy design, and India did not want to risk its newly won independence. Nehru, who was the linchpin in Indian foreign policy making from 1947 to 1964, considered American leaders condescending and, as a socialist, disapproved of American imperialist designs and materialism (Kux, 1992, p. 70). As a result, Indian leadership, and especially Nehru, viewed the Soviet Union to at least be an Asian power with legitimate security interests in the region. America was seen more as "the only foreign military in Asia" (Rotter, 2000, p. 70). In weighing relations between the United States and the USSR, Nehru found America more threatening than Soviet Union because of American military interventionalism.

The USSR and India forged close ties due in part to the Soviet Union's affirmation of Non-Alignment objectives and in part due to India's many socialist programs which included the nationalization of several large industries. Furthermore, Nehru's "Five Principles" for good relations: sovereignty, noninterference, independence, equality, and nonaggression, were also supported by the USSR (Young, 1993, p. 300). American suspicions of India were further heightened by Khrushchev's 1955 visit to New Delhi and the 1971 signing of the Soviet–India Friendship Treaty, which pledged mutual support against antagonistic powers (the US and China) (ibid., p. 134). The US retaliated by renewing relations with China, which included bestowing on China a permanent seat in the Security Council and the rejection of Taiwan, and second, in the 1972 Sino-American Summit, the Shanghai Communiqué, which stated their joint rejection of Soviet hegemony in Asia (ibid., p. 167). The United States had now allied with India's two main threats: China and Pakistan. The obvious irony in Indian and US policy was that both democracies had befriended proponents of communism. In addition, the US–India ties were further complicated by Anglo-American concerns as well as the US–Soviet competition and India–Pakistan enmity.

The foreign policy pursued by India during these significant international events further added to the negative perceptions among American foreign policy framers. During the first half of the 1980s, the US–India relations were also overshadowed by American perceptions about the implications of Soviet intervention in Afghanistan. The new Republican administration, led by Ronald Reagan, had a three-pronged strategy for South Asia. They would give military assistance to anti-Soviet Afghan guerrillas, would renew full economic and military assistance to Pakistan, and would provide humanitarian assistance to Afghan refugees in Pakistan. The United States had little interest in India except for the strategic consideration related to Soviet Union's presence in South Asia. The United States had a very jaded view of Indira Gandhi and a critical view of India because of its close links with the Soviet Union and its stance on presence of Soviet Union in Afghanistan (Dixit, 2003, pp. 150–151).

Pakistan and India have a volatile and tense relationship. The two nations have fought three wars over border disputes and Pakistan allied with the US during the Cold War. It offered the US a strategic foothold in the West Asian region, cooperation in an Islamic country, containment of the USSR from a southern vantage point, bases for American missiles to be targeted at points in Russia, and a very soft spoken Non-Alignment stance. India was not willing to offer America any of these strategic geopolitical advantages. Pakistan further allied with America by joining the nascent South East Asian Treaty Organization (SEATO) and the Central Treaty Organization (CENTO). SEATO was a grouping of nations including the Philippines and Thailand, where the purpose was to stop the spread of communism through joint intelligence. CENTO was a north middle-east grouping of nations including Iraq, which was also united against the influence of Communism.

The United States did not join these organizations but did initiate and coordinate joint military agreements with them (Young, 1993, pp. 204–205). India, with its policy of Non-Alignment, was naturally opposed to these organizations, as well as to NATO. Finally, the War for Bangladesh in 1971 further stressed the rift between India and the United States, and the US later sent the 7th Fleet into the Bay of Bengal to force India to adopt an early ceasefire (Gupta, 1995, p. 45). The Cold War brought about alliances that were simply geographical so as to counter military spheres of influence. National foreign policy agendas separated India and the United States as each nation pursued different goals: India, to protect its independence by respecting national independence via noninterference, and the United States, to protect and spread democracy. However, these territorial and ideological dynamics in international politics of the Cold War era began to take a backstage, and a path opened up that allowed focus on military alliances to shift toward a focus on economic partnerships in the post-Cold War era.

PERCEPTIONS ABOUT INDIA IN THE US CONGRESS AND THE US-INDIA RELATIONS DURING THE COLD WAR PERIOD

The above antipathy led to negative perceptions and unflattering images of India amongst US decision-making circles during the Cold War and the initial years of the post-Cold War period. Arthur G. Rubinoff did the pioneering work in this regard. Rubinoff is of the view that US policy makers often neglected India as their knowledge about India was based on ignorance and misinformation. Historically, there has been a basic congruence between the policies of the executive and legislative branches toward India, although Congressional bitterness surpassed that of the executive branch (Rubinoff, 2001, pp. 37–60). This insight is also emphasized by Norman Palmer, who argues that members of Congress, whether consciously or not, often gave offense to India and damaged bilateral relations by their outspoken criticisms of India's leaders, policies, and ways of life, particularly during the debates on foreign assistance and nuclear issues (Palmer, 1966, p. 10).

Prior to the World War II, India and America had only intermittent and ultimately insignificant interactions, barring some cultural and missionary contacts, such as the welcome address by Hindu Monk *Swami Vivekananda* at the World Parliament of Religion at

Chicago on September 11, 1893. This relative lack of interaction and uninformed and shallow knowledge about India and Indian society, and the international dynamics in which India and America had differing interests, prevented positive perceptions about India developing in the United States. As Stephen Cohen observes, the turning point in American policy, which foreshadowed later India–America disputes, was precipitated by the 1942 Indian decision of the Indian National Congress Party not to support the war effort and to launch the Quit India Movement. With allied fortunes then at their low point, the Congress action placed the Roosevelt administration in a position where it had to choose between Britain, the key ally, then under military attack, and India, a potential friend. Not surprisingly, Washington chose Britain (Cohen, 2000). At that time the US was also concerned about Indian nationalist friendship with Japan, especially in regard to Japan's march into South-east Asia and Burma.

Cohen further states that, while disappointing, the loss of American support was not critical for Indian nationalists. Their overseas lobbying efforts had been focused on Great Britain, especially the British Labor Party. Many Indian leaders had been educated in Britain or in British-oriented institutions in India, and they had little personal or intellectual interest in America. If anything, they had absorbed leftist British views that the United States was the epitome of capitalism and they shared a prejudice that Americans lacked the cultural refinements of the British. Only a few Indian leaders of these years had ever been to the United States—not including Nehru—and the most prominent of these (J.P. Narayan and B.R. Ambedkar) were not members of the Congress Party (ibid.).

On this lack of contact between India and America, Harold Isaacs observes that American "interaction with India occurs less dramatically, along a narrower arc, [and] in a smaller compass of awareness and interest" because the United States has much less shared history with that country than with China or Japan (Isaacs, 1980, p. 23). In fact, other than early humanitarian and missionary ties, and an interest in Mahatma Gandhi, the only important contacts between the United States and India began in 1942, five years before independence, when America first perceived a significant strategic stake in the Indian Subcontinent (Wainwright, 1994, p. 39). This relative lack of contact has been responsible for uninformed perceptions.

Misconceptions and negative images about India and Indians have been reflected consistently in public opinion surveys in America (Watts, 1982). Arthur G. Rubinoff assigns this outcome to the low level of interaction between India and America and the sporadic political and economic relations between them (2001, pp. 37–60).

This negative image of India in the US was further developed and reinforced by school textbooks, the media, and academic writings that depict it as a backward society. Rajiv Malhotra notes that India was lumped in a group of eight problematic countries whose nuisance value was to be contained. While India's accomplishments are nowadays being used to boost the image of its neighboring South Asian countries, in return, India gets associated with South Asian terrorism, violence, human rights problems, and backwardness. Ironically, India's culture gets blamed, and a rejection of Indianness by Indian students is encouraged as a marker of progressiveness (Malhotra, 2003). The Asia Society, in a review of some 300 school textbooks, found that the representation of India was the most negative among representations of all Asian countries (for detail, see Asia Society, 1976). According to a State Department analysis, American attitudes about India, more than about any other place, focus on disease, death, and illiteracy (Bureau of Educational and Cultural Affairs, 1982).

It is important to note, however, that during the formative years of the Cold War, America initially attempted to bring India into the anti-Communist fold. Washington suspected that in the wake of the Comintern's 1949 call for revolutionary revolts all over the world, internal weaknesses of India and Pakistan and India's leadership tilt toward socialism and the Soviet Union might lead them to move into the Soviet camp. The Cold War compelled the United States to look to South Asia in search of its allies in struggle against a comprehensive threat. Its containment policy in South Asia aimed at helping India and Pakistan defend themselves against external attack, obtain bases and from which the United States might strike the Soviet Union with its own forces, and help both countries meet the threat from internal (often Communist-led) insurrection and subversion. The US strategists saw India as the "pivotal" state of the region and Pakistan as a useful place to base long range US bombers as well as a potential ally in the tense Persian Gulf region (for detail insight, see McMahon, 1994). The US Secretary of State John

Foster Dulles initially saw democratic India as a nation which could bring plausible equilibrium to a Communist China in Asia. The US envoy to India during the Eisenhower and Johnson administrations, Chester Bowles, was a champion of the idea that India should be seen not as a quasi-ally of the USSR but as a vast developing country that, in contrast to China, had chosen democracy over communism.

Even in Congress there was some consideration of India's interests. Senators such as Fulbright openly criticized the Eisenhower's administration and especially John Foster Dulles' decision of bringing Pakistan into the US-led military alliances and military assistance to Pakistan and termed it as "an unfortunate mistake" and strategic blunder that would not serve the United States' interest in the region and would lead to alienation of India and push India more toward Communism (McMahon, 1994, p. 173; also see Kux, 1992, pp. 99–138). Even those who favored Pakistan, such as H. Alexander Smith (R-N.J.), had apprehension that military help and arming Pakistan would result into a permanent crack on United States relationship with India. A bipartisan coalition supporting enhanced relations, which included Presidential aspirant John F. Kennedy (D-Mass.), was forged by Senator John Sherman Cooper (R-Ky.), a former ambassador to India from 1955 to 1956. As a sign of improved relations, US President Dwight D. Eisenhower became the first American President to visit India in 1959.

The United States' initial tilt toward India resulted in a massive and multifaceted approach by the United States to counter Soviet influence. The US adopted a strategy of economic aid, developmental programs including technological and agricultural operations, and pursued an information and intelligence gathering strategy to offset Soviet influence. There was an increase in US economic aid to India between 1957 and 1964. Economic aid was considerable during Eisenhower's second term. American economic assistance grew from about $400 million in 1957, to $822 million in 1960. In May 1960, Washington signed a $1.27 billion PL 480 food agreement for a four-year period with India (Kux, 1992, p. 150). In the view of the State Department, "South Asia became a testing ground for the free world. In this area will be determined whether nations can surmount tremendous economic and social problems, can achieve far-reaching changes in their entire pattern of life without resorting to the totalitarian system of communism" (U.S. Department of State, 1959).

The peak of the US–India relationship during the Cold War could be considered as the US support to India during Indo-China border conflict in 1962. John F. Kennedy came to office determined to pursue closer relations with India, a country he viewed as pivotal in the struggle between east and west, without undermining the US alliance with Pakistan. Jacquline Kennedy's goodwill diplomacy visit to India in 1962 had charmed the Indian politicians, including the Prime Minister Jawaharlal Nehru (Talbott, 2004, pp. 10–11).

India, by virtue of its size and economic problems, had the greatest needs of any of the developing nations. The Kennedy administration had scarcely settled into office when India requested that the United States take the lead in organizing international support for its third Five-Year Plan. On April 22, President Kennedy approved in principle a two-year commitment of up to $1 billion in support of the Indian economic program and agreed on a program of economic assistance for fiscal years 1961–1962 and 1962–1963 in excess of $2 billion. Kennedy's foreign aid request to Congress in the spring of 1961 called for $500 million in Economic support for India for fiscal year 1962 and only $400 million for the rest of the world. Prime Minister Nehru expressed his gratitude in a letter to President Kennedy and personally to Vice President Johnson (ibid.). This was the short period when these two countries came together for a shared strategic purpose, but it could not stop humiliating defeat that India had to suffer from China.

Arguably, the India–US relations approached the point of becoming an alliance during the Sino-Indian Border War. John F. Kennedy responded favorably to India when the border war broke out between China and India in 1962, the United States provided military supplies to India (also see Steele, 2002; Thakar, 1999, p. 230). India received military equipment, though not of very high quality, from the United States during its border conflict with China in 1962. India purchased about $55 million in military equipment from the United States. New Delhi also received $80 million in American grant military assistance after the 1962 India–China War (Ganguly, 1990, p. 97). These developments took place alongside the Cuban Missile Crisis, and collected events saw the US relief programs to India being extended from the early 1950s to mid-1960s. In total, from 1954 to 1964 American aid to India totaled $10 billion (Rubinoff, 2001, pp. 37–60). At the end of 1963, US–India relations were somewhat closer than they had been before Kennedy came to office.[1]

The improvement of US–India relations had, however, caused a deterioration of the US–Pakistan connection (Rubinoff, 2001, pp. 37–60). Though Pakistan was included in the US military alliance system, for the American strategists India remained the main prize. They saw India as the key battlefield in the Cold War as they assumed that the most significant fight in Asia was between India, a democracy and China, a communist country. Sometimes the US aid to India even surpassed aid to Pakistan. This was to the immeasurable irritation of Pakistan, which deemed that it was natural for Pakistan to receive more American aid and favorable treatment than India because of Pakistan's military alliance with the United States.

Despite its refusal to join any of American-sponsored alliances and pursuing its foreign policy of Non-Alignment, India received considerably more military and economic aid than Pakistan in economic loans and grants (although much less on a per capita basis; Cohen, 2000). The Kennedy administration discovered in particular that, because of the Kashmir dispute, closer relations with India came at the expense of relations with Pakistan. Pakistan responded by seeking a rapprochement with China. Recognizing that the Kashmir problem stood in the way of the success of its policy toward South Asia, the administration tried to no avail to encourage India and Pakistan to find a solution.[2]

Ultimately, the negative points bubbling below the surface in the US–India relationship outweighed this short bonhomie even before the US normalization of relations with China. Prime Minister Jawaharlal Nehru had opted for Non-Alignment and later sided with the Soviet Union, despite US efforts to forge friendly ties with India. This added to the negative perception about India. Nehru was

---

[1] U.S. Department of State, *South Asia*, Office of the Historian. *FRUS, XIX*, 1961–1963.

[2] U.S. Department of State, *South Asia*, Office of the Historian. *FRUS, XIX*, 1961–1963.

branded a "Crypto-Communist," and along with many of his associates and successors, he was thought to suffer from Russophilia and Sinomania. Such perceptions in part can be attributed to constant pressure and statements from Indian leftist leaders that India should keep its distance from the United States (for the leftist pressure on Nehru's foreign policy, see Debnath, 2009). Pointing toward this negative attitude toward the United States, John P. Lewis, who served as a high-ranking Agency for International Development (AID) officer in New Delhi, noted that "a majority" of key players in the White House, the State Department, and Congress were fundamentally anti-Indian (Lewis, 1995, p. 87).

The annual Congressional debates on foreign aid appropriations constantly brought forth a spate of criticism directed at India, whose policies were seen by many Congressmen as contrary to the US interests. Although a wheat loan agreement was signed in 1951, followed by a $53 million package of direct assistance, the bitter comments made in the course of prolonged debates "counteracted the goodwill that American aid in time of crisis would have otherwise produced" (for an elaboration, see Rubinoff, 1992b, pp. 63–73). The 1951 debates were particularly acrimonious. India's opposition to a United Nation (UN) General Assembly resolution on February 1, 1951 that branded China as the aggressor in Korea antagonized many Congressmen. Among those who expressed reservations about providing aid to a country that was perceived as voting against American interests was Senator Tom Connolly (D-Tex.), Chairman of the SFRC (Palmer, 1966, p. 10). Responding to a special message from President Truman recommending emergency assistance for India, a bipartisan group of 40 senators and representatives brought legislation demanding the immediate dispatch of one million tons of American surplus wheat and authorizing the eventual shipment of another million tons. Although the House Foreign Affairs Committee reported the bill favorably, conservatives on the Rules Committee blocked the measure until it was rewritten in the form of a loan. Finally, the SFRC reported a bill that was partly a loan and partly a grant (McMahon, 1994, p. 93).

In fact India's bonhomie with China during the Korean War led many on Capitol Hill to deem India unworthy of American economic assistance. William Knowland (R-Calif.), who later became majority leader, accused India of "giving aid and comfort to the enemy" (ibid., p. 15). The Battle Act of 1953, which barred American aid to any country that traded in strategic goods with Communist China, targeted India and became a source of acrimony in bilateral relations.[3] Obviously the move of India to support China was driven by Nehru's foreign policy forging an Asian solidarity and anti-colonialism plank.

India's friendly gesture toward Soviet Union and Asian solidarity was not liked in US foreign policy-making circles. John Foster Dulles termed India's neutrality as immoral and responded to India's move by making friendship with Pakistan and entering into military pacts. Pakistan since its emergence in 1947 began to look for parity with India. It found itself in a disadvantageous position vis-a-vis India on every measure, including size, population, and wealth. Pakistan did not lose this opportunity to befriend the United States and responded positively to Dulles' initiatives. Consequently Pakistan strengthened its military ties with the United States and its allies such as Great Britain with a series of agreements, starting in 1954. In addition to the 1954 United States–Pakistani Mutual Security Agreement, Pakistan joined the SEATO in 1954, the Baghdad Pact (which became the CENTO, in 1958). India viewed the American defence relationship with Pakistan as a direct threat to its own security, which in turn had a detrimental effect on Indo-American relations. Congressmen were suspicious of India's democratic credentials as Indian leaders articulated a socialist form of democracy. The apparent sympathy many members of the Indian National Congress had for the Soviet Union. Doubts about India's sympathies were again raised in 1956 during the Suez crisis and the Soviet invasion of Hungary. Whereas the United States and India both condemned Britain, France, and Israel for their invasion of the Suez Canal, Nehru was reluctant to criticize Khrushchev's decision to use military force in Hungary. Most Americans inferred this as the height of hypocrisy on the part of Indian Government (Rotter, 2000, p. 70). As a result it was difficult task to convince Congressmen that it was in American interests to increase humanitarian aid to India in

---

[3] Prime Minister Nehru explicitly stated that his country could not allow "the United States to tell India with whom it could trade as a price of aid" (Kux, 1992, p. 124).

order to blunt Soviet influence in the region as well as to check India from falling behind China in economic development, which might lead to the loss of hundreds of millions of Indians to Communism (Thakar, 1999, p. 230).

In 1959 the United States and Pakistan signed a bilateral executive security agreement (Steele, 2002). Pakistan also received significant military and economic aid as a result of its inclusion American military alliances in the period 1954–1965. This included a $630 million in grant military assistance for weapons, $619 million for defence assistance (construction of facilities, and salary support for designated units), and $55 million worth of equipment purchased on a cash or concessional basis (Cohen, 1984, pp. 138–139; Kux, 1992, p. 150). Eisenhower's decision to strengthen relations with the Pakistani military Government rather than entering ties with Indian democratic Government was not in keeping with the rhetoric of the Cold War that democratic principles were to be defended no matter the cost (Brands, 1990, p. 99). Certainly the 1954 alliance with Pakistan reinforced Indian suspicions that "the Western countries themselves had combined with or opposed communism out of political expediency and not moral principle" (Singh, 1993, p. 161). The suspicion among the Indian policy makers about the imperialistic and hegemonic design of the United States resurfaced when the Washington reacted negatively to the merger of Goa in India on December 1961. Showing its disapproval, the SFRC tried, over the objections of President Kennedy, to cut the 1962 foreign aid appropriation to India by 25 percent (Rubinoff, 1971, p. 103).

Relations took a downturn after 1962 and came to a turning point in 1965. In 1963 Congressional conservatives, who had been hostile toward India, reneged on a $500 million public sector steel plant at Bokaro, in the state of Bihar (now in the separated state of Jharkhand), that was to be the showcase of Western aid. A seven-volume report-produced at a cost of $686,000 by a US Steel team for AID—had the effect of providing an opportunity for Congressional opponents of the Bokaro endeavor to embarrass the Kennedy administration. In August 1963, the House attached a provision to its foreign aid authorization bill forbidding any allocation of more than $100 million to a public sector project without specific Congressional authorization (Palmer, 1966, p. 150). The reluctance of the US Congress to build a "socialist" steel mill with capitalist dollars enabled the Soviet Union to fill the breach as it did in the case of the Aswan Dam in Egypt at the time of Suez Crisis. The American decision on Bokaro led India to cancel an agreement to share radio transmitters with Voice of America (Rubinoff, 2001, pp. 37–60).

In some respects, the 1965 Indo-Pak War, which resulted in the first of four arms embargoes to the region, was a turning point in Washington's dealings with the subcontinent. Due to the slow progress toward global détente after the Cuban Missile Crisis, for the first time regional considerations started acquiring importance and began to prevail over global Cold War equations. But it did not turnout in India's favor, and regional calculations worked against India. The United States tilted more definitely toward Pakistan in 1971 and the second arms embargo to the region during the Indo-Pak war leading to creation of Bangladesh (U.S. Congress, House Committee on Foreign Affairs, 1973). The United States also decided to send the carrier USS Enterprise into the Bay of Bengal in 1971. The United States aversion toward India at that time can best be understood from a conversation between President R. Nixon and national security advisor Henry Kissinger during Indo-Pak war of 1971. President Nixon, in fact, said that Indians were "a slippery, treacherous people." Kissinger's assessment in return was no better. "They are the most aggressive god-damn people around. They are plotting a war," he said. Despite horrifying reports of brutal repression unleashed by then Pakistani Army in the East Pakistan, the Nixon administration adopted a "hands off policy." Not only did the United States secretly encouraged China to move its military forces toward the Indian border, it assured China protection if the Soviet Union made any moves against it for menacing India.[4]

After 1971 Indo-Pak conflict, India and USSR entered into the treaty of peace, friendship, and cooperation in 1971. This led to further estrangement of the relationship between India and the United States. Washington showed uneasiness whenever Moscow

---

[4] The documents declassified and available at the US National Archives and the Presidential Library system detail how United States policy, directed by Richard Nixon and Henry Kissinger, followed a course that became infamously known as "The Tilt" (Gandhi, 2002; also see Pandit, 2005).

took a political or economic step indicating its closeness with New Delhi, but it was the 1971 treaty that determined the US perception of India for the next two decades (Mahapatra, 1998, p. 45). This strategic development not only alienated them, but also sustained the negative perception about India among many in US foreign policy-making circles. In the 1960s and 1970s, legislators such as Otto Passman (D-La.) and Clarence Long (D-Md.) ensured that the appropriations subcommittees that they chaired only grudgingly provided aid to a country that seldom agreed with American positions on global issues.

American interest in South Asia in general began to dwindle and US aid to the region went down (Valero, 1976). Ambassador Daniel Patrick Moynihan termed Washington's approach as one of "benign neglect" and as ambassador to India in the mid-1970s, he reduced the size of the US diplomatic establishment there, negotiated an agreement to forgive the significant sums that India owed the United States in payment for foodstuffs, and presided over American disengagement in the region. India invited the ire of members of Congress over issues such as the detonation of a nuclear device in May 1974 and human rights violations during Premiership of Indira Gandhi's Emergency rule, during the Khalistan movement and in reaction to Kashmir unrest (U.S. Congress, House Committee on International Relations, 1976). Both Democrats and Republicans criticized India's handling of these secessionist movements.

After the Vietnam War, Congress suffered from "foreign aid fatigue." Liberals, such as Representative Jonathan Bingham (D-N.Y.), began making arguments that had formerly been advanced by conservatives, such as Owen Brewster (R-Maine). They held that billions of dollars in American assistance to India had resulted in resentment rather than benefits, and had been responsible for a corresponding reduction in money for US domestic programs. Every consideration of an AID authorization became an occasion for Congress to demonstrate its displeasure with New Delhi's ungratefulness for US aid. Pakistan was portrayed as a frontline state with 2.5 million refugees, while India was seen as one of the most "persistently anti-United States members" of the UN, as it had endorsed Soviet positions on Cuba, Kampuchea, Nicaragua, and especially Afghanistan.

Several Democrats, resentful of India's support of the Soviet-backed regime in Kabul, joined Republicans to punish India for its stand on the Afghan issue. The conservative Representative William Broomfield (R-Mich.), a ranking member of the Foreign Affairs Committee and a critic of India for a generation, succeeded by a vote of 18–14 in pushing through an amendment that cut developmental assistance to New Delhi from $50 million to $35 million in 1987. Even after the end of the Cold War these perceptions lingered in the US legislative and executive branch well into the 1990s. The nuclear issues emerged as an important irritant in the last two decades of the Cold War. The situation of the Sikhs in the Punjab and the ensuing civil war in Kashmir added a human rights dimension to bilateral relations in the 1980s. Since 1993, Rep. William Goodling (R-Pa.) brought legislation each year aimed at denying assistance to countries that refuse to support American positions in the UN General Assembly. In 1992 Rep. Dan Burton won approval in the House for a bill to eliminate aid to India, but it never became law (Rubinoff, 2001, pp. 37–60). Burton, emerged as the strongest critic of India on Hill, every year introduced the bill to stop aid to India and has been vocal against India on many issues in Congressional debate.

During the Cold War the American military and economic aid to India was often debated and faced hurdles in the US legislative and executive branch. It was often attacked based on negative perceptions that were dominant among the US policy makers and in the American society at large. Robert Dahl has argued that the US legislative branch more often represents public perception attitudes more closely than the executive branch does. His finding showed that Congressional attitudes tend to be persistent, consistent, and shared (Dahl, 1950, p. 15). Harold Isaacs assigns perception to be a significant factor in the bilateral relationship between the two nations when they share a nominal common history or political interaction (Isaacs, 1980, p. xxxiii).

The common understanding about Indians among the general public had an influence on US policy makers. John Mellor notes that US policy is the product of stereotypes, in which India is portrayed "as poverty-stricken and helpless" (Mellor, 1979, p. 359). Nixon's personal disliking for India and Prime Minister Indira Gandhi during 1970s was also shaped by the negative perceptions about

India that existed among Americans in general. This is well known and the declassified Document 4 of his conversation with Chinese Prime Minister Zhou Enlai during the Bangladesh War in 1971 illustrates this. While reflecting upon the Germans, the Japanese, and the Chinese, who were seen to have qualities of drive and hard work, Nixon made derogatory remarks about the Indians' breeding habits, laziness, lack of sense of purpose, and determination. Nixon held that "the money goes down a rat hole in countries like India" and regretted that "the more aid we have given, the less influence we have."[5] Not surprising, during the 1971 Bangladesh crisis, President Richard Nixon's inclination toward Pakistan "was influenced by his long-standing disliking for India and the Indians" (Hoellen, 1980, p. 341). American Presidents had a disliking for India's neutralism (Castro versus the Eisenhower Administration, 2015) and they found it to be a weak and unethical stand in international politics. A similar sentiment was expressed by President Lyndon Johnson, who "regarded Indians as weak and indecisive" (Bjorkman, 1980, p. 234).

Arthur G. Rubinoff asserts that, like the general public, most members of Congress get their news and impressions from the media. Their information about India is neither adequate nor accurate (Rubinoff, 2001, pp. 37–60). It was further exacerbated by the ignorance by the American bureaucratic structure. The US Department of State's regional bureau, the European Bureau, was elevated in the internal hierarchy for almost for six decades. The Middle East, or as it was known, the "Far East," also attracted a great deal of attraction. South Asia was paired with the Far East in the State Department, but South Asia rarely attracted as much attention (Rudolph, L.I. and Rudolph, S., 2008, p. 37), except for negative and unflattering reasons.

The complaint has arisen that, although India had one of the world's largest populations and one of the largest military establishments, the United States does not take it seriously (Nayar, 1975, pp. 133–154). Also India did not figure as important in the strategic calculus around American foreign policy priorities, which was

---

[5] TopSecret/Sensitive/ExclusivelyEyesOnly. Retrieved 12 July 2015, from http://www.gwu.edu/~nsarchiv/nsa/publications/DOC_readers/kissinger/nixzhou/14-01.htm, Declassified Document 4, p. 28.

mainly the containment of communism. Furthermore, India hardly offered any significant natural resources such as oil reserves. Myron Weiner clearly explained why Americans accorded South Asia such a low priority:

> Its geo-political position raises no fundamental problems for American security...unlike China. India has no deep cultural or historic links with America, and unlike the countries of Western Europe, Israel and Greece, no significant segment of the American population originates from nor has an enduring association with the region. In short, none of the elements exist that attract the daily concerns of the President, Congress, the press, or the foreign policy publics (Myron Weiner, 1976, p. 65).

The negative perceptions about India in the US Congress, apart from the tradition of Indian and foreign scholars criticizing India for its crippling and disfiguring social and political ills,[6] can be attributed to the misunderstanding on the part of strategists and policy makers of both the countries. There was always a group in India who thought that India was already a great power and soon the whole world would acknowledge it and its emergence as the world power as a matter of course. The Americans failed to acknowledge this purported Indian greatness, which was inherently defined in civilizational terms. This failure can be attributed to American obsession with the Cold War, ignorance, cultural parochialism, and to the inability of the Indian Government to project a suitable image or to fully explain India's value as a major contributor to world history and development. In fact, the need of that period was that the Americans needed to be better informed and educated about the futility of the Cold War, and about the arts, culture, and history of India (Cohen, 2002, p. 3).

Sulochana Raghavan Glazer and Nathan Glazer are of the view that American perceptions—including indifference, hostility, resentment, and disdain have had even more effect than security interests

---

[6] India's stagnation, internal conflict, and disorder have been themes of many books, including those by number of American correspondents based in India (see Nossiter, 1970; Harrison, 1960; Crossette, 1993).

in shaping US policy toward South Asia. They assign this to India being on wrong side in the World War II and the Cold War. Despite millions of Indian soldiers serving in the British army, the Indian National Congress refused to support the war against the Axis powers as long as London would not promise independence. Prime Minister Jawaharlal Nehru was viewed as "clearly pro-Russian," and Indian nonalignment was seen as "a major obstacle to the US efforts to rally and unite the free nations of Asia in the struggle against Soviet world domination" (Glazer and Glazer, 1990, p. 4). On the Indian side, the government officials needed to make better use of lobbying process to convey the positive perceptions about India. The trace of any planned lobbying effort either by Indian Government, Indian American, or any prominent US Congressman to rectify this negative image of India was missing. From time to time, some Senators and Representatives did show concern about ignoring and alienating India at the cost of Pakistan or due to Cold War politics. However, the lobbying came from Congressmen such as Rep. Dalip Singh Saund of Indian origin and Rep. Stephen Solarz, and they focused on raising concern about ignoring India and raised voice for India.

AMERICAN INTERESTS, FOREIGN ASSISTANCE, AND LOBBYING

This negative perception about India was very much reflected during the debate on the two important issues of foreign assistance and nuclear power and weapons in the Cold War period. Such sentiments lingered until the last decade of the twentieth century. In the Cold War period there was hardly any significant lobbying effort by the Indian Government and by the Congressmen in the United States as well. The first voice of Indian–American community heard in the US Congress was that of Dalip Singh Saund. He was an immigrant to the Central Valley of California and represented a significant Sikh community who had migrated there in the 1930s and had become prosperous farmers over time. He was the first Asian American, Indian American, and Sikh member of the US House of Representatives and served the 29th district of the state of California from January 3, 1957–January 3, 1963. During his tenure as Congressman (1957–1958), Saund moved a resolution in the House of Representatives which read: "It is the desire, hope and expression of the Congress that nations receiving military assistance (from the USA) under the mutual security program guarantee to their people freedom of speech, freedom of religion and freedom of press." He cautioned that the fair face of the United States "as the champion of democratic way of life" would be blurred should she be "obliged to give military aid to countries ruled by dictators" (Saund, 1960, pp. 186–88).

In Saund's statement implied criticism of Washington giving arms and aid to Pakistan is traceable. Pakistan was seen to be a dictatorial country and where the freedom of religion had little space. This could be considered as the very first lobbying effort by an Indian American or lobbying on behalf of India in the US Congress. As an Indian–American activist, Saund utilized his political position and clout in countering anti-India lobbying as much as he could do under the constraints of the time.

Another Congressman who spoke for India and actively worked for the betterment of the US–India relations was Stephen Solarz (D-N.Y.), a nine-term Democratic Congressman who was first elected to the House in 1974 (Martin, 2010). Before his arrival on the foreign affairs committee due to a major reorganization of subcommittees in 1970, the House treated South Asia as an afterthought in many ways. Similar to the State Department, South Asia was often paired with the Near East as the domain of a subcommittee of the House Foreign Affairs Committee. This meant South Asia was generally overshadowed by Arab–Israeli matters. At other times South Asia was coupled with the Asia–Pacific region and consequently dwarfed by concerns such as the Vietnam War, and US bilateral relations with China and Japan. It was during Stephen Solarz Chairmanship (1981–1993) that committee interest in South Asian issues reached an all-time high (Rubinoff, 2001, pp. 37–60). Solarz had a positive outlook about India, and he was the sole voice for India in 1970s and 1980s in the US Congress who could be considered as a lobbyist for India. He had a positive impact on the US–India relations and often raised his voice for India when no other Congressman did. He was an influential Congressman whose voice mattered in foreign affairs and nuclear issues. He was given a standing ovation in the Indian Parliament for his contribution in redressing the negative perception about India in the US Congress, and for his constructive efforts toward the betterment of US–India relations.

However, in the 1980s India had to resort to lobbying after the US decision to sale of F-16 fighter aircrafts to Pakistan in the wake of Soviet invasion of Afghanistan. For a long time, the Government of India had a ubiquitous one-man lobbying operation in the capital— the late Janaki Nath Ganju served as India's on-again, off-again lobbyist. Rep. Stephen Solarz too played an active role in lobbying for India and opposing the sale of F-16 fighter aircraft to Pakistan. As India finally began to embrace the lobbying challenge on Capitol Hill, the Indian embassy hired a public relations outfit, Barron and Canning, to help it mount its anti-F-16 campaign (Keshavan, 1998). Though India lost its first lobbying battle, by this time it had started to realize the importance of lobbying in US foreign policy making. This was also the time when American Association of Physicians of Indian Origin (AAPI) had begun to show its presence as result of its growing economic clout and influence in the America. By the late 1980s the Indian lobbying effort had begun to register its presence at Hill and Stephen Solarz had emerged as lone but very vocal and powerful ally of India in the US foreign policy-making circle.

NUCLEAR NONPROLIFERATION TREATY, INDIA'S NUCLEAR INSUBORDINATION, AND LOBBYING

The nuclear issue, the Nuclear Non-Proliferation Treaty (NNPT), and India's nuclear test became an important issue in the US–India relations. In the post-Independence period India developed an excellent pool of nuclear scientists and could have soon tested a nuclear explosion. But it chose a policy of peaceful use of nuclear technology and made calls for complete nuclear disarmament. But during the Sino-India War in 1962, India suffered a humiliating defeat and its defence preparedness was badly exposed. The military support that came from the United States during the war was not sufficient to defend itself against Chinese attack. Finally the Chinese nuclear test in 1964 prompted India to rethink the nuclear option. When the NNPT was introduced to check nuclear proliferation,

India was from day one critical of it. India found it discriminatory in that it sought to create a nuclear order of "Nuclear Haves" and "Nuclear Have Nots." It allowed five countries, the United States, the USSR, England, France, and China, to continue to possess nuclear weapons while others would not be allowed to. India felt that the international community was unconcerned and unmindful of India's security threat. As a result, India opposed the NNPT and refused to sign it. Since then, the nuclear issue became a constant irritant in Indo-US relations. As the United States was in the forefront and was determined to make this nuclear regime successful, it found India a constant hurdle. As India did not sign NNPT, Pakistan also refused to sign the treaty.

The nuclear issue only added to further negative perceptions about India in the United States. Debates in Congress since 1970s reflected this perception among the Congressman. India's nuclear dalliance with the United States actually goes back to 1950s and in 1963 a 30-year nuclear cooperation agreement was signed with India in 1963 under which the United States pledged to help with the construction and provide for the refueling of the twin reactors at Tarapur near Bombay. But when India and Pakistan refused to sign the NNPT in 1968, alarm bells went off both in the White House and on Capitol Hill, resulting in calls for sanctions and restrictions designed to compel Indian and Pakistani conformity to the treaty. The din reached a crescendo after the 1974 Pokhran explosion. Ever since India's 1974 detonation, its possession of nuclear weapons has been the dominant issue in relations with the United States.

Since the 1974 Pokhran nuclear test, the US policy toward India has been centered on nonproliferation, and primarily it has not been focused on economic aid, diplomacy, or military sales or assistance, but on technological embargoes and economic sanctions (Cohen, 2002, p. 283). In the 1980s, many of India's friends in Congress felt compelled to advance the cause of nuclear nonproliferation at the expense of bilateral ties with New Delhi. South Asia became a testing ground for global nonproliferation aspirations (Palmer, 1966, p. 216). The United States threatened to cut off foreign aid and reliable supplies of nuclear materials if international safeguards were violated. India argued that the United States has not applied similar standards to China and Israel. Successive US administrations offered incentives to India, while Congress imposed sanctions (Galbraith, 1990). In 1974 the Ford administration withheld fuel shipments to the Tarapur nuclear plant until it could determine that American materials had not been used in the Indian detonation. In a move that embarrassed the administration, Congress instructed the US representative to the International Development Agency to refrain from voting for loans to countries that had exploded nuclear weapons but had not signed the NNPT—a provision that applied exclusively to India. When Prime Minister Morarji Desai, of the short-lived Janata government, promised that India would not develop nuclear weapons or conduct further tests, Congress repealed the prohibition, and aid to India resumed (Rubinoff, 2001, pp. 37–60).

Jimmy Carter made nonproliferation the center piece of his foreign policy (until the Soviet invasion of Afghanistan). South Asia became the target of US nonproliferation legislation that included technology denials and sanctions (Cohen, 2002, p. 283). Congress passed the Symington and Glenn Amendments, sections 669 and 670 of the Foreign Assistance Acts of 1976 and 1977, which prohibited aid or arms sales to countries that delivered or received nuclear enrichment equipment or technology and did not accept International Atomic Energy Agency (IAEA) safeguards. As a result of evidence that Pakistan—which had just undergone a military coup—was engaged in such activities, the United States terminated assistance to that country for the third time in April 1979 (Rubinoff, 2001, pp. 37–60). However, in the wake of Soviet invasion of Afghanistan, the nuclear proliferation concern took a backstage in terms of policy priority on Capitol Hill, and the United States ignored clandestine Chinese proliferation and transfer of nuclear technology to Pakistan, and the secret development of a Pakistani nuclear weapons program.

To compensate for the sale of F-16 fighter jets aircraft to Pakistan, Carter administration approved export licenses for two fuel shipments and spare parts for India's Tarapur reactor, notwithstanding a claim by the Nuclear Regulatory Commission that India had not met the criteria set forth by the 1978 Nuclear Nonproliferation Act. The Reagan administration in 1982 helped negotiate an end to the Tarapur stalemate by getting France to shoulder the commitment to supply fuel. In 1983, Secretary of State George Shultz guaranteed that Washington would be the supplier of last resort. But the negative perception that existed on Capitol Hill again resurfaced during a Senate effort to overturn Shultz's commitment. Stephen Solarz lobbied for India by thwarting it in conference. Solarz, also weakened an amendment by Senator Rudolph Boschwitz (R.-Minn.) that would have undermined the Reagan administration's decision of supply of fuel to India (ibid., pp. 37–60).

In the 1980s, a change in Indo-US relations was visible, especially in the defence sector. In the wake of Soviet intervention in Afghanistan, the United States offered to sell American military hardware to India as well. An Indian team visited the United States in 1980 to explore the possibility of buying tube-launched, optically tracked, wire-guided (TOW) anti-tank missiles and long range howitzers. The Carter administration reversed its earlier policy of disapproving the use of an advanced American electronic guidance system in India's Jaguar aircraft (Sharma, 2008). In the nuclear field it approved two more enriched uranium fuel shipments to Tararpur. It appeared as if Carter was providing incentives to India in the wake of the Afghanistan crisis so that India did not move further toward the Soviet Union. This worry was salient as a result of improving Sino–US ties, and the rearming of Pakistan with US weapons. As India was seeking to diversify its sources of military acquisition, scientific, and technical co-operation and trade and investment destinations, improvement of relations with the United States was considered to be important. A Memorandum of Understanding was signed between the United States and India in 1984 on transfer of technology. In exchange for alterations to India's own export-control regulations, the United States would begin allowing access to civilian and dual-use technologies as well as some military assistance, subject to previous restrictions imposed by US law. Under this agreement, sensitive technology transfer took place (for detail, see, Mahapatra, 1998). India received Super Computers, General Electric F-404 engines for the light combat aircrafts (LCA) program (Cupitt and Gahlaut, 1999), LM-2500 gas turbine engines for upgrading Indian naval vessels, night vision devices for tanks (as well as permission to co-produce the devices), co-production of the Northrop Corporation TF-5 aircraft in India, and a F-5 tooling facility for 5 percent of original cost. In terms of export licenses issued by the US in 1987, India ranked number seven (Saksena and

Grillot, 1999, pp. 154–155). In the period 1984–1988, there was a five-fold increase in US Government approvals of civilian technology exports to India (for details, see Chellaney, 1993, p. 202). The MoU led to a surge of technology licenses to Indian Companies and government institutions, but mainly for the items that were below the level of state-of-the-art technology.

Since 1985, policy makers in the Reagan Administration began to use the term "opening to India" to improve relations with India. The US Defence Secretary C. Weinberger visited India in 1986 and 1987, and C. Weinberger's successor Frank Carlucci in 1988 indicated a US desire to forge closer ties with India. A new beginning started in Indo-US defence co-operation in 1989 when along with the official dialogue India also resorted to Track II diplomacy. The Defence Minister of India in his visit to the United States was accompanied by high-level civilian and armed services officials. This visits served as a major effort to remove mutual misperceptions and enhance understanding among the strategic communities in both the countries.

However, this 1980s development in the US–India relations was more because of strategic consideration than change in perception due to lobbying. The negative perception about India still existed on the Hill. It was obvious from the fact that despite Pakistani nuclear weapon development, its Pro-Pakistani lobbyists were able to harm India's interests. Pakistani atomic development had become a serious issue in the US legislative and executive branch after and a Pakistani-born Canadian citizen, Arshad Parvez, and a Pakistani citizen, Nazir Vaid were found purchasing special steel alloys for nuclear purposes and smuggling krytons. Congress passed a measure in 1985 jointly introduced by Representative [Stephen] Solarz and Senator Larry Pressler stipulating that American assistance should immediately be cut off if the president found that a country had tried to illegally acquire American material for making nuclear weapons (Rubinoff, 1992a). The Pressler Amendment of 1985 (Section 620E of the Foreign Assistance Act of 1961), required annual presidential certification that Pakistan did not possess a nuclear device and the US assistance to Pakistan would immediately be cut off if the president found that Pakistan had attempted to illegally acquire American material for making nuclear weapons. When press reports, including claims by Pakistani scientists and officials, and independent evidence indicated that Islamabad's bomb was near completion, some members of Congress, including John Glenn, Chairman of the Senate Government Operations Committee, attempted to terminate the administration's six-year, $4.02 billion Pakistani aid package. Working through Senate appropriations subcommittee that was dominated by its chair, Robert Kasten (R-Wis.), and his predecessor, Daniel Inouye (D-Hawaii), lobbyists for the Pakistani embassy succeeded in cutting off all aid to India until foreign assistance to Islamabad was restored. The ability of Pakistan to induce Congress temporarily to cut off aid to India in 1987, when its own funding was in jeopardy for embarking on a nuclear weapons program, was testimony to the strength of its influence on Capitol Hill and New Delhi's lack of influence (ibid., pp. 167–73). It demonstrated India's ignorance of the importance of lobbying in the US foreign policy making, which its adversary had realized from the beginning.

It has been pointed out by foreign policy analysts and Congressional sources that the political wing of the Indian Embassy in Washington was not as knowledgeable as one would expect, and their understanding and grasp of the US policy process was superficial. In fact, they adopted a short-term knee-jerk reaction approach to many intricate and important issues that eventually affected India negatively in the long run. Despite being aware of the significance of lobbying in US policy making, the Indian Government and diplomats ignored the need of lobbying and displayed a curious antipathy toward the very idea of lobbying on Capitol Hill to shape US policy toward India. Perhaps Indian strategists needed to realize that, despite not being in US military pacts and alliances, they could still have at least mitigated the negative perception about India and thwarted anti-Indian lobbying. It could be also considered as sheer arrogance and a symptom of an unprofessional attitude among the Indian Government and its diplomats that they considered taking the help of lobbying firms to tackle their diplomatic hurdles in Washington as being equal to confessing their personal ineptness. They should have learnt from the past positive role of American President such as Franklin D. Roosevelt in pressurizing Britain for expediting the Indian Independence process by appealing to the liberal audience of America, and they could have attempted to change the negative perception about India. It can be also interpreted that the moral and civilizational-based sense of superiority that Indian political elites harbored in their attitude did not allow them to resort to such tactics of lobbying.

THE END OF THE COLD WAR AND THE EMERGENCE OF INDIAN LOBBYING

The defeat of Soviet forces in Afghanistan and breakdown of the Soviet Union brought an end to the Cold War, thus bringing an end to the ideological divide between the United States and India. The fallout of this development was the declining strategic importance of Pakistan in the US strategic framework, and a better convergence of interests between India and the United States. The disintegration of the Soviet Union and the end of the Cold War changed much of the international alliance structures of the Cold War era leading to the establishment of US unipolar primacy.

The implications became increasingly clear. During the Gulf War, in a significant departure from the Cold War paradigm, India allowed US military planes to refuel at Bombay's Sahar Airport to liberate Kuwait from Iraqi military occupation. Despite good relations with Iraq, India took a firm position and condemned the Iraqi invasion of Kuwait and demanded immediate withdrawal of Iraqi forces from Kuwait. India also adhered to all 12 mandatory UNSC resolutions on sanctions against Iraq and took effective steps to implement them. A positive trend emerged in the defence relationship between the US and India, and efforts were undertaken to increase the reciprocal exchange of information and personnel. This was part of an envisaged attempt to improve defence cooperation between the Army, Navy, and Air force and to enhance greater US–India military-to-military interaction. This military-to-military relationship developed in the April 1991 under "Kickleighter Proposals," so named because of the support of Commander of the US Army in the Pacific, Claude Kickleighter. These proposals were further formalized by the "Agreed Minute on Defence Cooperation" in January 1995. The changing perception was visible in the White House too, as President George Bush turned down a proposal which sought to verify that Pakistan was not involved in making and acquiring nuclear weapons and as a result US assistance to Islamabad was deferred.

However, if one looks at the immediate post-Cold War attitude of US policy makers toward India, it did not much change, despite new Russia no longer being seen as an immediate threat to the United States. The Cold War mindset still lingered in the minds of many who mattered in US foreign policy-making circles, especially in the legislative branch. This was obvious from Congressman Dan Burton still continuing his annual bills to cut down aid to India, the first Assistant Secretary of State for South Asian Affairs Robin Raphel's controversial remarks on Kashmir, and the passing of the Brown Amendment which provided relaxation to the rules in Pressler Amendment. The issues such as the signing of the Comprehensive Test Ban Treaty (CTBT), the Kashmir issue, and alleged human rights violations by the Indian armed forces provided fodder to those Congressmen to continue with their negative attitude toward India.

However, it began to change in the mid-1990s due to the formation of India Caucus, the increasing political activism by Indian Americans, and the lobbying firms hired by India. In the meantime, India's economic liberalization allowed increased interaction between the business communities of both the nations. It not only infused trust and confidence, but also paved the way for a better perception about India in America. This growing political activism of Indian Americans in US politics combined with supposed business opportunities for US companies brought a fundamental change in Congressional attitudes and policy approach toward New Delhi. It was the beginning of positive and constructive approach among the Congressmen about India. By this time the Congressmen began to realize that an engaged bilateral ties with India could bring better prospects for America economically and politically as well. As observed by James A. Robinson, the changed perception had two instant outcomes: It prompted greater Congressional interest in South Asia, and it led to a dramatic shift in Congressional outlook toward India (Robinson, 1967, p. 7).

India had lost its political and military ally with the demise of the Soviet Union and the economy was on the threshold of bankruptcy. Against this background, India was forced to reorient its foreign and economic policy in the newly changed international system that was a unipolar world led by the United States (Pant, 2009). One of the most striking features of this reformulation of foreign and economic policy was India's opening up of economy and engagement with the United States. The structural changes in the international order provided a platform for the United States and India to converge. The Indian economic liberalization of 1990s led to the opening of its market, and allowed greater interaction between the Indian and the US business communities. It built on the professional success of Indian Americans, and lobbying efforts by Indian lobbying firms, Indian Americans and India Caucus members, began to change much of the negative perceptions about India among US policy makers (see Hathaway, 2001), which in turn cemented the improving trajectory of the US–India bilateral relations.

In fact the importance of lobbying in US foreign policy was better understood around this time. There emerged a consensus among both leading national parties, the Indian National Congress and the Bharatiya Janata Party (BJP), to improve the relationship with the US. Prime Minister P.V. Narsimha Rao and Finance Minister Man Mohan Singh were both instrumental in shaping India's foreign and economic policy toward the US in the beginning of the post-Cold War period. The ostrich attitude, that abhorred the idea of lobbying in the United States, changed when the Indian Government posted Sidhartha Shankar Ray, a hardnosed politician, as the Indian envoy at Washington. He was instrumental in hiring a professional outfit, Rafaelli, Springer, Spees, and Smith, which later came to be known as the Washington Group. Also with the help of Stephen Solarz, initiatives were taken to establish Political Action Committee (PAC) for India on the pattern of American Israel Public Affairs Committee (AIPAC). By this time, the Indian–American community had emerged as a professionally successful community and had begun to show their willingness to transform its economic and professional achievements into political activism by lobbying for the Indian–American community interests and contributing toward the India–US relations.

It was in 1990s when Indian Americans took the anti-India lobbying activities by Pakistani Americans seriously. Consequently, they also started making use of their economic and political clout in America to lobby for India in the United States. In the beginning phase, roughly 1990 up to 1998 when India conducted its nuclear test, Indian lobbying did not achieve significant success, but made its presence felt for the first time. Indian lobbying was new and was not able to stop its adversary Pakistani lobbying. The India Caucus that was formed with just six members was too small in number and had yet to attract significant number of members in the House. The Indian–Americans had begun to assert themselves politically, but there was not enough political participation. There was still too few influential Indian–American political organizations dedicated to the cause of lobbying for the US–India relations. The US–India relationship was still struggling to come out of the Cold War prism, issues like signing of CTBT, Kashmir issue, human rights, and lingering negative perceptions about India, kept creating a political environment which was not vey conducive and favorable for Indian lobbying efforts. Nevertheless, Indian–American lobbying efforts did achieve some success in countering anti-India legislation. This was true in the case of Dan Burton's legislation and anti-Indian public relations efforts undertaken by Pakistani American lobbying groups.

However, despite apparent positive developments, the US–India relationship did not improve quickly, except perhaps in the field of defence cooperation. That too was limited to exchange of military personals and a couple of exercises. It was expected that the Clinton administration would build on the foundation established by its predecessor, welcome India's economic liberalization, and improve the US–India relations.

Contrary to this expectation, the United States reduced its foreign aid appropriations by 20 percent, reneged on the delivery of promised cryogenic rocket engines to India, and began renewing certain types of commercial sales to Pakistan that Congress had previously prohibited by the Pressler Amendment. A notable reason for this low level of improvement in the relationship was due to the Clinton administration's emphasis on nuclear nonproliferation and the signing of CTBT, on which India was not ready to sign. Other barriers included the passage of Brownback Amendment that would allow the sale of F-16 fighter aircrafts to Pakistan; the election of Benazir Bhutto as Prime minister of Pakistan, who was well connected in Washington; India's left and socialist mixed government in 1996, which was not very inclined toward the relationship with the United

States; the human rights issues in Kashmir and Punjab; the lack of diplomatic contact in 1990s; and Robin Raphel's unfriendly remarks against India. To top this off, India's nuclear test in 1998 kept the relationship between the United States and India from blossoming.

Nevertheless, Indian lobbying began to consolidate and take shape on three fronts. The professional success and economic achievement of Indian Americans led to their growing interest in political activism. The formation of the India Caucus was critical, as were the lobbying firms hired by India. It seemed that India had realized the importance of lobbying to engage the lone super power. This could be considered as the first phase of Indian lobbying. Their strategy was mainly focused on tackling anti-India lobbying on Capitol Hill and changing the negative image of India that persisted in US policy-making circles for the last four decades. The next chapter deals with the final arrival of Indian lobbying after India's nuclear defiance in 1998, during the negotiations over a US–India nuclear deal, and the overall impact of lobbying on the US–India relations.

6

Achievements and Actions of Indian Lobbying toward a Transformed and Robust US–India Relation

One of the critical outcomes of the fall of the Soviet Union and its absence from global strategic framework was the necessity for India to engage with the United States in a more effective manner. Other factors were also responsible for this development, such as the dire economic situation the country found itself in the early 1990s. Economic liberalization resulted in the opening of the market in India, which in turn allowed for greater interaction between the Indian and the US business communities. This was a factor that cemented the new bilateral relationship as India's rapidly growing economy would make India a more attractive economic partner for the US business.

Furthermore, amidst the hopes created in new strategic environment after the end of the Cold War (Thakur, 1996), both India and the US began to carve out a new relationship in the defence and strategic arena too. The concurrent growth of India's military capability has resulted in many American analysts starting to see India as a potential balancer in the Asian region. The US also faces threats relating to Islamic terrorism and thus has a common cause to fight against the terrorism in South Asia, in particular. These developments have together created a platform for the United States and India to come together and forge a sound partnership.

But the role of lobbying has been critical in accelerating and facilitating the development of a strategically robust bilateral relationship. This includes lobbying by economically affluent and professionally successful Indian Americans, by their political organizations such as the US–India Political Action Committee (USINPAC), Indian American Forum for Political Education (IAFPE), Indian-American

Committee for Political Awareness, the members of the Indo-American Chambers of Commerce (IACC) in several major cities such as Dallas, Houston, Detroit, Texas, and so on, the US–India Business Council (USIBC) as well as lobbying by the India Caucus in US Congress and the lobbyists and lobbying firms hired by the Indian Government. Their lobbying activities collectively have played a significant role in creating an environment that is conducive to the development of positive perceptions about India among US foreign policy makers in the post-Cold War era, and, thus, have played a significant role in facilitating the US–India relations.

The combined Indian lobbying efforts have had positive impacts by highlighting the democratic credentials and political and economic viability of India in the changed world scenario. The influence of these groups began to become clear after India's atomic explosion in 1998. After this event, Indian lobbying effort acquired pace and momentum. These efforts began to show effectiveness and landed a significant blow with the passage of the US–India nuclear deal. As a result, today there is a growing and stable strategic partnership between the world's two largest democracies that is reflected in all aspects of bilateral relations, including the collaborations in economic, science and high-technology, joint military exercises, defence commerce, defence industry, defence agreement, counter-terrorism cooperation, civilian nuclear deal, energy security, civil society interaction, and the global commons.

This chapter focuses on lobbying related to foreign aid, India's nuclear test and the US–India civilian nuclear deal, combating terrorism, economic cooperation, including issues such as Kashmir. An examination of the role that Indian lobbying played in aftermath of India's nuclear defiance in 1998 and the Kargil incident is undertaken. This is important as this was a watershed moment in the history of Indian lobbying in the US and the first incidence of noticeable arrival of Indian lobbying at Capitol Hill. This chapter also places emphasis on two important dimensions of Indian lobbying activities in the US. The first dimension is countering Pakistani–American lobbying activities. The second dimension is alignment with the Israel lobby, especially on the passage of many crucial bills, with a special focus on the lobbying during the passage of the US–India civilian nuclear deal, considered as the final arrival of Indian lobbying in Washington. The aim of this chapter is to show how

Indian lobbying has been a major factor in changing the US foreign policy priorities concerning India, which has resulted in a deepening US–India strategic partnership.

NUCLEAR DEFIANCE: LOBBYING AND THE POST-POKHRAN US–INDIA RELATIONS

Certain developments in 1990s activated the Indian–American lobbying. The passage of the Brown Amendment, signed into law by the then President Clinton on January 27, 1996, caused outrage in India, worsened its relations with the United States, and embarrassed Washington's friends in New Delhi.[1] Politicians from across the political spectrum urged renewed acceleration of India's short-range Prithvi and medium-range Agni missile delivery systems. The BJP, then the main opposition party, renewed its call for a nuclear option. The passage of the Brown Amendment and the Indian Parliament's reaction to it showed the delicate nature of the then still nascent Indo-American rapprochement. By resurrecting Cold War slogans, American members of Congress and Indian parliamentarians demonstrated their inability to adjust to the realities of the new unipolar international system. Contrary to predictions that bilateral ties would worsen when the BJP—on record as opposing the Comprehensive Nuclear-Test- Ban Treaty (CTBT)—came to power in March 1998, the US–India relations began to move in a positive direction. For the

---

[1] *Congressional Record,* vol. 141, no. 147, 20 September 1995, pp. S13909–13971; and vol. 141, no. 147, 21 September 1995, pp. S13995–14005; *Indian Express* (1995); The setback to India–US relations was signaled by a speech that Home Minister S.B. Chavan addressed to the Rajya Sabha on November 29, 1995. According to Chavan, the selling of arms to Pakistan indicated "evil designs" that the United States had on the subcontinent. The BJP opposition leader endorsed his unfounded assertion that the United States was interested in acquiring a "foot hold" in Kashmir, *The Hindu,* 16 December 1995. Foreign Minister Pranab Mukherjee declared that, by selling arms to Pakistan, the United States was once again forcing India to divert scarce resources to the military sector. Commerce Minister P. Chidambaram claimed that the Brown Amendment "cast a shadow over commercial ties" because higher military spending undermined the free enterprise economy the United States desired to see established in India, *Indian Express,* 8 December 1995.

first time, American domestic considerations worked to New Delhi's advantage in Washington's formulation of foreign policy.

Never had India confronted the dominant discourse of the international system so directly as when it walked out of the CTBT negotiations and then challenged existing international norms when India embarked on five underground nuclear tests on May 11 and 13, 1998, ending a 24-year self-imposed ban on nuclear testing. The fear of the reprisals from the United States stopped India from testing nuclear devices during Narasimha Rao-led Congress Government in 1995, but the Atal Bihari Vajpayee-led BJP/National Democratic Alliance (NDA) Government went ahead with the decision to go nuclear in 1998.

Various reasons have been cited for India's nuclear test including the deteriorating security environment in the region. In a May 12, 1998, letter to the then President Clinton and other world leaders, Prime Minister Vajpayee listed concerns about the "deteriorating security [and] nuclear environment"—with oblique references to China and Pakistan—as the impetus for India's conducting the May 1998 nuclear tests (*New York Times*, 1998). The United States' second honeymoon with China was obvious from the transfer of US missile technology to China. Furthermore, the growing nuclear collaboration between China and Pakistan, India's two main adversaries, and the United States' connivance in it, aggravated the Indian perception of a national security threat (for details, see Kamath, 1999a). Different insights have been given to explain the timing and reason for India's nuclear test, such as BJP' revivalist agenda and the quest for India's great power status contained within it. Others have cited the domestic political consideration for the timing of the test, as BJP-led NDA Government was a coalition of 13 parties and BJP wanted to consolidate its position by creating a pro-nuclear environment in the country (for details, see Cohen, 2002; Ganguly, 2001).

The Indian nuclear tests completely surprised US intelligence and the policy community and set off a world-wide storm of criticism. President Clinton announced, on May 13, 1998, that he was imposing economic and military sanctions mandated by Section 102 of the Arms Export Control Act. The administration applied the same sanctions to Pakistan on May 30, which had responded to India's nuclear test by conducting its own nuclear test (LePoer, Medalia,

Rennack, and Cronin, 1998). The Indian nuclear test had also brought embarrassment to the American intelligence community as there had been a serious intelligence failure in detecting the preparations for the test (Weiner, 2013).

The United States imposed mandatory sanctions and mobilized other nations, in particular, Japan, to cut economic assistance to India. France and Russia were more sympathetic to India but could not stop the United States creating an international framework under UNSC Resolution 1172 in June 1998, which demanded the signing of the Nuclear Non-Proliferation Treaty (NNPT) and attempted to address the root cause of Indo-Pakistan tension—the Kashmir dispute. Also during his visit to China in June 1998, Clinton announced a new strategic partnership with China and condemned India's nuclear test. These developments seemed to worry India and put it on the back foot as the UN resolution seemed to internationalize the Kashmir dispute, leading to the UN intervention that Pakistan had always wanted. The US–China convergence of interest for putting down India was another disturbing factor for India (Mohan, 2003, pp. 90–91).

Unlike the Republicans, in general, the Democrats were more concerned for the nuclear nonproliferation agenda. As was expected, the Clinton administration came down heavily on India's nuclear test. Clinton, Calling India "a perfectly wonderful country," said that not any rational calculation of security needs, but chauvinism and vainglory had prompted the decision to test. "It is not necessary for them to manifest national greatness by doing this," he said. "It is a terrible decision" (Burns, 1998). Madeleine Albright, then Secretary of State, lamenting the test said "India has dug itself into a big hole which it will find difficult to climb out from" (Chengappa, 2015). The State Department spokesman, James Rubin, accused the Indian Government of being deceitful in its dealing with the United States on nuclear issues. He accused India of lying and conducting a "campaign of duplicity" during 20 high-level meetings between the two countries (Kamath, 1999b).

Most of the criticism came from friends of India who were also opponents of proliferation. Many members of Congress were outraged at New Delhi for not honoring assurances, supposedly made to Energy Secretary Bill Richardson in April, that it would not test nuclear weapons. Congress seemed more willing to excuse Pakistan for following India's example and conducting its own explosions. Edward Markey (D-Mass.), one of the few remaining opponents of nuclear proliferation in the House, denounced New Delhi's actions as "reckless, shameful and irresponsible." Dan Burton, unsurprisingly, insisted that the United States "stop subsidizing" India's nuclear program by cutting foreign aid. In the testimony before the House International Relations Committee(HIRC), Karl Inderfurth (1998), Assistant Secretary of State, said: "More than $1 billion worth loans have been postponed... having a ripple effect in the Indian economy and resulting in decreased investor confidence". Congressman Frank Pallone, then Co-Chairman of the Congressional India Caucus, said that he did not approve of India' nuclear test, but, he also lamented China–Pakistan strategic and nuclear collaboration, including the Pakistani test firing of Ghauri which had "placed India in a vulnerable position" which may have led to the Indian tests (*Hindustan Times*, 1998; also see Kamath, 1999).

In the Senate, Tom Harkin, drawing on President Franklin D. Roosevelt's remarks on the bombing of Pearl Harbor, referred to a day of "infamy" in condemning the Indian tests. Pakistan was promised the repealing of the Pressler Amendment if it refrained from testing. But once Pakistan followed the suit 17 days after the Indian test, pro-Pakistani Congressmen's attack on India paused for some time. But there was a common understanding in Washington that Pakistan was much less at fault than its neighbor, because New Delhi had initiated the nuclear test and had historically advocated nonviolence (Rubinoff, 2001).

Expressing a widely shared sentiment, Richard Lugar, the Senate's leading Republican authority on foreign affairs, asserted that the administration shared the blame for India's tests because it had not seriously engaged New Delhi. Senators Moynihan and Joseph Biden called for an end to America's benign neglect of South Asia (ibid.). Newt Gingrich, then speaker of the House blamed Clinton's dangerous policy of the transfer of American missile technology to China. He further added that China conducted 45 tests, but Clinton continued to accommodate it. On the other hand, the administration roared with outrage when a democratic Indian Government chose to test its capability. Chairman of the Senate Foreign Relations Committee (SFRC), Jesse Helms, characterized China as the one-third of the problem in the proliferation of nuclear weapons. In the same fashion

Connie Mack (R-Fla.) pointed out that India—unlike China—was not a nuclear proliferator and had broken no American laws.[2]

The Indian nuclear test once again antagonized the United States, and it was clear from the criticism in US executive and legislative branch. The Clinton administration and the proponents of nuclear nonproliferation had doubts about India's nuclear posture. This situation required delicate handling as it was also the time when the Indian mission in the United States was having an exceptionally difficult and tough time looking for support to counter anti-India propaganda and justify its action.[3] India's nuclear defiance of the United States in 1998, and the lobbying and reconciliation after that could be considered as the most complex, daring, and successful political maneuvers the nation ever initiated. A massive and conscious lobbying effort was made by the Indian mission in Washington to put forward to defend India's case for a nuclear test. They lobbied before the people whose opinion mattered in the US policy-making circle and could understand India's security concern and view it objectively.

Expressing his views on CNN on May 13, Henry Kissinger, the former US Secretary of State, said that India lived in a troubled neighborhood and if he were in the position of the Prime Minister Atal Bihari Vajpayee, he would have done the same thing.[4] Kissinger's views carried weight in the Republican Party members and encouraged other opposition members to speak out on the same lines. The President of the Republican National Committee, Jim Nicholson, supported India's stand and said that the US Government should have known that it was in the BJP's manifesto.[5] Former US National Security Advisor Zbigniew Brezsinski and Dalai Lama expressed their views in a helpful way related to India's security concern for the nuclear test. Former President Jimmy Carter gave another statement in favor of India that helped India get support from both Republicans and Democrats. On May 14, 1998, Richard Hass, Director of Foreign Policy Studies at the Brookings Institution,

---

[2] *Congressional Record*, vol. 144, no. 98, 23 July 1998, pp. S8685–S8687.
[3] Interview with Lalit Mansingh, and Former Secretaries of MEA June 2004–June 2005.
[4] Quoted by the Ambassador of India to the US Naresh Chandra in an interview with *India Abroad,* 25 October 2002.
[5] Ibid.

came out with a balanced view in the Washington Times. He said that although the timing of the tests was a surprise to the US, it was consistent with India's prior position, that is, longstanding refusal to sign the NNPT, and its reservations regarding the CTBT, and the political agenda of the BJP.[6] According to him, it only made India's nuclear weapons status more explicit. He suggested that isolating India would not serve the economic and strategic interests and purposes of the United States, and hence the US should pursue only minimum economic sanctions.[7]

An analysis of the statements of the people who lobbied for India and countered anti-India propaganda suggests that these views later were reflected in the administrations understanding. One example of this can be seen when the US Assistant Secretary of State Karl Inderfurth made a statement during his briefing on India and Pakistan on June 26, 1998,

> I would like to make a fundamental point. While we do not accept the rationales given by India and Pakistan for testing or possessing nuclear weapons and believe that the tests have diminished their security, we must continue to recognize that as sovereign nations, both India and Pakistan have legitimate security concerns and interests, and we must bear that in mind as we move forward. We have far too many national interests at stake to do anything other than engage under these terms.[8]

The sanctions announced by the Clinton administration also highlighted sharp rifts in the American establishment and not on just along party lines, with differences of opinion also surfacing within the Clinton administration itself. And the Indian–American community lobbied Congress to lift sanctions and put considerable pressure on the administration.

---

[6] Richard Hass, Director, Foreign Policy Studies, Brookings Institution in *The Washington Times*, 14 May 1998.

[7] Ibid.

[8] Text: Karl Inderfurth's June 26, 1998 briefing on India and Pakistan. Retrieved 22 July 2004, from http//www.state.gov

Support for India came from some unexpected sources. The Speaker of the House, Newt Gingrich, who had not normally been considered a great friend of India, spoke out in favor of India and blasted the Clinton Administration for its double standards vis-a-vis China.

Noting that the administration knowingly transferred nuclear missile technology to China, Gingrich declared:

In stark contrast to the Clinton policy of accommodation toward Communist China, the Administration roared with outrage when a democratic Indian government chose to test its nuclear capability. India faces a potential threat from China. China has deployed nuclear missiles in Tibet, improved its missile capabilities with US assistance, and never renounced its claim to part of eastern India. As India's defence minister George Fernandis noted, "China is potential threat No 1" (Joseph, 1998).

Democrat Frank Pallone, then Co-Chairman of the India Caucus in the House, spoke up in India's favor. On May 19, 1998, he made a statement before the Rules Committee opposing the Markey Amendment to the Defence Authorization Bill, seeking to revoke the MFN status from India for textile and apparel products. According to Pallone, the Amendment would have "an entirely inappropriate and counter-productive approach, with the unintended consequence of punishing poor and working class people in India who have nothing to do with nuclear testing" and that "in light of the extremely severe sanctions already imposed on India," the Markey Amendment would constitute "a form of piling-on" (Rubinoff, 2001, pp. 37–60).

Nevertheless, President Clinton went ahead with the Glenn Amendment, 1994 of Nuclear Proliferation Prevention Act and imposed sanctions on New Delhi on May 13, two days after India's nuclear test. Similar sanctions were imposed on Islamabad after the Pakistani nuclear explosion on May 28 and 30. However, the sanctions did not last long. Considerations such as Pakistan's weak economy, its dependency on international aid, and Pakistan being the third largest foreign purchaser of US wheat at a time when the US farming industry was in a desperate crisis, worked in Pakistan's favor. The India–Pakistan Relief Act of 1998 passed in the Senate granted authority to the president to waive all sanctions except those pertaining to military assistance, dual-use exports, and military sales for one year (ibid.).

The Brownback Amendment II approved by Congress in October 1999 gave President Clinton the authority to waive permanently (an earlier version was limited to five years) all sanctions against India, including the provisions of Pressler Amendment, Glenn Amendment and all sections of the Symington Amendment. But Frank Pallone opposed the lifting of the sanction of the Pressler Amendment (for detail, see Sreenivasan, 2008, p. 157). Pakistan—through the efforts of its principal lobbyist, former Texas representative Charles Wilson—was restored to pre-October 1990 status under American nonproliferation law (*New York Times*, 2000). India was able to piggyback on the waiver through the efforts of Senator Pat Roberts (R-Kans.), whose State had Boeing contracts in India that were affected by the sanctions legislation (Rubinoff, 2001, pp. 37–60). Pakistan received more lenient and favorable treatment than India. The deep-rooted negative perception about India in Washington foreign policy-making circle was arguably still alive. Though India was able to piggyback on the waiver, the substantial influence of Indian lobbying had yet to be reflected at policy level.

POST-KARGIL DEVELOPMENT AND LOBBYING

However, developments in 1999 went in favor of New Delhi. Pakistan's unprovoked armed incursion in the Kargil area of Kashmir and the military coup in Islamabad led Congress to reauthorize the Clinton administration to lift indefinitely most remaining sanctions against New Delhi, while retaining the Glenn Amendment prohibitions that were directed against Islamabad. For the first time, according to Representative Gary Ackerman, Congress viewed India and Pakistan as distinct entities (Representative Gary Ackerman, Spoken Remarks, 2000). Representative Benjamin Gilman, the Chairman of the HIRC, led a Congressional effort to oppose the resumption of military aid to Islamabad. By a vote of 21-4, his committee passed a resolution introduced by Representatives Sam Gejdneson (D-Conn.) and Sherrod Brown (D-Ohio) that "condemned" the military coup in Pakistan and went on record as opposing the resumption of military assistance and training programs to Islamabad until a civilian government was restored (*Indian Express*, 1999). There was support for any further waivers of the Pressler Amendment provisions being made contingent upon democracy being restored in Pakistan.

Realizing the fact that Pokhran II nuclear tests had created enough antagonism in the United States to dismantle the improving bilateral relationship, India resorted to all types of lobbying efforts aimed at important segments of the US foreign policy-making process. The lobbying effort tried to reach out to the Clinton administration as well as grassroots level public in the United States to make India's security concerns well heard. While Jaswant Singh and Strobe Talbot were engaged in intensive official dialogue, the Government of India sent many individual delegates bearing high credentials to lobby for India in the United States. These individuals were provided access to high-level officials through India's mission in Washington to lobby for India by engaging former diplomats, think tanks, former policy makers, former Congressmen, members of the business community, and academia in the United States.[9]

The Pokhran test in May 1998 brought a significant change in the Indian lobbying. It was a watershed in the way India sought to engage, cultivate, and lobby the US Government. The Kargil intrusion by Pakistan in 1999 further activated the Indian lobbying. Since the nuclear test and Kargil War the Indian–American community mobilized themselves in a more efficient and focused way than ever before. Indian Americans flooded the Congressmen and Senators with emails and letters. Some people even suggested that the Washington agreement signed between Bill Clinton and Nawaz Sharif in July 1999 (Talbott, 2002; for detail, see Talbott, 2004), which put an end to the conflict, was partly a result of the Indian lobbying. One of the most prominent newspapers, *The Washington Post*, reported that this pro-India tilt in Washington was made possible in no small measure because of the political activism and the lobbying efforts of Indian Americans. The newspaper further stated that Indian Americans had figured prominently in the efforts to

---

[9] Interview with ex-foreign secretaries and ambassadors of India to the US, June 2004–June 2005.

bring India and the United States closer that they had generously donated to political campaigns and had met with lawmakers and administration officials to explain the security rationale behind the Indian tests.[10]

Though in the beginning there was debate about the futility of India's nuclear tests among the Indian–American community, eventually nuclear tests were perceived as warranted and explained to the American officials that circumstances made the nuclear test inevitable. Many felt that it was their duty to defend their homeland even if the Indian case was difficult to defend, as India's relations with US traditionally have not been compatible.

Initially condemned by the Clinton administration, the tests precipitated the longest series of high-level bilateral talks in the history of the US–India relationship. These talks were led by the US Deputy Secretary of State Strobe Talbot and Indian Foreign Minister Jaswant Singh (which started on June 11, 1998). For the first time, there was a mutual attempt to structure the relationship independent of Indo-Pakistani or Indo-Russian concerns. In all, the US had 11 round of talks with India and this dialogue covered broad issues from the questions of proliferation and nuclear policy to larger issues such as the shape of the international system, terrorism, and strategic cooperation between the two States (Cohen, 2002, p. 285).

Lobbying activities that were running parallel to the Jaswant–Talbot talks helped clarify the US apprehensions, misconceptions, and misperceptions about India's nuclear posture. The Confederation of Indian Industry (CII), Federation of Indian Chambers of Commerce and Industry (FICCI), and National Association of Software and Service Companies (NASSCOM) delegations ably articulated the adverse impact of economic sanctions on the US–India relations. They lobbied and convinced their counterparts and some prominent Congressmen in the US that economic sanctions imposed on India was affecting the United States more than India.

In addition, the Indian lobbying effort included hiring of Stephen Solarz to lobby for India in the United States, as the Indian Government had sacked two old lobbyist firms and retained the services of APCO Associates, a company represented by Solarz in

---

[10] *The International News*, Pakistan, 11 October 2000.

Washington. The services of David Springer's firms were dispensed with in the wake of the post-nuclear test development as Springer, who had represented India on the Capitol Hill for the last five years, was not convincing enough in selling India's case for going nuclear. Apart from APCO Associates, India retained the services of another influential lobbying firm. The two firms combined cost India a tidy $75,000 per month,[11] a worthwhile expenditure for defending India's nuclear case among the US lawmakers. It helped clear up misperceptions and misunderstanding and countered the anti-India propaganda by Pakistan through their own lobbying firms on Capitol Hill.

Consequently, in the Kargil case, for the first time the US administration saw the Kashmir problem objectively. The policy makers viewed the whole episode of Kargil in an impartial way and found that Pakistan was guilty. Furthermore, President Clinton's visit to India in 2000 symbolized changing and improving relations between the two nations. All this could not have been possible without lobbying, among other things.[12] Despite an inconclusive nuclear dialogue, Clinton went ahead with his visit to India in March 2000 and initiated a political rapprochement with New Delhi. He changed his position from punishing India for the alleged nuclear transgressions to building a new partnership (Clinton Speech to the Joint Session of the Parliament, 2000). India's lobbying effort and campaign on Capitol Hill was showing its impact.

A new India–US bilateral relationship was proclaimed in a vision statement signed by President Bill Clinton and Prime Minister Vajpayee during the President's March 2000 visit to the subcontinent. In his address to the Parliament on March 22, 2000, Clinton offered an extended critique of India's decision to go nuclear, but his tone was respectful and implied the sense of debate among equals. Moreover, refusal of the BJP Government to sign the CTBT faded as an issue when the Republican-controlled Senate also rejected US ratification.

---

[11] http://www.rediff.com/news/1999/jam/09buzz.htm, accessed on 22 June 2002.
[12] Interview with Lalit Mansingh, the former Indian ambassador to the US, June 2005.

A positive change occurred in the US–India relations after the 1998 nuclear test and Kargil period. The focus of the relationship between the two States shifted from nuclear nonproliferation to nuclear stability, nuclear deterrence, trade and commerce, energy security, fighting international terrorism, promoting democracy, and improving governance. This constructive engagement between the United States and India has been the result of the effect of symbiotic combination of official dialogues as well as lobbying efforts.

A clear example of the lobbying efforts was reflected when a Congressional panel urged "President Clinton to broaden the US special relationship (with India) into a strategic partnership" (*Indian Express*, 1999). and by a vote of 396-4 the House lauded India as "a shining example of democracy for all of Asia to follow" (*Times of India*, 1999). The Indian lobbying made US policy makers more sensitive to Indian interests. It highlighted the problems faced by India because of terrorism and a tough neighborhood. According to Representative Gilman, also a vocal India Caucus member, Congress (especially the Republican majority) recognized that India, because of its conflicts with China and Pakistan and because it is surrounded by Islamic terrorism, "is living in a tough neighbour-hood" (*India Today*, 1999). India's economic liberalization was showing results and its increasing economic importance, especially as an emerging market, and as a destination for American busi-nesses, worked in favor of India as Republicans gave more priority to economic issues than nuclear nonproliferation issues. For the first time, economic opportunity figured in Congressional thinking about India. US Congressmen had started to visit India's commer-cial cities frequently and the stakes and the investment of American firms had begun to increase. Pepsico and General Electric, which have major investments in India, became important lobbyists for India in Washington. As American investment in India began to increase, the influence of India lobbying also began to increase. The combined lobbying effort of Indian lobbying was showing results. By the time Clinton left White House, the platform for a better US–India relation in the twenty-first century was already set and the Congressional members were no longer averse to the idea of a deeper US–India bonding.

PRESIDENT GEORGE W. BUSH AND THE TRANSFORMATION OF THE US-INDIA RELATION

In early 1999, when asked about the reasons for his obvious and noteworthy interest in India, Bush immediately responded, "a billion people in a functioning democracy. Isn't that something?" This was a signal for the dawn of a new US-India relation which saw a significant change during the George W. Bush Administration.

President Bush reportedly had a "big idea" of transforming the US-India relationship based on the enduring foundation of shared democratic values and congruent vital national interests. Often mentioned during his presidential campaign, this "big idea" was that by working together more intensely than ever before, the United States and India, two vibrant democracies, could transform the very essence of their bilateral bonds, thereby making the world "freer, more peaceful, and more prosperous" (U.S. Department of State, 2003). In short, President Bush understood the rise of India to be one befitting world power. Knowing that Prime Minister Vajpayee believed that the United States and India were natural allies, a roadmap was developed in early January 2001.

The Bush administration also understood that there was no way to reverse the nuclear weapons programs of India and Pakistan. At the political level, President Bush made an early decision to build a long-term strategic partnership with India, one that would go beyond the change of atmosphere cultivated under Clinton. The Bush administration promised that it would lift the sanctions imposed on India at the earliest possible opportunity without reference to the CTBT or the other benchmarks imposed by Clinton. That decision ended the nuclear dispute that had long-haunted India-US relations, quietly and without great fanfare. By the time the internal consultations were completed on lifting the sanctions against India, the United States was in the post-9/11 era, an event that would further transform the India-US relationship (Mohan, 2003, pp. 95–96). But before 9/11 the foundation for a strong US-India partnership amidst the rise of a military China was already being laid under Bush administration.

The Bush administration, and especially Pentagon, was determined to redefine the defence cooperation with India. They saw the strategically important India as a potential partner in providing peace and stability in the Indian Ocean and in shaping a new Asian balance of power. When the Bush administration surveyed the strategic landscape it saw China looming large. Consequently, in May 2001, the US Deputy Secretary of State Richard Armitage came to India to explain President Bush's strategic framework that included a missile defence program and hinted at a new beginning with India and the countering of rogue states by naming Iran, Iraq, Libya, North Korea, and some in India's neighborhood (Trikha, 2001). In a speech delivered in New Delhi in September, the US ambassador to India, Robert Blackwill, reiterated the earlier US position saying that "President Bush has a global approach to US–India relations, consistent with the rise of India as a world power" adding that this was "because no nation can promote its values and advance its interests without the help of allies and friends" (Washington File, 2001). There was now a detectable sense of a transformed perception about India in the United States.

The road map for US–India engagement gained a new sense of urgency after Islamic terrorists attacked the Twin Towers and Pentagon in America on September 11, 2001, and the Indian Parliament on December 13, 2001. Since these attacks, both the nations have been more intensely working jointly to counter the Islamic terrorism.

India also responded to the positive gesture shown by the Bush administration. It responded positively to the Bush administration missile defence initiatives. Even before the President announced his missile defence initiative on May 1, 2001, Foreign Minister Jaswant Singh, in his meeting at the White House on April 6, 2001, expressed his understanding of the imperatives of the coming transformation of the deterrence calculus in favor of defensive technologies. India supported the Bush administration's missile defence plan, which was attacked ferociously in China, Russia, and Europe. In the same vein, India was also among the first nations to back the American war against terrorism after September 11 attack and offered the full use of India's military facilities to the United States to pursue its military and political objectives in Afghanistan. These two Indian positions invited criticism especially in India and were considered controversial, but also defined a new paradigm in India's approach to the United States.

India's support for missile defence systems and full cooperation with the United States after 9/11 was seen positively by the Pentagon. The India–US Defence Policy Group—moribund since India's 1998 nuclear tests and the ensuing US sanctions—was revived in late 2001 and began meeting frequently. There was an increased frequency of high-level military and political leaders' visits to each other' capital (Rediff.com, 2003). The dialogue on defence cooperation focused on institutional dialogue and included other areas of defence cooperation between the two countries. The perception about each other, both in the United States and India, had begun to change. Now Washington no longer considered India to be an acute and abiding international proliferation risk that must be carefully managed and constantly lectured. Marking the first time in five years that a senior US official had come to India to discuss civil nuclear collaboration, in February 2003 Nuclear Regulatory Commission Chairman Richard Meserve toured the Tarapur Atomic Power Station and the Bhabha Atomic Research Center.

Cooperation in the defence and military sector emerged as one of the most intense and fastest growing aspects of the US–India bilateral relationship, paving the way for another breakthrough in the form of Next Step in Strategic Partnership (NSSP). The NSSP would guide and transform the US–India relations in the coming years. Parallel efforts regarding high-technology transfer and civil space cooperation bore fruit when Prime Minister Man Mohan Singh visited Washington in July 2005 and signed an agreement to promote cooperation on civilian use of nuclear technology.

The changing geo-strategic landscape and the growing military and economic significance of India in the United States helped the Indian lobbying gain more influence on Capitol Hill, and vice versa. This change in perception infused a new confidence into Indian lobbying. Their focus became less about a reactively countering its adversary lobby in the form of Pakistan, and more about directly how to enhance the US–India relationship on a grand level. After the year 2000, India Caucus members lobbied extensively in the US Congress and executive branch by giving statements, issuing press releases and introducing legislation in the House to increase foreign assistance programs for India, and economic and trade-related issues.

Pallone issued a press release and urged the Bush Administration to support India's effort to support a natural disaster management program in India.[13] Then Co-Chairmen of the India Caucus, McDermott and Ed Royce, in a letter to President Bush, urged US aid to India for the Gujarat earthquake relief effort.[14] Prominent member of India Caucus Ackerman also issued a press release urging the Bush administration to explore the rehabilitation and reconstruction of Gujarat.[15] The House Committee on International Relations also urged the Bush administration to help India in relief work.[16] Congressman Wexler, Helms, and Biden also urged Bush administration to increase disaster aid to India for Gujarat earthquake.

On July 24, 2001, the US House of Representatives voted to increase funding for the South Asia office of USAID's Office of Foreign Disaster Assistance. In a voice vote on the amendment that McDermott (then Co-Chairman of India Caucus) helped promote, the House voted unanimously to spend $10 million of funds on South Asia in an attempt to help those countries increase their disaster response capability.[17]

In December 2004, Pallone announced plans to introduce an aid package for victims of South Asian earthquake[18] and Congressman Joseph Crowley sent a letter to Colin Powell urging the US administration to take the lead in providing emergency aid relief to South Asia.[19] In February 2005, United States, Sen. Jon S. Corzine (D-NJ) and US Rep. Frank Pallone, Jr. (D-NJ) introduced comprehensive legislation in the US Senate and US House of Representatives,

---

[13] Pallone Maintain Support for Programs in India, *Pallone Press Release*, 30 March 2000.

[14] To President Bush: McDermott, Royce, Letter on India's Earthquake Day, 25 January 2001.

[15] Ackerman to Explore Reconstruction Assistance for Gujarat, *Press Release*, 31 January 2001.

[16] Letter from House Committee on International Relations, 29 January 2001.

[17] McDermott Statement on Increased Funding for USAID's Office for Foreign Disaster Assistance, *Press Release*, 24 July 2001.

[18] Pallone Announces Plans to Introduce Aid Package for Victims of South Asian Earthquake, *Press Release*, 28 December 2004.

[19] Congressman Joseph Crowley to Send Letter to Collin Powell Urging US to be Leader in Emergency Aid Relief in South Asia, *Press Release*, 27 December 2004.

respectively, that established a global tsunami warning system and called for long-term assistance and relief to victims of the Indian-Ocean tsunami in South Asia. After the system is set up, the legislation provided $32 million annually to maintain the worldwide system, making it the only legislation that authorizes continual annual funds for a global system.[20]

In April 2005, at a Committee Hearing on the US Response to the Global Aids Crisis, Congressman Joseph Crowley (Chief Deputy Whip) expressed his grave concern over the absence of India from the President's Emergency Plan for AIDS Relief (PEPFAR). He urged the Bush administration to expand PEPFAR to include India as the 16th eligible country in order to avert an impending crisis. Crowley said "India not only needs our vast experience and know-how in fighting this deadly disease, but as a friend in the world, they also deserve our assistance in combating this epidemic for their people."[21]

The above examples of India Caucus members advocating for India showed how favorably India began to be treated at Capitol Hill. Even on the controversial issues such as outsourcing of jobs which had created anger American against India for taking their jobs the Indian lobbying was able to defend India against the BPO backlash.

The lobbying campaign was launched to counter a BPO backlash and anger among the United States. In the past, China had been Americans' favorite scapegoat for many of the US economy's ills, but due to BPO, which resulted in job scarcity for Americans, there was a growing perception among Americans that India was snatching their jobs. This time India was being targeted and the lobbyists for India moved to counter this backlash.

Washington Alliance of Technology Workers, a unit of the Communications Workers Union pressurized the States to pass legislation that would block government contract work from being performed overseas and lobbied Congress to put new limits on guest

---

[20] Corzine and Pallone to Introduce Legislation to Create Global Tsunami Early Warning System, *Press Release*, 17 February 2005.
[21] Crowley calls for administration to include India in Presidents Emergency Plan for AIDS relief, *Press Release*, 13 April 2005.

visas granted to high-technology workers. While China and the Philippines were also the union's targets, India—with its low wages and highly educated English-speaking labor pool—increasingly was seen as the major rival for US high-tech jobs. A lobbying campaign was launched to change the perception that India was taking an unfair number of high-end US jobs by a coalition of Indian Government officials, business groups, and Indian Americans.

On Capitol Hill, lawmakers proposed half-dozen bills to limit the number of guest-worker visas. Connecticut's Democratic Sen. Christopher Dodd and Republican Rep. Nancy Johnson sponsored a bill that required companies using so-called H-1B guest visas to prove Americans are not available to fill a job before bringing in foreign workers. Colorado Republican Rep. Tom Tancredo proposed legislation to eliminate the H-1B program outright. Meanwhile, at least nine States considered anti-outsourcing legislation.

To fight back, the Indian Government paid several high-priced Washington lobbying and law firms to craft an "education" campaign extolling the benefits to the United States of closer economic ties with India. They argued that sending some jobs overseas more than repays the United States with lower prices for imported goods, expanded markets for US products, and fatter profits that US companies can put back into more-innovative businesses.

Instead of relying on television ads and newspapers, they relied on a lobbying coalition that included Washington-based law firm Akin, Gump, Strauss, Hauer & Feld with former House Speaker Tom Foley, and other former diplomats and lawmakers, along with well-known international advisor Edward von Kloberg at the firm, who campaigned and lobbied for the cause. India's NASSCOM, a New Delhi trade group representing 850 international companies, shared the load: it hired Hill and Knowlton, an influential public relations and lobbying firm. According to Senate lobbying records, NASSCOM paid the company $100,000 for the first six months of 2004 year. The India alliance, working with Hill and Knowlton and a few local Indian–American lawmakers, succeeded in temporarily blocking passage of outsourcing bills in New Jersey and Maryland. To bolster India's lobbying muscle, coalition members urged Indian Americans—many of who are well-paid technical workers and professionals—to get more involved politically. Rep. Jay Inslee and

Rep. Joseph Crowley advocated in favor of the outsourcing of job to India and their view was that would not harm America. They said that outsourcing is the reality in today's world of free trade (Schroeder, 2011).

The Indian private sectors such as FICCI and CII, NASSCOM, and Ananta Aspen Center actively lobbied for India. Their lobbying techniques also involved inviting American businessmen and the influential voices of America to India tour. Till 2012 FICCI had organized 14 study tours of India and in one such tour it invited the influential Americans such as Henry Kissinger and Joseph Nye, and Ratan Tata from Indian side in 2001 in Udaipur. These apex bodies of Indian industries invited a number of Congressmen and American business delegates to India to showcase the benefits of engaging India and prospects for businesses in energy, defence, and technology sectors.

By this time the weight of the Indian lobbying was being felt on Capitol Hill. They were successful on many occasions in getting pro-India and pro-Indian American legislation passed in the US Congress. In 2004, the Indian lobbying became more consolidated and strengthened with the formation of the India Caucus in the US Senate. It was the US–India Civilian nuclear deal for which the stage was already setup during the NSSP talks between President Bush and Prime Minister Vajpayee in 2004, and later on between President Bush and Prime Minister Manmohan Singh.

By now the emerging geo-strategic scenario and increasing business ties backed by Indian lobbying had taken the US–India relationship to a new level. The collaboration in the field of joint military exercises, counter-terrorism cooperation, missile defence cooperation, defence commerce, and economic ties were making significant progress.

THE INDIAN LOBBYING AND THE US–INDIA CIVILIAN NUCLEAR DEAL

Nothing demonstrated the growing influence of combined Indian lobbying efforts better than when the India Caucus, Indian–American community and lobbying firms hired by the Indian Government began to lobby for the safe passage of the US–India civilian nuclear deal in the US Congress. This ultimately resulted in the Henry J. Hyde United States–India Peaceful Atomic Cooperation Act 2006. The nuclear deal, signed on July 18, 2005 between the United States and India, alarmed nations like China and Pakistan and the non-proliferation community. They criticized Bush administration for the nuclear exception to India by offering full civilian nuclear energy cooperations without India having signed the NNPT.

China perceived nuclear deal as part of a US designed containment policy in the context of great power politics (for the latest and detailed insights into the US–India nuclear deal, see Pant, 2011), and Pakistan opposed the deal from the beginning. To demonstrate its desire to maintain parity with nuclear rival India, Pakistan test fired a nuclear-capable, surface-to-surface ballistic missile with a range of 2,000 km (*The Times of India, 2006*). The anti-nuclear deal groups tried their best to block the deal in Congress on the pre-text of arms race. Moreover, there were consistent lobbying efforts by Pakistan together with other opponents of the US–India nuclear deal to block it in Congress.

The Republicans having a majority in the US Congress and the nuclear deal being backed by the Bush Administration was not enough to guarantee its passage through the US Congress. There were still deeply entrenched mindsets within the US State Department and the nonproliferation lobby that were against the US decision of nuclear exception to India (Haniffa, 2005b). The anti-US–India nuclear lobby groups and nonproliferation activists like David Albright resisted the nuclear pact. The deal faced resistance in the 49-member HIRC headed by Illinois Republican Henry Hyde. Out of 26 Republicans on the committee, prominent Republicans like Indiana's Dan Burton and California's Dana Rohrabacher were not ready to support the deal, unless changes were made. Pakistan and China were also putting in their best efforts to block it in Congress on the pre-text of arms race in Asia.

Some of the India Caucus members of Democratic Party, who were strong advocates of nonproliferation from the beginning, were opposed to nuclear agreement. In fact it was the most embarrassing situation for India that of the 18 lawmakers who introduced a motion against the nuclear deal, 10 were members of India Caucus.

The resolution was presented on the floor by Republican Fred Upton in association with Democrat Edward Markey, who described the deal as a "historic nuclear failure" that threatens to endanger US national security. A group of American scientists also maintained that the deal is bad for long-term security interests in the United States, India, and elsewhere.[22]

The concerns regarding the Iranian nuclear program had both negative as well as positive effects on the deal. India's voting against Iran in the UN resolution helped those favoring the US–India nuclear deal to muster support on the Capitol Hill. But Iran's threat of nuclear defiance by conducting nuclear tests kept on obstructing debate on the nuclear deal in the favor of India, since nonproliferation groups cited the Iranian example and blamed the Bush administration for making nuclear favor to India. India's nuclear weapon status and its refusal to sign the NNPT were also cited by the opponents of the nuclear deal to block the nuclear deal.

Though the leadership of both the Republican and Democratic Party agreed to bring in the nuclear legislation in the House of Representatives, they were explicit that they did not essentially support the legislation. *The Time* wrote about the scepticism over the Congressional support to the nuclear bill:

Even though it is too early to tell whether opponents will build enough momentum to block the landmark agreement, what is already striking is how silent—and unenthusiastic—Congress seems over an agreement the Bush Administration hails as critical for cementing a strategic alliance with the world's largest democracy. Similarly the *New York Times* reported uncertainty over the fate of bill on Capitol Hill and an emerging "alliance of conservative Republicans, who are concerned that the [nuclear] deal will encourage Iranian intransigence, and liberal Democrats, who charge that the Bush administration has effectively scrapped the Nuclear Nonproliferation Treaty" (see Kjølseth, 2009).

However, the opponents of the US–India civilian nuclear agreement, and the nonproliferation lobbyists in both the United States and in India, could not compete with the well-funded efforts by

---

[22] Indo-US Nuke Deal in Trouble in Congress. Retrieved 22 July 2008, from http://www.isn.ethz.ch/news/sw/details.cfm?id=15562

Indian Americans, the business associations, the Indian embassy, and the PACs formed by affluent Indian Americans. Given the opposition from various interests, the Indian Government and the Indian–American community knew that easy passage of the nuclear agreement would not be possible. As a result, the various combined pro-nuclear deal lobbying activities was taken during both the legislative steps of the nuclear deal resolution in Congress. First in 2006 the bill was introduced to make nuclear exception to, a non-NNPT member. This step also introduced some of the amendments to kill the nuclear deal bill by attaching the conditions under which Congress was to grant this exemption. Before the second step in September 2008 which would put the bill for final voting in Congress, the executive branch had to negotiate the final, technical aspects of the nuclear agreement with India and get endorsement from the International Atomic Energy Agency (IAEA) and Nuclear Suppliers Group (NSG). During both the stage, the Indian lobbying was well-coordinated, unrelenting, well-funded, intense, and massive.

The nuclear deal, meant to address India's looming energy crisis, reduce dependency on fossil fuel, end India's nuclear apartheid and enhance US–India relations to a new level, energized the Indian community. In the last few months their intensive drive to support the nuclear pact included heavy spending on lobbying, campaign contributions, and public relations to persuade Congress to approve the deal. They hired lobbyists, organized fund raisers and blanketed Capitol Hill with briefings, phone calls, and petitions. They organized a round of meetings with the prominent Congress members to muster maximum support for the deal. They first targeted members of the Foreign Relations Committees of both houses to get the bill on the floor of the house. The lobbyists lobbied the SFRC head Richard Lugar and HIRC head Henry Hyde for their support of the nuclear bill.

Community leaders like Dr Barai, Swadesh Chatterji, and Sanjay Puri, Chairman of USINPAC, lobbied hard for Henry Hyde's support. Looking at the division within the India Caucus members in Congress over the intrinsic worth of the nuclear deal, the Indian Government, Indian Americans along with leading India Caucus members like Gary Ackerman, Frank Pallone, and John Cornyn, and Indian–American organizations like USINPAC and

Indian–American Friendship Council (IAFC) lobbied to ensure the support of 39 members of India Caucus in the US Senate and more than 180 members of Indian Caucus in the House of Representatives in favor of deal. For many Indian Americans this increasingly contentious battle in Congress came as a unique opportunity to demonstrate their budding political influence in their adopted country. In fact, Indian–American lobbyists worked energetically to highlight the business potential for the US nuclear industry to take part in the projected build-up of nuclear power plants in India. They also sponsored numerous trips to India by the Congressmen and their staff (Sharma, 2006).

Much of the lobbying was focused on lawmakers from the New York metropolitan region, with its heavy concentration of Indian Americans. USINPAC organized a fund raiser for Senator Hillary Clinton, Co-Chairwoman of the Senate's 39-member India Caucus. Her position on the deal and her support was crucial for the nuclear pact. Most of the members of India Caucus are Democrats and many of them showed reluctance in supporting the bill, since they took the nuclear nonproliferation agenda very seriously. The support of Hillary Clinton and her husband Bill Clinton, former US President and a prominent Democratic leader who pursued nonproliferation policy seriously, was important to ensure support of majority of the Democrats for nuclear bill in the crucial vote ahead in the US Congress (ibid.).

The Indian–American community played a very active role. In every state the Indian–American community did their bit by well-coordinated lobbying and tried to convince their Congressional representatives about the worth of nuclear deal. The role of Congressmen from Texas was prominent. In the Senate, the bill had 10 co-sponsors, all Republican in House, 16 out of 45 co-sponsors were from Texas. This was due to massive lobbying effort by the Indian–American community and individual efforts put by A.K. Mago in Dallas and Durga Agarwal in Houston. During the killer amendments, the US–India Friendship Council sensing that the stakes were high amendments could derail the nuclear deal process, lobbied by sending out "SOS" messages to Congressmen to reject any amendments. The leaders such as Swadesh Chatterji personally went eight times to persuade his Congressman to support the nuclear deal. The lobbying by Indian–American community was a display of the persistence, coordination, and endurance (for a detailed insight into Indian American lobbying for nuclear deal, see Kjølseth, 2009; Andersen, 2006; Haniffa, 2006; Mistry, 2013).

There have been reports that suggested that Government of India spent around $5 million on lobbying for the safe passage of the nuclear deal in the US Congress.[23] In Washington, the Indian Government mounted a multi-faceted lobbying campaign, expending large sums of money—for example, $1.3 million on two lobbying firms—with the aim of pushing the deal through Congress. One of the firms it hired is Barbour, Griffith, and Rogers, which is headed by Robert Blackwill—a former US ambassador to India. Stumping for the deal and soliciting support from the US business community was none other than Dr Montek Singh Ahluwalia, the Deputy Chairman of India's Planning Commission and a close confidant of Prime Minister Singh. In his enthusiasm to woo US business, Dr Ahluwalia emphasized that any opening up of international trade would give the United States a "terrific advantage." And referring to an order placed by Air India for 68 aircraft from Boeing, he predicted that the Air India deal was only one example. It was expected that there would be many others.[24]

A significant push in lobbying efforts for the deal came from the business lobbies. The lobbying on the business front was taken up by the Confederation of Indian Industries and the USIBC. That there is much more at stake behind the nuclear deal is apparent from the worth given to it by the business leaders in both countries.

The USIBC and the IAFC were also involved in lobbying for the nuclear deal. The USIBC hired Patton Boggs, one of the leading and most expensive lobbying firms in Washington, D.C., to lobby for nuclear agreement. Patton Boggs is supposed to have banded with the new lobbying firms hired by the Indian Government—Barbour, Griffith, and Rogers, headed by the former US ambassador

---

[23] "India Spends $5 Million on Nuclear Deal Lobbying," 29 June 2006 Retrieved 22 July 2006, from http://www.india-defence.com/reports/2164
[24] "US Repot on Indo-US Nuclear Deal," June 2006. Retrieved 22 July 2006, from http://www.ciionline.org/common/92/pages/88/Images/US%20Report%20June%2006.pdf

to India Robert Blackwill, and the Venable Law firm—to begin a concerted lobbying campaign to convince US Congressmen that approving the necessary changes in US nonproliferation law was essential if the strategic partnership between the United States and India was to be realized. The CII was supposed to have contributed for Congressional travel between 2000 and 2005, spending some $538,000.

In fact, the business lobbies such as the USIBC targeted and showed the prospects of energy market of $20–$40 billion that India was planning to spend by 2020. It would also open the door for large-scale sale of American military hardware and defence industry business to India. For example, Lockheed Martin could get a contract between $4 billion and $9 billion to supply 126 fighter planes India was planning to buy. As if on cue, the *New York Times* wrote that the Bush administration was organizing a business delegation to India that fall at the time was potentially the largest such mission ever to a single country.

The lobbyists defended the nuclear agreement from the business point of view by emphasizing the billions of dollars of business opportunities in the Indian energy sector. They also claimed that the partnership would boost India's economic reforms, which would open markets to US investment in vital areas such as information technology, telecommunications, and pharmaceuticals.

The powerful Israeli lobby worked less conspicuously, but made its substantial network available to the relatively neophytes in the embassy and the Indian lobbies. Even the American-Jewish Committee (AJC) expressed its strong support for the deal by sending a letter to influential lawmakers. Collectively, both Indian lobby groups and Jewish lobby groups launched a massive lobbying effort by blanketing Capitol Hill with receptions, meetings, and briefings, and the like and highlighted the commercial potential for the US nuclear industry to participate in the projected build-up of nuclear power in India.

In a bid to expand the legislative support India reached out to 43 members of the Black Caucus and 20 members of the Hispanic Caucus. Black Caucus at the time had become leery of India's growing closeness to the Republican administration and Jewish groups. There has been traditional antipathy between African Americans and Jewish Americans (Rajghatta, 2006). India's vote against Iranian nuclear program strengthened the support from the powerful Jewish lobby group. The American Israel Public Affairs Committee (AIPAC) and USINPAC sometimes collaborated on issues like countering terrorism, security, and sale of high-technology weapons to India. The passage of the nuclear deal bill in both the houses of the US Congress with overwhelming support demonstrated the reach, strength, and impact of Indian lobbying which, apart from the Israeli lobbying, no other ethnic lobbying group could match.[25]

On July 26, 2006, the House passed its version of the legislation by a vote of 359–68. On November 16, 2006, the Senate approved a similar bill by a vote of 85–12. In 2008, after the IAEA and NSG approval the nuclear bill was again put to final voting in Congress. The civilian nuclear deal was passed in to law with the two-third majority in both the Houses of the US Congress on September 28, 2008 in the House of Representatives with a vote of 298–117 and on October 1, 2008 in the Senate with a vote of 86–12. After receiving the Presidential assent the law is now called United States–India Nuclear Cooperation Approval and Nonproliferation Enhancement Act.

After the nuclear deal, the presence of Indian lobbying has been missing on Capitol Hill, which can be attributed to several factors. One reason could be seen that after the nuclear deal there has not been an issue of similar magnitude that has required the India lobbying to be mobilized on a similar scale. The priority of the Obama administration in addition to fixing the economic crisis at home, shifted to other major international issues such as Af-Pak region and Iraq War, dealing with a rising and assertive China and the larger strategic issues in the Asia-Pacific region became the top priority. In addition, the deadlock over nuclear liability bill in the Indian Parliament, an ineffective Indian foreign policy under the second term of the Congress-led United Progressive Alliance Government and its failure to reach out to the Indian–American community and negligence of the importance of lobbying were equally responsible. As result, Indian lobbying could not do much such as in terms of

---

[25] Sharma (2006); also see for the impact of the Indian American lobbying on the nuclear deal Kirk (2008) and Sharma (2008a).

handling the diplomatic row on the Devyani Khobragade issue, blocking US military aid to Pakistan or maintaining the pace of the India–US strategic partnership.

However, there were a couple of issues on which Indian lobbying was active such as the US military aid to Pakistan, bringing the culprits of Mumbai terror attack to the justice, Pakistan's noncooperative approach on the Mumbai terror attack investigation, and Islamabad's passivity in cracking down on Pakistan-based terrorist organizations such as the Lashkar-e-Taeba, which has been masterminding the terrorist attacks in India. The civilian nuclear deal was one such issue which was the biggest stumbling block for a comprehensive US–India strategic partnership. The nuclear exception to India not only ended the nuclear apartheid against India, but it also opened the avenues for defence industry relationship, high-tech cooperation, civilian nuclear energy cooperation, energy security, and above all underpinned the US–India strategic partnership in the context of Asian balance of power.

However, since his first September 2014 United States visit as the Prime Minister of India, Narendra Modi has reinvigorated and re-energized both the India–US relation and Indian–American lobbying. Modi's two visits to the United States, his meeting with various Indian–American organizations and professionals, who form the core of Indian lobbying, have reactivated the India lobbying. The India lobbying could be seen the way India–US strategic partnership is picking its momentum and the kind of positive welcome, reception, and approval that Modi and his initiatives to enhance the India–US relationship at a comprehensive level are receiving among the Indian–American community and in the US policy-making circle at Capitol Hill.

THE SUCCESS OF THE INDIAN LOBBYING: THE FACTORS AND STRATEGY

A combination of factors seems to have played an important role in the success of Indian lobbying. The first is the role of the India Caucus in changing the Congressional perception toward India, which has been already discussed in the previous chapters (Hathaway,

2001). In which the affluence, organization, and leadership of the Indian–American community and their desire to shape the US policy toward India have been significant. Another factor is the strategy that has been adopted by Indian lobbying. The Indian lobbying strategy included countering of its adversary Pakistani lobby group, aligning with Israeli lobby and hiring of professional lobbying firms to enhance their lobbying effectiveness.

Countering Pakistani Lobbying

Since the creation of Pakistan, India's relationship with Pakistan has been strained. An enduring conflict and mutual suspicion characterized by border disputes, two high-intensity wars between India and Pakistan, respectively, in 1965 and in 1971, Pakistan's sponsoring of terrorism in Indian States of Jammu and Kashmir and Punjab, and Pakistani intrusion into Kargil in 1999 have defined the strained and tense relationship for India in particular (Sharma, 2012b). During the Cold War period Pakistan was a close ally of the United States and received significant economic and military aid. The nature of US–Pak strategic ties were of utmost importance for India (Kanjilal, 1989).

There has been an active pro-Pakistan lobby among the Congressmen as well as among officials in the US executive departments. The aim of Pakistani propaganda and lobbying efforts has been often to counter Indian interests and advance Pakistan's own interests, mainly US military and economic aid and pursuing its own stand on Kashmir. Some Pakistani Americans have acquired economic clout and political leverage, with which they have sought to influence American policy makers to adopt certain policies conducive to Pakistani interests.

Although the practice of lobbying the US Government existed beforehand, it was only in 1971 that the Pakistani League of America was formed to organize Pakistani Americans and lobby for Pakistan's interests. But effective lobbying by Pakistani Americans and the Pakistani Government was visible in the late 1980s and early 1990s. For example, the Pakistani Physician's Public Affairs Committee (PAK-PAC) was formed in 1989, and the Pakistani–American Congress was formed in 1991.

The lobbying efforts by Pakistani Americans in the case of the Brown Amendment and the waiver of the restrictions of the Pressler Amendment point to the effectiveness of a strong Pakistani lobby in America. The Pakistani lobbying usually allowed Pakistan to gain the upper hand in terms of framing the US policy approach over disputes between the two nations, and India's interests were often thwarted.

Indian Americans became aware of the anti-India lobbying by Pakistani Americans and realized that they could not stay away from the lobbying process. The passion for countering the Pakistani lobbying seems to have motivated the Indian Americans to lobby for India in the United States. The origin of this idea could be traced back in 1950s when Mr. D.S. Saund, the first Indian–American Congressman (1957–1958), moved a resolution in the House of Representatives in which he had warned the military aid to Pakistan might damage the image of the United States as a champion of democracy (Saund, 1960, pp. 186–188). That plea by Saund could be considered as the very first lobbying effort by an Indian American in the US Congress to counter Pakistani lobbying. As an Indian–American activist, Saund utilized his political position and clout in countering Pakistani lobbies the way he could best do.

But Indian lobbying began to overcome Pakistani lobbying only in the post-Cold War era and particularly after the Kargil War. Not long ago, the Pakistan lobbying was accustomed to steamrolling over the weak Indian lobby in Washington. But since 9/11 terrorists attacks, Capitol Hill has hardly a good word to say about Pakistan. The steady deterioration of Pakistan's internal security situation and the American realization that both the Taliban and Al-Qaeda—the two much-feared enemies of the Americans—enjoyed the patronage of many, including the most powerful, in Pakistan for many years. Not to be underestimated is the fear of Islamic terrorism drummed into American minds since September 11, 2001. But in the case of India, some events in India, which would have angered US Congressmen in bygone days and would have led them to issue strong verbal denunciations, if not demand the imposition of sanctions, go virtually unnoticed. This drastic transformation was neither automatic nor magical. It was the Indian lobbying strategy that played a major role in bringing about this change.

In 1990s, when the Pakistani propaganda about Kashmir was at peak, the *Friends of India Forum* was formed in England to counter the Pakistani propaganda. So too was the *Indo-American Kashmir Forum* by immigrant Kashmiri Pundits and backed by some Congressmen in the United States, to garner support for the community, lobby for India's stand on Kashmir and to check the Pakistani lobby. The forum worked for bringing the plight of Pundits in Kashmir brought to the notice of the Congress that because of militancy more than 250,000 Pundits were driven out of Kashmir. The forum in its meeting in 1994 moved a resolution and urged President Clinton to take action against Pakistan and declare it a terrorist state. Vinay Sazawal, the President of the Indo-American Kashmir Forum, asked the State Department to declare Pakistan a terrorist state for sponsoring terrorism in India. While welcoming the US decision to designate the Pakistan-based militant group Harkat Ul-Ansar as a "terrorist organisation," Sazawal-led delegation wanted the action on Jammu and Kashmir Liberation Front and the Hizbul Mujahideen. The members of the forum also met Karl Inderfurth, Assistant Secretary of State for South Asia, to lobby for Kashmiri Pundits and also requested from him US humanitarian aid for Kashmiri Pundits living in refugee camps (Rediff On The Net, 1997a, 1997b).

During the nuclear tests Indian Americans mobilized themselves in a much better way than Pakistanis, partly because Indians were economically more affluent and greater in number than Pakistanis and also because Washington had become increasingly interested in India's economic and strategic potential. Furthermore, India's democracy appeared stable, while Pakistan was increasingly becoming a locus of instability and insecurity.[26]

Before the 2000 visit of Indian Prime Minister Vajpayee to the United States, the pro-Pakistani lobby of 20 US lawmakers led by India bashers, such as Dan Burton, Edolphus Towns, Major Owens, and Gary Condit, became vigorously active on the Hill. They wrote a letter to President Clinton demanding that India be declared a "terrorist state" because of alleged atrocities against Christian, Muslim, and Sikh minorities (Chandran, 2000).

---

[26] *The International News*, Pakistan, 11 October 2000.

But they suffered a setback when one of the 20 Congressmen, Eva Clayton from North Carolina, withdrew her signature and wrote to Clinton that her name was included in the two letters sent to the President inadvertently or by mistake. The move to declare India a terrorist state was inconsistent with her views and Rep. Clayton further maintained that the Government of India has consistently been moving at a rapid pace to strengthen its ties with the United States and the world. The economic and diplomatic relationship between the United States, the world's oldest democracy, and India, the world's largest democracy, is growing. She further added that the United States cannot and must not ignore the important progress and mutual benefits that both the nations have achieved in the recent years (ibid.). This move by Eva Clayton took place because of the pro-India lobbying. Indian American community was taken aback by the inclusion of her name. Under the leadership of Swadesh Chatterjee, the President of IAFPE, the Indian Americans actively lobbied and persuaded the Democratic Congresswoman to change her mind (ibid.).

There has been a number of pro-Khalistani and pro-Pakistani moves by Dan Burton and Ed Towns but have repeatedly suffered defeats in the Congress because of the lobbying by India Caucus members like Gary Ackerman, Jim McDermott, Ed Royce, Sherrod Brown, Frank Pallone, and others.

Now Indian supporters are not only able to defend Indian lobbying interests but also counter the anti-Indian moves made by adversaries. In April 2004, indirectly blaming the Indian lobby in the US Congress for piloting a new Bill calling for stringent monitoring of its adherence to nonproliferation, Pakistan said it hoped the legislation would not be as abrasive as it initially looked. That Bill called for a provision for annual certification by the US President about Pakistanis' adherence to nonproliferation and vested him with powers to cut down US aid in the case of any violations (*Indian Express*, 2004).

Another example of Indian lobbyists at work could be seen when in 2004 when the United States declared a $3 billion aid package to Pakistan. The announcement of $3 billion aid package activated the Indian American community leaders, and as a result they started lobbying through their different political organizations in the United

States. The USINPAC, which deals with the India Caucus members in the US Congress, successfully lobbied for an amendment to the House's $3 billion aid package for Pakistan. They sought to link the provision of aid with the prevention of Islamic militants crossing into India. The amendment was proposed by then Co-Chairman of the India Caucus, Gary Ackerman (D-NY), calling for an end to US assistance until Pakistan stopped cross-border attacks in the disputed state of Jammu and Kashmir and gave up weapons of mass destruction (Maitra, 2003b). After persuasion, Gary Ackerman withdrew the proposed amendment. But what is important to note is that Ackerman and the USINPAC were not making empty threats: they had the capability to push through the amendment, but backed out in favor of US interests.

In place of the Ackerman Amendment, the India Caucus, led by Eni Faleomavaega (D-AK), sponsored an amendment titled "Section 708". Report on "Actions Taken By Pakistan" which was adopted by the House. Accordingly, for the next two years, the President was required to prepare and transmit to Congress a report describing the extent to which the Government of Pakistan had closed all known terrorist training camps operating in Pakistan and Pakistan-held Kashmir. It also required reporting on Pakistan's efforts to establish serious and identifiable measures to prohibit the infiltration of Islamic extremists across the LOC into India, and efforts to cease the transfer of weapons of mass destruction, including any associated technologies, to any third country or terrorist organization (ibid.).

In a historic vote on June 9, 2005, the HIRC passed the State Department Authorization Bill in which a provision in the bill added by Congressman Brad Sherman (D-CA) acknowledged the dangers of the ongoing close military partnership between China and Pakistan, and also noted the fact that the technology peddled by Pakistani scientist Abdul Qader Khan to rogue countries had originated in China. A second provision, added by Congressman Tom Lantos (D-CA) and Congresswoman Ileana Ros-Lehtinen (R-FL), conditioned military sales to Pakistan on that country's full compliance on terrorism and proliferation of weapons of mass destruction. Congresswoman Ros-Lehtinen remarked, "The issue of WMD in the hands of terrorists and rogue nations in the current day world is very real. We need to work together to ensure that this threat is contained and diminished on time" (USINPAC, 2003). Congressman Tom Lantos (D-CA), while praising USINPAC's work, emphasized that "this measure is not aimed at any specific country, but addresses the global threat of nuclear black market activities because it is in our vital interest to shut them down" (ibid.).

After the 1999 Kargil incident, India and Pakistan took their rivalry for the favor of the United States to Washington's Capitol Hill to the next level. The Pakistani lobbying attempted to appoint a special envoy for Kashmir, but was foiled by Indian lobbying when Benjamin Gilman, Chairman of the HIRC, and his Democratic counterpart, Sam Gejdenson, sent a letter to the US President urging him to spurn any call for the US to appoint a special envoy for Kashmir. They demanded, "Instead of appointing a special envoy we should be urging Pakistan to stop sending infiltrators across the LOC into India" (Jones, 1999). As a consequence, the Indian efforts prevailed and there was no direct US intervention in Kashmir conflict.

Similarly, the master stroke foreign policy acts of Obama's first week in office in 2009 was announcement of Richard Holbrooke as the formidable new US envoy to South Asia—"A special representative for Afghanistan and Pakistan." India was conspicuous by its absence. But the omission of India from Holbrooke's title was not a mistake. In fact, when they came to know about Holbrooke was going to deal with India–Pakistan, the Indian lobbying got alerted and vigorously—and successfully— lobbied the Obama transition team to make sure that neither India nor Kashmir was included in Holbrooke's official brief (Rozen, 2009).

While the Pakistani lobby and the Indian lobby are active players, there is a popular misperception that Pakistan does better at lobbying than India. In fact, Pakistani lobbying activities seem to be less effective and its achievements rather dismal, compared to similar activities by the Indian lobbying in the post-Cold War period.

For instance, Pakistanis contended that two pro-Indian–American politicians were defeated, respectively, in 1992 and 1995, thanks to their mobilizing efforts: Stephen Solarz, a staunch supporter of

India, and Larry Pressler of the Pressler Amendment. But in reality, Stephen Solarz lost the election at best due to an effective alliance between Pakistanis and Hispanics, but more probably because of redrawing of constituency boundaries. There were also some financial irregularities when his wife had issued some checks, which bounced. His rival was a Hispanic candidate who massively attracted the votes of South American electors. In the same vein, Larry Pressler lost his election primarily because he was perceived as being out of touch of his constituency. His opponent, Tim Johnson, who was financially supported by Pakistani American, was considered to be a grassroots politician, and this factor more than financial backing apparently is what played the decisive role in his victory.[27]

Pakistan's claim of victory over the Brown Amendment passed in 1995 which allowed the United States to sell to Pakistan weapons that were until then embargoed under the provision of Pressler Amendment is also contested. These weapons included the 28 F-16 planes for which Pakistan had already paid money. But the sale of F-16, a contentious issue, was successfully held up for one decade before the Bush administration announced the resumption of sales. Also the US Government deducted $60 million from Pakistan's F-16 account saying that it had been adjusted against 400,000 tons of wheat supplied in 1999 under its aid program.[28] Although the sale of F-16 resumed, then Secretary of State Condoleezza Rice soon announced the possibility of the F-18, an upgraded version of F-16, to be passed to India, a proposal by the United States to produce planes as per Indian security requirements. Moreover, after the signing of a 10-year Defence Agreement in June 2005 and extended further for 10 years in 2015 and conclusion of nuclear deal this victory of Pakistani lobby became irrelevant, as these two agreements ultimately have opened gateway for a much enhanced and comprehensive US–India defence collaboration, which includes co-production of all sorts of high-end defence products.

As far as Clinton's visit to Pakistan is concerned, for which the Pakistani Americans had lobbied for, Pakistani Americans raised

---

[27] Interview with Lalit Mansingh, the former Indian ambassador to the US, June 2005, also see Hathaway (2000).

[28] *Dawn*, 30 November 2000.

$50,000 for the Senate campaign of his wife Hillary Clinton.[29] Clinton's five-hour visit was more of a lecture to Pakistan, to stop terrorism, and to express concerns that Pakistan was becoming a rogue State.[30] In this sense, the visit was more of a negative than a positive.

However, there have been limits to the power of Indian–American lobby. It became apparent when they tried to put its riders in the US Aid Bill for Pakistan and the executive branch opposed it (Kapur, 2010, p. 199). Another agenda that Indian–American lobbying has not been able to achieve is to declare Pakistan as a terrorist state. Pakistani lobbying have so far successfully lobbied for Pakistan not to be declared a terrorist State by the United States. But this too can be attributed to the fact that United States needed Pakistan in its counter-terrorism agenda, and strategically, the United States did not want to antagonize Pakistan and push it further in China's lap.

Alliance with Israeli Lobby

Aligning with an Israel lobby has been one of the major strategic moves that have helped Indian lobbying in Washington. Indian lobbying has followed the American–Jewish lobby serves as a model for developing an effective lobby organization and achieving success within the American political system. The primary organization dedicated to lobbying on behalf of a good US–Israeli relation is the AIPAC. AIPAC's membership is approximately 60,000 and its annual budget is over $14 million. Its headquarters is in Washington, D.C. experts have described AIPAC as "King of the Hill" and the "preeminent power in the Washington lobbying." Plenty of Senators and House Members regard AIPAC political power as awesome (for the Jewish lobby in detail, see Tivnan, 1985).

The remarkable level of material and diplomatic support that the United States provides to Israel cannot be fully explained on either strategic or moral grounds. Rather, the power of Israeli lobby is also an essential factor to consider, and it has a far-reaching impact on

---

[29] *The International Herald Tribune*, 15 March 2000.
[30] Interview with Lalit Mansingh, former Indian ambassador to the US, June 2005.

America's posture throughout the Middle East and policy that affects or concerns Israel (for detail on Israel Lobby, see Mearsheimer and Walt, 2007). In fact, it would not be an overstatement to say that AIPAC effectively frames the debate on Capitol Hill's with regard to Middle East policy. Almost without exception, House and Senate members do its bidding. Whether based on fact or fancy, the perception is what counts. AIPAC means power—raw intimidating power.

One of AIPAC's primary objectives is to secure American foreign assistance for Israel on the most favorable terms possible. AIPAC has worked closely with successive presidents and virtually with every member of the Congress to ensure a continuous flow of aid. Israel has been the single largest recipient of American foreign aid for decades—exceeding $3 billion per annum. AIPAC has successfully promoted increased cooperation between America and Israel, such as joint works on various weapon systems, and intelligence sharing. Working with its allies in Congress, it has blocked a number of weapons sales to Arab nations that might have posed threats to Israel's security. On rare occasions, those supporting a close US relationship with Israel have come into direct conflict with American presidents. Such incidents provide a remarkable view of the power of the pro-Israel lobby.

Despite their obvious differences on Palestine issue, the teaming up of Indian lobbying and Israel lobbying has exerted greater influence on the legislators on the Capitol Hill. In July 2002, the pro-Israel and pro-India lobbies in Washington, D.C., held a joint reception for senators from both sides of the aisle. Tom Lantos, the Democratic Congressman from California, a Holocaust survivor, greeted the reception, emphasizing the commitment of Jews and Indians to respecting others, rule of law and democracy, and adding that lately the two lobbies have grown closer, because of a shared opposition to terrorism (Barkat, 2003). In the post 9/11 environment, the Indian lobby has been working in coordination with the Israel lobby not only in terms of their shared concern about terrorism, but also due to the growing and deepening strategic partnership between India and Israel that encompasses almost all areas of bilateral relations.

Although both countries gained independence from Britain at about the same time in 1947–1948, they were wary of each other for decades. But in the immediate post-Cold War period, the majority of India's political establishment realized that it was imperative for India to build sound relations with the United States, the sole hegemonic power in the changed international system. India comprehended that normalization with Israel would facilitate India's rapprochement with the United States, since they believed that the American–Jewish lobby had a major influence on the foreign policy decisions of Washington. Indian Prime Minister Rao, in particular, was convinced that normalization with Israel was necessary to improve India's standing vis-à-vis the American–Jewish community and the US political establishment. Amidst these international scenarios and perceptions India decided to change its earlier stance toward Israel and entered into diplomatic relationship with it. India was ready to rectify its West Asian policy distortion and inconsistency.

As a result, on January 29, 1992, India accorded full diplomatic recognition to Israel and both the nations established embassies in each other's countries. India entered into a strategic partnership with Israel for 10 years. Trips by Israeli officials to weigh the diplomatic and political mood in New Delhi culminated with the visit of Israel Deputy Director of Israel Foreign Ministry Moshe Yaeger in 1992. Before 1992, India made the formal diplomatic relationship with Israel conditional on the solution of the Palestinian problem. The relationship with Israel was no longer dependent on Palestinian independence. This departure from the India under the Congress Government was a paradigm shift from Nehruvian anathema to a more practical and realistic approach. Since then, the India–Israel relationship has been strengthening (for detail, see Sharma and Bing, 2015; Kandel, 2010).

The bonding between the two nations further became stronger during the BJP-led NDA Government (1999–2004) when the two high-profile ministers belonging to the BJP, Deputy Prime Minister L.K. Advani and Foreign Minister Jaswant Singh visited Israel in 2000. The prominent leaders of the BJP, Prime Minister Atal Bihari Vajpayee and Deputy Prime Minister and Home Minister L.K. Advani, had an admiration for Israel for its survival in a hostile neighborhood and their view on the threat of global Islamist terrorism coincided with that of Israel (Sharma and Bing, 2015, pp. 620–632).

In the year 2000, Israel was in its second year of fighting a Palestinian uprising and India was in a tense military standoff with Pakistan over extremist Muslim separatists in Kashmir. The two countries agreed to increase mutual military cooperation at this point. Since then, India and Israel have built a close economic and strategic relationship and India has become one of Israel's largest business and defence partners (Ramer, 2002). This development appears to have had a positive influence on the cooperation between Israeli and Indian lobbies.

Although population-wise they are small—about 6.5 million Jewish Americans and about 3.18 million Indian Americans—the coming together of two highly educated and economically affluent communities has the potential to magnify the voices of two communities seeking to promote the interests of their democratic homelands.

Indian–American and Jewish–American lobbyists together gained the passage of an amendment, sponsored by Del. Eni F.H. Faleomavaega (D-American Samoa), pressuring Pakistan to stop Islamic militants from crossing into India when the House passed a $3 billion aid package for Pakistan in July 2003. When the amendment's supporters gathered in a Capitol Hill reception room to celebrate the burgeoning political alliance between Indians and Jews in the United States, Rep. Tom Lantos (D-Calif.), a Hungarian-born Holocaust survivor, said to the triumphant crowd "Indians and Jews share a passionate commitment to respect for others, for the rule of law and for democracy, and lately we have been drawn together by our joint fight against mindless, vicious, fanatic Islamic terrorism" (Alan, 2003). Also, Indian and Israeli lobbyists successfully worked together to gain the Bush administration's approval for Israel to sell four Phalcon early warning radar planes to India for about $1 billion. Three years ago, the United States blocked a nearly identical proposal for Israel to sell radar planes to China. The same coalition of groups—including the USINPAC, AIPAC, and AJC—worked for US approval for India to purchase Israel's Arrow ballistic missile defence system.

The AIPAC and the AJC are also drawing on their considerable lobbying experience in helping Indian lobbying groups. On the domestic political front, the AJC held two training sessions in

New York in 2000, in which grassroots lobbying techniques were taught to about 80 Indian Americans. Many Indian–American lobbying groups are blunt about their desire to emulate American–Jewish groups.

The AJC, for example, has sent seven delegations to India since 1995, and in 1998 it took a group of Indian–American leaders to visit Israel. AJC has opened a permanent liaison office in India and has indulged itself in completing renovations to an earthquake-damaged school that serves mostly Muslim children in the Indian State of Gujarat, according to Jason Isaacson, AJC's director of Government and international affairs (Alan, 2003; also see Kutty, 2000).

So far, the Jewish–Indian alliance in the United States has focused on foreign policy. But the two communities also have combined forces on electoral politics. They worked to defeat former House member Cynthia McKinney (D-Ga.), whom they perceived as antagonistic both to Israel and to India. When McKinney was bashing both India and Israel, both Indians and Jews communities took their existing business and social connections to political level.[31] Jeffrey Colman, AIPAC's deputy legislative director, is of the opinion that cooperation between American Jews and Indians mirrors the growing relations between Israel and India.

The support of Israeli lobby to their neophyte partner was significant during successful passage of the landmark US–India civilian nuclear deal bill and it has helped Indian lobbying grow stronger on Capitol Hill, consequently impacting the US–India relations.

Lobbying Firms Hired by India

Last but not the least strategy in the success of Indian lobbying has been hiring of the high-profile lobbying firms by India. During the late 1980s and early 1990s, the Indian Government realized the need for hiring lobbying firms to put forward India's case in Washington. They knew that lobbyists have entry to multiple access points of power. Their inadequate knowledge of how Washington functions

---

[31] Barkat (2003); also see http://gotofindit.com/results.php?qq=india%20israel%20lobby%20in%20us, accessed on 23 March 2004.

made it necessary for India to hire lobbying firms to supplement the work of Indian embassy in the United States.[32]

The large and powerful lobbying firms such as Verner and Akin have lobbied for India at a contract often exceeding $50,000 per month. Both Verner and Akin are public relations giants, with connections going to the highest levels of the US political establishment, and that is saying something in Washington. According to one series of statistics, some 70,000 people are employed influencing or monitoring Government actions in the Capital. Among themselves, this brigade of influence-peddlers mops up annually about US$8 billion, if not more. They have lobbied for India by providing India, for instance, some sense of security in dealing with the anti-India lobby within the United States. These lobbying firms have guided India's policymakers on how to deal with adverse forces in the United States and how to maximize the benefit from those who are willing to consider India a "friend." Lobbying firms are also expected to deflect criticism against their client country and defend its client's point by putting its case forward (Maitra, 2003a).

In 1997, Verner, Liipfert, Bernhard, Mcpherson & Hand, Chartered, was the biggest grossing lobbying practice. Verner Liipfert is far less exposed to variations in the market. Just 26 percent of its income comes from its top five clients, and no sector accounts for more than a quarter of Verner Liipfert's income. Verner Liipfert employed 85 lobbyists in 1999.[33]

The former Senator Robert Dole (Republican-Kansas) and former Brooklyn Congressman Stephen Solarz (Democrat-New York) were the people who ignited the lobbying effort of India. Solarz, an important pillar of the Israeli lobby and once a powerful Congressman, helped facilitate India's rapprochement with Israel. Solarz is a showman who went on to the extent of putting on a sleeveless jacket—popularized by India's first Prime Minister

---

[32] Interview with Lalit Mansingh, the former Indian ambassador to the US, June 2005.
[33] Data released by the Federal Election Commission, 1 April 2001. Also see http://www.opensecrets.org/pubs/lobby00/toplobby03.asp, accessed on 14 April 2005.

Jawaharlal Nehru and since called the "Jawahar coat" in India—and calling himself the "Congressman from Bombay."

Dole, a Republican presidential contender and the former Senate minority leader, was not the only power player who lured India to hire Verner in 1998. President Bill Clinton's former Treasury Secretary Lloyd Bentsen, former Texas Governor Ann Richards (another Clintonite), and former Senate Majority Leader George J. Mitchell, all were on the Verner roster and helped the firm, at least indirectly, to get prized contracts.[34]

Then again, in March 2003, India went onto hiring Akin Gump to focus on Congress and draw attention to the terrorism emanating from Pakistan for substantive results. Akin Gump, Strauss, Hauer & Feld, won over $600,000 contract from India's traditional lobbying firm of Verner, Liipfert, Bernhard, McPherson & Hand, now called Piper Rudnick.

Founded in 1945, it is the 10th largest law firm in the United States and has a great deal of interest in improving mineral-extraction methods in the Central Asian nations and China, developing port facilities in Central America, building a global satellite network and investing in virtually every emerging market (Maitra, 2003a). The company boasts top corporate clients such as America Online, AT&T, Dow Jones, Pfizer, Time Warner, Motion Pictures Association of America, and the Saudi royal family (Dutt, 2003).

---

[34] In fact, Verner, founded in 1960, has deep roots in the Democratic Party and is definitely not a favorite with Republican presidents. One of its partners, McPherson, was White House counsel to President Lyndon Baines Johnson. Another partner of the firm and a former assistant secretary of state, Bert Bernhard, who directed Maine Democratic senator Edmund Muskie's failed 1972 presidential campaign, served as special advisor to secretary of state Dean Rusk during the Johnson presidency.

Yet another important insider at Verner is Leonard Garment, an AIPAC member and a wheeler-dealer within Washington's powerful Israeli lobby. Garment was a counsel with Richard Nixon's White House and he also provided legal assistance to Clinton in the Monica Lewinsky affair. Garment has another asterisk beside his name: he was hired by Mark Rich, the billionaire criminal living in exile in Switzerland for almost 20 years who was pardoned by the departing Clinton as his last act of clemency. Rich is also acknowledged to be a major financier of Prime Minister Ariel Sharon's Likud Party in Israel (see Maitra, 2003a).

In 2003, as the relationship with United States was witnessing a transformation during the Bush–Vajpayee era, Indian lobbying aimed at facilitating that growing trend by hiring a lobbying firm which was well connected with the party in power. Akin fit the criteria as it was also very well connected with the Bush family and the Republican Party. Nine officials from this lobbying shop served as members of the Bush administration's Transition Advisory Teams, including Bill Paxon, the former Congressman from New York, who remains close to the House Republican leadership. The lobbying firm had the added advantage of being close to the Democratic Party as well.[35]

In Washington, power players do have party affiliations, but such affiliations do not put them in exclusive corners. In fact, firms such as Akin have on their roster lawyers from both the Democratic and Republican parties. Still, power players change with the changing of the guard at the White House, and countries change lobbying firms in sync. This change by the Indian foreign office was in accordance with the unwritten rules of the lobbying game.

Several top lobbying firms had been wooing the Indian embassy but six were enlisted. But Akin Gump, Strauss, Hauer & Feld was able to grab the Indian lobbying task on the ground that it is considered as one of the three biggest firms lobbying Washington, won and ranked top among the leading 10 lobbying firms in the United States according to the US National Journal, and had the highest revenue among all the six evaluated firms.[36]

As discussed in this chapter, during the passage of the nuclear bill, Indian lobbying efforts focused on hiring the best and most powerful in the lobbying business. USIBC hired lobbying firm Patton Boggs, one of the leading and most expensive lobbying firms in Washington, which together with Indian Government hired lobbying firm—Barbour, Griffith & Rogers, headed by former US

---

[35] The new firm, Akin, Gump, Strauss, has its own Israel reps and Clinton men: first and foremost is Vernon Jordan, now chairman of the Wall Street firm, Lazard Freres, and Bob Strauss, former US ambassador to Russia and former chairman of the Democratic National Committee.

[36] "India appoints new lobbying firm in US," *Hindu*, 14 April 2003.

ambassador to India Robert Blackwill, and the Venable Law firm—did a concerted lobbying campaign to lobby for the deal.

The resources, organizational strength, the leadership, and focused strategy have made the Indian lobbying one of the most powerful ethnic lobbying in Washington policy circle. No doubt, the Indian lobbying has come a long way from its insignificant presence during the Cold War period to one of the most to be watched out ethnic lobbying influencing the US foreign policy toward a country with a considerable geo-strategic impact.

Summing up, the US–India relationship has evolved from a wary association during the Cold War period to a strategic partnership. This tremendous transformation could not have been imagined during the Cold War period. Their relationship has reached to a level from where derailment seems impossible.

The US–India relations entered in a new era with NSSP launched by President Bush and Prime Minister Vajpayee in January 2004. The United States and India agreed to expand cooperation in three specific areas: civilian nuclear activities, civilian space programs, and high-technology trade. In addition, the two countries agreed to expand dialogue on missile defence. These areas of cooperation have strengthened and progressed through a series of reciprocal steps. The result has been reflected in the landmark US–India civilian nuclear deal, a 10-Year Defence Agreement in 2005 further extended for 10 years in 2015 (U.S. Department of Defense, 2015), counter-terrorism cooperation, energy security, high-tech and space, and the growing defence industry and commercial ties.

The trade between the United States and India has grown significantly in recent years. Constituting a crucial element of US–India relations, bilateral trade in merchandise goods has witnessed a 10-fold increase from $5.6 billion in 1990 to $103 billion in 2015.

The remarkable change in the US–India relations can be seen in the joint military and defence ties between the two nations. The United States and Indian military and law enforcement officials now participate in joint military and training exercises and they collaborate on the counter-terrorism fronts. High-level political and military meetings have marked the improving US–Indian relations since late 2001 and it has progressed further. Today every year they engage in around 50 military and defence-related exercises, talks, and seminars. This has built the mutual confidence, trust, and interoperability. Today India conducts more joint military exercises with the United States than any other country in the world (Sharma, 2008b).

In fact the US–India relationship has become so comprehensive that there is no imaginable area where either both the nations' government, companies, or people are not involved. At present the US–India relation is moving in a positive direction and both area cooperating on the series of bilateral, multilateral, and global issues. Both are engaged in counter-terrorism[37] and frequent joint exercises between the two military forces have become commonplace. Both collaborate on stopping the spread of Islamic radicalism and illiberal democracies and preventing the proliferation of weapons of mass destruction. They are working to strengthen the global trading system. High-ranking officials on both sides regularly consult on regional and global diplomatic and security issues. Both sides are working to eliminate infectious diseases and trafficking in persons. They are in close consultation on environmental and climate-change issues, energy security and protecting the sea lanes of communication. India's long drawn battle to get into United Nations Security Council (UNSC) as a permanent member has bi-partisan support in the United States. At the same time, people-to-people contacts between India and the United States have grown stronger. Last, but not least, the top US officials, President George W. Bush and President Obama have publicly and consistently stated that they want to see India as great power with a global role in the emerging geo-strategic and geo-economic scenarios of the twenty-first century.[38]

All this has been achieved not by the whims and desires of heads of two political establishments, but the positive and conducive environment that has been created in the post-Cold War era in the United States, in general, and among policy makers and Congressmen, in particular. The credit for this goes to the combined lobbying efforts

---

[37] For the detailed analysis and development in the US–India cooperation on counter-terrorism, see Sharma (2012a); Bruce Riedel (2015);; Hyot (2009, pp. 73–98).

[38] For the recent developments and US–India strategic partnership in the post-Cold War era, see Sharma (2010) and Ganguly (2006).

of India Caucus, Indian Americans, and the lobbying firms hired by Indian Government.

The present geo-strategic and geo-economic significance of the emerging India fits into the US foreign policy goal and this gives Indian lobbying a strong leverage in US policy-making circles. India's growing economic importance and its lucrative energy and defence market, its strategic importance in Asia-Pacific region, and for the balance of power in Asia, for maritime security in the Asia-Pacific region, for tackling terrorism, and India's credentials as democracy, all make New Delhi significant in the United States' broader foreign policy design.

However, Indian Americans (along with India Caucus and other Indian–American lobby groups) with their high-level professional success, growing numbers, political clout, self-confidence, and their admiration for high-achieving Jewish Americans and following consciously in AIPAC's footsteps will continue to get the results in their favor which adversary groups might find it difficult to stop. This will further underpin the ongoing US–India strategic partnership but with a profound impact on the US policy, with important strategic consequences for the future of Asia and the world.

Conclusion

It is obvious that lobbying plays a significant role in the policy formulation in the Unites States, both at domestic and foreign policy levels. While lobbying is as old as the nation-states, significance of lobbying in the US foreign policy process considerably increased with the emergence of the United States as a super power after the World War II. The importance of lobbying in the foreign policy can be judged from the fact that every nation in the world maintains either friendly or inimical relations with the US leaders in office and in opposition in other countries realize that understanding and influencing the decision-making processes and domestic opinion in the US capital can lead to substantial military and economic aid, opportunity to buy weapons, garner support in the United Nations as well as in multilateral lending agencies. Undemocratic regimes know that failure to gain sympathy from American official and public audiences could mean unwanted criticism and bring outside probing into their internal affairs. Accordingly, the domestic agencies, interest groups and foreign governments seek to involve in lobbying activities in Washington to further their respective interests. Various socio-economic, political, legal, institutional, and cultural factors have contributed to the proliferation of lobbying groups in the United States and have given them a unique space in the country's policy process both at the domestic and foreign policy levels.

The very First Amendment to the US Constitution, which incorporates the freedom of assembly clause, upholds the right to organize such groups. The existence of three levels of government—federal, state, and local—and the separation of powers at each level among the legislative, executive, and judiciary branches of government produces many points at which policy making can be influenced. Legislative Acts regulating lobbying such as Utilities Holding Company Act 1935, Merchant Marine Act 1936, Foreign Agents Registration Act 1938, Federal Regulation of Lobbying Act of 1946, Federal Election Campaign Act 1972, and Lobby Disclosure Act 1995 amended by the Honest Leadership and Open Government Act of 2007, have further legitimized the lobbying activities at the federal and state levels of American politics. The weak and decentralized political party system has enabled the interest groups to automatically come forward to influence the policy making process by lobbying practices. The fundamental changes within the Congress marked by the creation of various committees and subcommittees have given additional space to lobbying groups. Socio-political, economic, and cultural values in a nation of immigrants have considerably facilitated the existence of interest groups and have legitimized their lobbying undertakings in the United States.

The interest groups' lobbying activities have been explained by various theories related to group formation. David Truman, Mancur Olson, Robert Salisbury, and Jack Walker are principal theorists of group formation in the United States. The lobbying activities by Indian Americans and the formation of Indian–American political-pressure groups can be explained with the help of group theories, advocated by the prominent group theorists.

David Truman suggests that group activity is characterized by successive waves of mobilization and counter mobilization. According to him people whose interests are adversely affected by major disturbance within the political environment will band together to improve their lot. It fits into the case of Indian–American community's lobbying case that resorted to counter Pakistani lobbying in the 1990s and lobbied extensively to counter Pakistani lobbying. The formation of India Caucus and other political organizations such as Indian–American Forum for Political Education (IAFPE), Indian–American Committee for Political Awareness (IACPA), and US–India Political Action Committee (USINPAC) could be clearly seen in that context as they needed to counter their adversary group to get their voice heard on Capitol Hill. The Indian government had almost neglected the lobbying in the United States for a long period, but it began to lobbying by engaging the Indian American community groups and by hiring lobbying firms to counter anti-India lobby groups in the 1990s in the US.

Another theorist of group formation *Mancur Olson*, an economist, advocates that principal incentive for joining a group is the *selective benefits* that people receive from being members. He says that a key to group formation and especially group survival is the provision of selective benefits. The formation of American Association of Physicians from India (AAPI) is a case in point. Indian doctors joined AAPI for their own benefits. They were racially discriminated, as they faced "glass ceiling" in employment opportunities in the 1980s. Consequently, AAPI came into existence and today it is the only nonpolitical organization of Indian Americans that is involved in extensive lobbying and has survived till now. Many other professional interest groups of Indian Americans came into existence, and the explanation of their formation too lies in the fact that they wanted to improve their lot in American professional life.

Robert Salisbury, a political scientist, says that a group, which has a valuable product and ability to promote that, would probably succeed in creating and maintaining its organization. He gives the credit to the role of a leader or entrepreneur for group formation. In the case of Indian–American organizations, the role of leaders is quite visible. For example and by no means exhaustive, the leadership role of Joy Cherian and Swadesh Chatterjee of IAFPE, Kapil Sharma, Gopal Raju of IACPA, Sanjay Puri of USINPAC, and Ashok Mago of US–India Chamber of Commerce have been significant in the successful lobbying efforts of these organizations. Similarly, Congressmen such as Frank Pallone, Gary Ackerman, Jim McDermott and Ed Royce of India Caucus in the House of Representatives and John Cornyn and Hillary Clinton in the Senate Caucus are worth mentioning. In this context, the leadership provided by Stephen Solarz, Gary Ackerman and Frank Pallone who took immense interests and initiatives in promoting the cause of Indian Americans and India on many crucial times is noteworthy. It was also the continuous efforts of various Co-Chairpersons of India Caucus that saw the number of Caucus members grow from just six to around 180–200. One of the toughest challenges of lobbying for India was in the wake of the nuclear test in 1999. Frank Pallone defended India's nuclear test in 1998 by highlighting the security threat that India was facing due to the China–Pakistan nuclear nexus. He highlighted India's democratic credentials and economic reforms and the business opportunities that it provided in the future for American investors and businesses.

The leadership factor has been an important factor in the prominent Indian–American lobby groups. Another example of leadership was demonstrated during the passage of the nuclear deal bill in the

US Congress. The role of community leaders such as Dr Barai and Sanjay Puri, Chairman of the USINPAC was significant. Looking at the division within the India Caucus in Congress over intrinsic worth of the nuclear deal, leading India Caucus members like Gary Ackerman, Frank Pallone, Senators John Cornyn, and Hillary Clinton took the initiative and lobbied to ensure the support of 39 members of India Caucus in the US Senate and more than 180 members of Indian Caucus in the House of Representatives in favor of deal. They focused on highlighting India's democratic credentials, business opportunities for American companies as result of nuclear deal in the field of energy and defence sector, and emphasized on India's non-proliferation record to counter those questioning India's non-signatory status of NNPT.

Whereas political scientist Jack Walker explains the interest group's success by emphasizing the resources available to the various groups that are not equal. According to him, the group formation and activity, that too in contemporary times, depends very much on the nature of groups' financial base. Start-up funds need to be sufficient to begin the group and support its operations. At least initially these funds need to be obtained from outside the membership base, although over time the membership may be able to sustain itself (Walker, 1983). In the case of Indian–American lobbying groups this is very much evident. When measured in per capita income terms the Indian–American community is richest ethnic community in the United States. In the past two decades, they have been generously raising funds and contributing to Presidential and other elections and their political organizations for the cause of Indian Americans and betterment of US–India relations. Most of these active Indian–American interest groups are well funded, and it is one of the important factors in their survival and their effectiveness. It was very much evident from the lobbying during the nuclear deal that the opponents of the nuclear deal could not compete with the well-funded Indian lobbying efforts which were taken by India Caucus, USINPAC, and the organization such as AAPI, IAFPE, IACPA, and so on. They have survived long and have effectively lobbied for their cause. Obviously they have been supported generously by the affluent Indian–American community. It is obvious that these theories of group formation explains the formation, proliferation, and success of Indian–American political and lobby groups.

Indian Americans' success in protecting group interests in areas, such as immigration policy, anti-discrimination legislation, and countering pro-Pakistani tendencies, is also due to their focused and dedicated lobbying efforts. However, looking at the professional success and achievements of Indian Americans in the United States in comparatively shorter duration than several other ethnic immigrants (who took several generations to achieve the same) one can say that their level of political activities is not that impressive. The Indian–American community is a way behind the Hispanics, Jews, and African Americans.

Political inactivity or low level of political participation by the Indian community can be attributed to many factors. Their brown skin and alien culture might have inhibited Indian American from playing an active role in American political process largely dominated by White Anglo-Saxon Community. Another great impediment comes from within the community itself. Indians are not well organized and are a divided lot by language, religion, region, and caste. Third reason seems to have emanated from their economic success. As a prosperous community, most Indians in the United States appear quite content with the *status quo* and show little interest in politics.

Nonetheless, there has been gradual progress in the political activities of Indian Americans since early 1990s. The political inactivity of Indian Americans is increasingly becoming things of the past. The new activism was caused by perceived discrimination in employment opportunities and restrictive immigration policies. As a result, the professional and material advancement, initially as immigrants, have finally made the Indian–American community active and awaken. Commensurate to their success in professional life they are now eager to assert in the political arena of America life. There seems to be a realization among the Indian American community that the political activism must accompany their professional and economic success and their growing population in the United States to protect and enhance the community's interest.

The political activism of Indian Americans was initially limited to protest against the restrictive US immigration and naturalization laws. Subsequently, the force was against the racial discrimination and ethnic violence. During the 1970s and 1980s, Indian Americans organized themselves against glass ceiling and racial discrimination, and for the protection of minority rights.

But after 1990s there has been a significant increase in their participation in direct politics, fund raising activities, and indirect and direct lobbying through various Indian–American organizations. The success of lobbying efforts of India and Indian Americans in recent years is largely due to professional success especially in the medical field and information technology; their growing number in the United States; the end of the Cold War allowing more space for the lobbying activities; the opening up of Indian economy which grabbed the attention of American businessman and investors; and the convergence of world views of America and India on many of the strategic, security, and international issues.

All these developments enabled Indian Americans to prevail over Pakistani lobbyists in the new context of the post-Cold War era except in few instances, such as amendment to Pressler law, aid to Pakistan and declaring Pakistan as a terrorist state. The change in the US policy toward India after the Cold War; the crumbling of Pakistan as a state both institutionally and economically; the linkages of almost all the terrorist organizations with Pakistan have also put hindrances in the way of successful lobbying by Pakistani Americans and Pakistan in recent years. Some of the significant developments over the past couple of years have further weakened Pakistan's lobbying. For instance, in 2011 the American forces were able to track down and kill Osama bin Laden in Abbotabad near Pakistani military headquarters. The declaration by the US Government about a bounty of $10 million on Hafiz Muhammad Saeed, the founder of Jamat-ul-Dawa, a cover organization for the most dreaded Islamic terrorist organization Lashkar-e-Taeba, for his role in Mumbai terror attack in 2008 in which the US citizens were targeted and killed. These incidents have raised suspicion on the role of Pakistan in the US-led war on terrorism in Afghanistan, and have further weakened the already slackening Pakistan lobby in Washington.

Part of the success of Indian lobby groups can be explained by their approach. Indian Americans are known as "Model Minority" group, not because of high level of education and influences, but because of their approach toward American political system and society. They have lobbied for the community and India without being critical of the American political system, and have always shown the respect to democratic norms prevalent in the United States. They have lobbied through institutional channels and exercising moderation coupled with their affluent status has resulted in the favorable response for Indian association from the US Government.

The success is, however, relative as there are enormous hurdles on the way. For example, there are more than 1,000 Indian–American registered organizations but only very few are active in the politics. Indian lobby, which has emulated lobbying techniques of the Jewish lobby and has been getting considerable support from the Jewish lobby as well, is a way behind Jewish lobby's outstanding success in gaining so much goodwill and support for Israel in the US.

The American Israel Public Affairs Committee (AIPAC) is the strongest ethnic lobby groups in the United States and it has effectively gained control of virtually all of Capitol Hill's action on the Middle-East policy. The AIPAC has been successful to secure American foreign assistance for Israel on the most favorable terms possible and Israel has been the single largest recipient of American foreign aid for decades—$3 billion in direct foreign assistance each year.

The AIPAC has successfully promoted increased cooperation between America and Israel, such as joint works on various weapon systems, and intelligence sharing. It has blocked a number of weapons sales to Arab nations that might have posed threats to Israel's security and to America's interest in the region.

But, despite its strong hold on Capitol Hill, Jews–American lobby groups have failed in its lobbying effort at certain instance. For example, in the early 1980s AIPAC could not stop the United States by selling Airborne Warning and Control System (AWACS) to Saudi Arabia. Jews Americans lobbied hard to stop the weapon missile system sale to Saudi Arabia by the US administration but failed. Again in 1991 they had to face the defeat with regard to loan grant. Israeli lobby failed to persuade President Bush for $10 billion loan grant for Israel. This was a severe blow to the Jews lobby in the United States. But these are rare occasions in the history of Israeli lobby and the record shows that they have been simply unchallenged when it comes to their lobbying impact on many matters which affect Jews American and Israel.

Indian Americans appear are in the process of transforming their professional success into political capital. Indian Americans are also increasingly developing contacts with individual senators, representatives, and Congressional staff even although there is a long way to go. Any group that seeks to influence the US national public policy needs to establish an office in Washington, D.C. Till recently only two Indian–American professional organizations, AAPI and the Asian–American Hotel Owners Association had so far started that process.

One of the major obstacles preventing the creation of effective public affairs organization is that some Indian–American groups are eager to assume this role for themselves, but are not willing to cooperate on behalf of the welfare of the entire community. Too many Indian–American organizations, many with similar names and objectives, send confusing signals to the members of Congress. The members do not know which organization is really reflective or representative of the community. Basically, too many organizations dilute the effectiveness. The Indian–American community has presence in all the 50 states. There is not a single Congressional district that does not have at least 100 Indians. However, they have not established constituent-based relations with every member of Congress.

The Congressional Caucus on India and Indian Americans is one of the largest of its kind in the US Congress. Since its inception in 1993 it has been lobbying for the cause of Indian Americans and for the betterment of US–India relations. India Caucus has also supported the cause of India and Indian Americans on matters, such as immigration, family reunification, and civil rights. Lobbying efforts by Caucus members have focused on economic development and foreign assistance too. Their lobbying effort not only countered anti-India measures, but also fought for foreign assistance to India for meeting natural calamities, agricultural development, and other purposes, such as medical, energy and environment, science and technology. They have done so through debating in the US Congress, by press releases and statements, by enlisting floor speakers, lining up votes, and placing materials in the Congressional Record.

India Caucus members have lobbied extensively by giving statements, issuing press releases and introducing legislations in the House by applauding India's democratic credentials, praising

India's economic reforms and highlighting India's security concerns in a volatile region. The influential Caucus members such as Frank Pallone, Jim McDermott, Ed Royce, Gary Ackerman, Wexler, Helms, Biden have been very vocal on these matters. Even India Caucus has limitation and its share of criticisms too. It has been criticized on the ground that a majority of India Caucus members hardly attend Caucus meetings or Indian–American events, and have not made any comments in the Congress on issues of importance to the community. Essentially a few members of Caucus carry the load of the entire organization. This is because Indian Americans, who convinced their representatives to join the Caucus, failed to question them for not being active. Robert Hathaway, Policy Fellow and the former Director Asia Program of Woodrow Wilson International Centre Asia and who has observed the Caucus since its inception, pointed out that may be only 20 members are active and suggested that members needed to be pushed to be more serious in their role to make the Caucus more effective in the House.

In fact, although the India Caucus is one of the largest of its kind, only a fraction of its members are concerned for helping the Indian–American community or making a tangible contribution to improving India–US relations. In the late 1990s, the Caucus was criticized for not doing anything substantial for advancing the US–India relations and especially for the Indian-American community's matters. The Caucus also received flak for their being at ease to just add more names to the India Caucus list and make public statements about their claim through press releases and media bites. The Indian American community was taken presupposed, as suggested by a prominent India Caucus member.

For example, Representative McDermott revealed that he along with Robert Menendez had tried to garner the support for the Congressional appropriation of $120 million for earthquake relief in Gujarat in 2001. The difficulty in getting Congressional support on India issue, he noted that even an amendment seeking $20 million failed to get the necessary nod in the House. The influential Republicans and prominent members of India Caucus refused to co-sponsor it since the administration convinced them that seeking such an appropriation would complicate

President George W Bush's tax bill.[1] Although Caucus claims a membership of more than hundred, only a couple dozen of these members take an active interest in the affairs of the Indian American community and very few about India. Personal rivalries have also affected the Caucus' efficacy, although by its very nature this development is difficult to document. Besides, the efficiency of Caucus in getting things done at Hill was confined to the House of Representatives only.

But past 2002 and especially after the formation of India Caucus in the US Senate in 2004, these criticisms began to take a backstage as the contribution of the lobbying efforts of India Caucus began to be reflected in the way India was perceived in the US policy making circle and progress towards the US–India strategic partnership. Lalit Mansingh, then Chief of the Mission of India in the US and former Foreign Secretary of India, who was pivotal in foresight and initiative to shape the events that ultimately led to the formation of India Caucus in the US Senate, noted that the idea of a Caucus in the Senate dedicated to a single country was new and needed to overcome several hurdles.[2] The formation of the India Caucus with more than 25 percent of the Senate members was possible because of the positive perceptions about India in the US Congress which was very much the combined efforts of the India lobbying represented by the India Caucus and Indian American community and India's growing strategic and economic importance. Their role in the successful passage of the US–India nuclear deal in both the Houses of the Congress put all the ineffectiveness and other criticism of India Caucus on the backstage. The strengthening and deepening of the US–India strategic partnership continue to endorse their lobbying efforts and credentials.

The very presence of India Caucus in both the Houses of Congress has given India and Indian Americans a strong platform in the US policymaking system. Hathaway too concedes that the India Caucus to an important extent is responsible for a sea-change in the attitude

---

[1] Ramatanu Maitra, "Indian diaspora gains muscle in Washington,"Asia Times online, http://www.atimes.com/atimes/South_Asia/EI23Df03.html, accessed on 14 October 2004.
[2] Interview with Lalit Mansingh, the Former Indian Ambassador to US and Foreign Secretary of India, 24 May 2005.

of members of Congress about India and about the importance of the US–India relationship. In fact, the India Caucus has indeed come a long way since its formation and has provided an institutional base at Hill which was totally negligible during the Cold War period.

The importance and role of lobbying in the process cannot be underestimated. The US–India relations used to be very strained during the Cold War years. The US legislators used to have very little knowledge of India or interest in India. Indian Republic seldom got the attention of America lawmakers during the first 45–50 years of its existence. Ironically, there was not such respect and recognition for India as the world's largest democracy in the US Congress. But today there is a positive image of India in the US Congress. Today one can find a substantial number of legislators in both the Houses of Congress declaring their friendship for India. They defend India on many issues and applaud it for its commitment toward democratic principles, a successful democratic government, for its economic progress and reforms, and so on. The India Caucus members regularly visit India to show their friendship, concern, and to better ties between the two countries. Legislative attempts to cut US foreign aid to India—long an annual tradition in the House of Representatives—is now a story of the past. India Caucus members have been able to curb anti-India moves and have substantially marginalized the anti-India lobby in Washington. They try to ensure that there are no adverse comments on India based on Indian voting record in UN, human rights condition at home or on Kashmir issue or for any other matter which is motivated by the opposition lobbying groups to demean India.

The net result of lobbying effort of India Caucus is that there is significant and remarkable change in the perceptions and attitudes of Congress toward India. And with the formation of India Caucus in the US Senate, Indian lobby has grown in strength and their lobbying strategy has evolved too.

The Indian lobbying strategy has evolved over a period. In the beginning, Indian lobbying primarily aimed at countering the anti-India propaganda by its adversary, the Pakistani lobby groups and some staunch anti-India Congressmen such as Congressman Dan Burton. But the real testing time for lobbying was visible after nuclear test by India and the Kargil War in 1999. India's nuclear test in May 1998 brought a significant change in Indian lobbying. It was a watershed moment for the way India sought to cultivate the US Government. Intensive lobbying effort involved for the first time the US administration to see India–Pak conflict more objectively. The Indian–American community mobilized themselves in a more efficient and focused manner than ever before. Indian lobby successfully defended the nuclear test on ground of the security threat faced by India, cleared apprehensions about India's nuclear posture, put forth New Delhi's standpoint on Kashmir issue and highlighted Pakistan's unprovoked armed intrusion in Kargil.

The policy makers viewed the whole episode of Kargil in impartial way and found that Pakistan was guilty in the conflict. Clinton's visit to India in 2000 improved relations between the two nations perhaps would not have been possible without lobbying efforts in the United States. Clinton changed his position from punishing India for the nuclear "transgressions" to building a new partnership, despite the continuing differences over the nuclear issues, is evidence of lobbying effort. The US–India strategic engagement began to unfold under the Clinton–Vajpayee and Bush–Vajpayee governments. However, it was during the passage of the US–India Civilian Nuclear Agreement Bill in the US Congress that the real clout of Indian lobbying was witnessed and its final arrival was stamped. Indian lobbying, during the passage of the nuclear deal bill, was a well-coordinated lobbying effort by the Manmohan Singh Government in which the Indian American community and their leaders, India Caucus, business groups and lobbying firms, and Prime Minister's special envoy for the nuclear deal Shyam Saran, then Foreign Secretary of India put a united lobbying endeavor. The positive aspects of the nuclear deal were highlighted, those opposing the bill were snubbed and the safe passage of the bill at every stage in the US legislature was ensured (Sharma).[3]

---

[3] Ashok Sharma, "Indo-US Nuclear Deal: Intense Lobbying," Institute of Peace and Conflict Studies, 24 June 2006, http://www.ipcs.org/article/india/indo-us-nuclear-deal-intense-lobbying-2049.html, accessed 24 June 2006; Jason Kirk, "Indian-Americans and the U.S.–India Nuclear Agreement: Consolidation of an Ethnic Lobby?" Foreign Policy Analysis, Vol.4, Issue 3 (2008), Pp:275–300; Ashok Sharma, "Indo-American Lobby boosted ties," *The Sunday Guardian, 25 January 2015*, http://www.sunday-guardian.com/extra/indo-american-lobby-boosted-ties, accessed on 25 January 2015.

Over the past decade and a half, the US–India relation has been moving in a positive direction. Both the countries have been cooperating on the issue of counter terrorism, their views converge on stopping the proliferation of weapons of mass destruction, protecting the sea lanes of communication, energy security, and other human security issues. They have been working to strengthen the global trading system, though differences are there. High-ranking officials on both sides regularly consult on regional and global diplomatic issues. Frequent joint exercises between the two military forces have become commonplace. Both sides work to eliminate infectious diseases and trafficking in persons. They have been sharing their views and been in close consultation on environmental and climate-change issues. India's aspiration to become a great power and its pro-active foreign policy for a bigger role in the international order is encouraged and supported by the United States. India's bid for the permanent membership in the UN Security Council is supported by the US, first endorsed by the George W. Bush administration and then openly supported by the President Barack Obama in the Indian Parliament during his visit to India in November 2010. The latest Modi-Obama meeting in 2016 reaffirmed the deepening partnership with the US–India joint statement covered a broad range of issues including the US continued open support to India's bid for the UNSC permanent seat, membership to the international organizations such as Nuclear Suppliers Group and Asia-Pacific Economic Cooperation. At the same time, people-to-people contacts and cultural links between India and the United States have grown stronger.

No longer does the United States fixate on India's nuclear weapons and missile programs. American nagging is silent on these subjects and India has been incorporated in the global nuclear order in indirect way by the nuclear exception in the form of nuclear deal. Washington no longer views its relationship with India through a prism that must always include Pakistan–India's next-door neighbor. In short, the United States perceives India as a strategic partner and not as an "irritating recalcitrant." In fact, there have been few instances in history in which the conceptualization and core components of a bilateral relationship, especially between two democracies, have been so transformed in so short a time by peaceful means.

However, in the post-nuclear deal phase, the US–India relationship went backstage, so did the Indian lobby. The expected momentum in the progress on the various issues of the US–India strategic partnership slowed down. The Congress-led UPA II government failed to reach out to the Indian–American community and the importance of lobbying was neglected. As a result, there were issues which could not attract the Indian lobbying attention. For example, despite the 2008 Mumbai terror attack and a series of terrorist attacks in the Indian cities, the most of which were backed Pakistan-backed terrorist organizations, the Indian lobby coalition seemed unmoved. Neither the Indian–American organizations nor India Caucus members were able to bring any pressure on the US administration in this regard. Unlike the lapsed Kerry–Lugar bill, the India Caucus members could not make provision in the American military aid to Pakistan to stop supporting terror outfits in Pakistan involved in terror attacks in India. Indian lobbying also could not do much in terms of resolving the diplomatic row on Devyani Khobragade issue, impasse over the nuclear liability bill or act when the US manufacturing association and big pharmaceutical companies unleashed a severe campaign against India in 2014. On top of that, India's ineffective foreign policy could not maintain the rate of knots of the India–US strategic partnership. And from the United States side, the priority of the Obama administration had also shifted to other major international issues.

However, the resounding victory of Prime Minister Narendra Modi-led Bharatiya Janata Party (BJP) government has created hope and expectations in the nation of around 1.2 billion people. Modi is faced with the challenge of reviving India's economy and creating jobs for its young demography. India needs foreign investment and a comprehensive international collaboration for its development agenda. In this India's relationship with the United States is vital. Modi has rejuvenated the India–US relationship and introduced a new approach to the Indian lobbying. This new modus operandi can be seen in Modi's diplomacy by establishing personal rapport with foreign leaders and unprecedented ability to connect with Indian Diaspora by addressing them directly which began with the United States at Madison Square Garden, and is being replicated in almost all parts of the globe where there is a sizeable number of the Indian Diaspora. Modi's September 2014 Madison Square Garden appearance was unique which was received by a thumping applaud from around 20,000 Indian Americans and 40 Congressmen—the two main pillars of the Indian lobbying in the United States.

In addition, Modi's leadership style of establishing personal rapport with President Barack Obama has not only helped India and the United States to reach on a common and acceptable point on some of the most pressing and challenging issues confronting the US–India bilateral ties but also the world. For example, during the Paris Climate Conference held in December 2015, India's opposition to Paris climate change issue prior to the debate was seen as India being a stumbling block to the resolution on climate change (Davenport and Barry, 2015; Davenport and Harris, 2015). But it was Modi who went his own way to strike the deal on agreeable terms with Obama in the Paris Conference on climate change resolution. Unlike the other world leaders who go for the media and press release to connect with people in America, Modi has taken a different approach reflected in his penchant for addressing the community gathering in a big number. Modi has taken advantage of Indian Americans' increased political awareness and activism to enhance India's presence in the United States, and is giving an image of India that is being welcomed by American society, business, and political circles. Modi is leveraging the Indian lobbying to put India's position on the global stage where the United States nod matters.

The enthusiasm generated among the Indian–American community could be seen in Narula, who came to the United States 17 years ago, first working in the garment industry, now has his own company with more than, 200 employees who was part of the host committee for PM Modi's visit to the United States in September 2014, who expressed "We attempted to do business in India. I hope Modi will look into streamlining issues such as VAT, the role of FDI (foreign direct investment) and find a way for American businesses to not have to go through 19 red tape bureaucracies" (*The Times of India*, 2014b). Not only Narula, but this expectation is visible across the Indian–American community, and the community leaders, the US–India business lobby, as well as the Congressmen, especially who are in the list of India Caucus in the US Congress.

Under Modi government, many Indian Americans have seen a hope in the revival of India's economy and the way toward development. Indian Americans have often complained about the red tapism, obstinate bureaucracy, corruption, the tax system, and the dilapidated infrastructure, the obstacles that they have been facing for doing business in India. Modi' government's "Make in India" and "Digital India" initiatives, and the measures taken in regard to economic reforms and attract FDIs in India have created a positive environment among Indian–American community, who are also interested in doing business in India. The recent visits of Prime Minister Narendra Modi, Foreign Minsiter Sushma Swaraj and and Indian finance Minister Arun Jaitely, and their meetings with US business community and movers and shakers of India–US relations have further added to their confidence.

However, in the above context, it would be equally important how Prime Minister Modi deals with the controversies surrounding the lobbying in India. The concept of lobbying in India is totally misunderstood including among the political class. There is a negative perception about lobbying in India which surfaced during the Wal-Mart disclosure of its money spent in total of $25 million over the four years on lobbying in the United States which also included on the matters related to its access to India market. But it became a big issue of corruption in the Indian Parliament and the BJP then leading opposition party alleged that Wal-Mart bribed the Indian Government officials for getting access to Indian market. But the investigation found that Wal-Mart's disclosure report was totally in compliance with US lobbying regulations acts. In fact, there is a fundamental difference between the United States and India on the way the concept of lobbying is perceived. This issue would become important as more US companies are going to invest in India. Not only there is an absence of the law on lobbying in India, but the concept of lobbying is not even acknowledged in the Indian political system. The misperception about lobbying in India might hamper US-based efforts to enhance economic ties. There is a need of better understanding of the concept of lobbying as more and more United States and foreign companies would be looking to invest in India. The provision of a law dealing with the concept of lobbying on dealings between private sector and the Government of India would make conducive environment for the foreign investment and bring transparency to the system.

Prime Minister Modi's three visits to the United States and President Obama's India visit on Republic Day on 26 January 2015 have rejuvenated the India–US strategic partnership, with emphasis on enhancing the economic and trade relationship in addition to deepening strategic and defence ties. This has brought a new enthusiasm in the various modules of Indian lobbying.

During his US visits, Modi not only met the Indian lobbying modules, but also engaged with the Jewish lobby and the Jewish community leaders. The power of the Jewish lobby in terms of its organizational strength, financial capability, and its impact on the US foreign policy in the Middle East and especially the US policy toward Israel is well known and well documented. Though India–Israel relation has bi-partisan approval (a full-fledged diplomatic ties was established in 1992 by the PM Narsimha Rao-led Congress government), but the ties deepened during Prime Minister Vajpayee-led BJP/NDA government (for detail on the evolving India–Israel relations, see Sharma and Bing, 2015). Modi was the second Prime Minister after Prime Minister Vajpayee who held meetings with Jewish community in the United States and is going to be the first Indian Prime Minister to visit Israel. As discussed in the previous chapter, it is clear that Indian lobbying considers Jewish lobby as a "Model" to be followed and the Jewish lobby has supported the Indian lobbying on most of the crucial issues and helped Indian lobbying for their cause toward the betterment of India-US relations. Modi's meeting with the Jewish community and his impending visit to Israel is all set to enhance Indian lobby in the United States. His meeting with the different segments of Indian lobbying with special focus on highly successful professional and business class of Indian Americans has re-energized the Indian lobby. After all, the interest groups lobby continues to be of utmost importance, and it is the powerful lobby groups that ultimately decide the fate of many policies in the United States.

In this context, it is important to acknowledge that success of Indian–American lobby is also due to the changing perception about India in the American corporate sector which wields the profound influence in the American political system. Arun Sharma, who was educated in the United States, a past National Chair of the Australia India Business Council and a long-time keen observer of America, suggests that the emergence of CEOs of Indian origin in the mid-1990s added greater credibility to the Indian–American lobbying effort. Though in 1980s Indians had demonstrated great professional success as doctors, engineers, academics, and small business owners, and were beginning to make a mark in the Information Technology sector, they were absent from the highest levels of mainstream corporate America. This began to change with the emergence of Indian origin Chief Executive Officers (CEO) such as Rajat Gupta at Mckinsey & Company and Gangwal at US Airway in mid-1990s to Indra Noovi at PepsiCo and Vikram Pandit at Citigroup in the 2000s. This was because the revenues of the American companies from outside America started becoming significant and that provided opportunities for corporate leaders with the global outlook in which the Indian origin corporate leaders became very competitive. This provided an added level of credibility to the Indian lobbying effort which had started to change the perception at corporate level which ultimately helped the overall Indian lobbying effort. The presence of Indian Americans in top rank of corporate America is being replicated in the Information Technology companies sector with CEOs such as Sunder Pichai at Google and Satya Nadela at Microsoft. The emergence of Indian origin CEOs in Information Technology companies further likely to strengthen the Indian lobbying as both the nations are keen to enhance their economic engagement.

Obama–Modi may have co-authored a column in *The Washington Post* and pledged to walk together in the Twenty-First century, in reality the US foreign policy is not what it looks like. This famous reply to a delegation of industrialist by President Franklin D. Roosevelt remains relevant, "Okay, you've convinced me. Now go out there and bring pressure on me," Modi is not unfamiliar with this. Once again the lobbying has acquired an importance in the US–India relationship under the new approach of Prime Minister Narendra Modi.

Above all, the change in perception about India in the United States could be seen from the top US officials and the recent two Presidents namely George W. Bush and President Barack Obama openly advocating their support for India as a great power in the Twenty-First century. The 2016 Presidential election front runner from both the parties Hillary Clinton and Donald Trump have welcomed India's progress and look forward to engage India constructively. The support for the US–India relations is bipartisan and is institutionalized on many fronts. Both the nations' perceptions converge on the emerging strategic geometry in the context of a rising military China in the Indo-Pacific region, the security threats emanating from the Islamic radicalism and on many global commons. Today the US India relation, based on democratic values and principles, is marked by unprecedented convergence of interests in the emerging geo-strategic and geo-economic realities of the present world which will define the global order in the twenty-first century.

Notwithstanding ceaseless efforts of Indian and American Governments to forge a strategic partnership between the two countries, the process can be de-railed by lobbyists. To give further concrete shape and strengthen the strategic partnership between the world's two largest democracies, the lobbying—an inescapable reality of the American political system—will continue to be relevant, indispensable, and unavoidable.

Bibliography

Adherents.com (2014). *Composite US demographics.* Retrieved 20 July 2014 from http://www.adherents.com/adh_dem.html

Ahrari, M.E. (1987). Conclusion. In M.E. Ahrari (ed.), *Ethnic groups and U.S. foreign policy.* New York: Greenwood

Almond, G., and Verba, S. (1963). *The civic culture.* Boston: Little, Brown.

America's Asian Population Demographic Patterns & Trends. (2015). Retrieved 9 December 2015 from http://proximityone.com/asian_demographics.htm

American Israel Public Affairs Committee. (2001). *AIPAC: About us, who we are.* Retrieved 20 October 2004 from http://www.usisraelorgpower usisraellobby html

American Israel Public Affairs Committee. (2004). Retrieved 20 October 2004 from http://www.aipac.org/

Anand, R.S. (1992). *Indo American begin to flow in the mainstream politics.* Indian American Forum for Political Education, 10th Annual Convention, Washington, DC.

Andersen, W.K. (2006). The Indian-American community comes into its political own. *India Abroad,* 1 September.

Arnold, F., Minocha, U., and Fawcett, J. (1987). The changing face of Asian immigration to the U.S. In J. Fawcett and B. Cairno (eds), *Pacific bridges: The new immigration from Asia and the Pacific Islands* (p. 105). New York: Centre for Migration Studies.

Arora, V. (1995). AAPI Opens PAC in Washington. *India West,* December 22 and 29, 1995 in a Report of Indian Embassy in the U.S., 2003. California: Emery Ville.

Asian Indians a Success Story. (2011). Retrieved 10 March 2011 from http://www.indianembassy.org./indusrd/comm.htm

Asia Society. (1976). *Asia and American textbooks.* New York: Asia Society.

Assisi, F.C. (2007). Skilled Indian immigrants create wealth for America. *INDOlink.* Retrieved 20 November 2012 from http://www.indolink.com/displayArticleS.php?id=010307105012

Bahri, D. (2001). The digital diaspora: South Asians in the New Pax Electronica. In M. Paranjape (ed.), *Indian diaspora: Theories, histories and texts* (p. 223). New Delhi: Indialog Publications.

Banerjee, K.K. (1969). *Indian freedom movement in America.* Calcutta: Signals.

Barkat, A. (2003). Pro-Israel, pro-India lobbies now working together in U.S. *Harretz,* 8 September.

Bentley, A. (1949). *The process of government.* Texas: Principia Press of Trinity University.

Berry, J.M. (1977). *Lobbying for the people: The political behavior of public interest groups.* Princeton: Princeton University Press.

Bjorkman, J.W. (1980). Public Law 480 and the policies of self-help and short-tether: Indo-American relations, 1965–68. In L.I. Rudolph and S.H. Rudolph (eds.), *The administration of U.S. Foreign Policy towards South Asia under Presidents Johnson and Nixon.* New Jersey: Humanities Press.

Boroder, D.S. (1978). Introduction. In S.M. Lipset (ed.), *Emerging conditions in American politics* (p. 3). San Francisco: Institute for Contemporary Studies.

Brands, H.W. (1990). *India and the United States: The cold peace.* Boston: Twayne.

Budde, B.A. (1980). Business political action committees. In M.J. Malbin (ed.), *Parties, interest groups, campaign finance act laws* (pp. 10–11). Washington, D.C.: American Enterprise Institute for Public Policy Research.

Bureau of Educational and Cultural Affairs. (1982). *United States-Indian cultural relations.* Washington, D.C.: Bureau of Educational and Cultural Affairs.

Burns, J.F. (1998). The world: Riding the tiger; India charts a Pariah's path to glory. *New York Times,* May 17. Retrieved 22 May 2005 from http://www.nytimes.com/1998/05/17/weekinreview/the-world-riding-the-tiger-india-charts-a-pariah-s-path-to-glory.html?pagewanted=all

Castro versus the Eisenhower Administration. (2015). *Macrohistory and world war report.* Retrieved 12 July 2015 from http://www.fsmitha.com/h2/ch24t-cuba2.htm

Chandran, R. (1999). Anti-India amendment suffers resounding defeat in US Congress. *The Times of India,* 23 July.

Chandran, R. (2000). Setback for pro-Pakistani lobby in the US Congress. *Times of India,* 28 July.

Chatwood, C. (2005). *Why is there a great sucking sound to India?* Retrieved 12 February 2005 from http://www.aea.org/documents/040715SuckingSoundFromIndia.html

Chaudhari, P.P. (2000). India and America: The knowledge partners. *SPAN,* 41(6), 52.

Chea, T. (2003). *New generation of Indian Americans looks to politics,* 26 July. Retrieved 12 March 2005 from http://www.modelminority.com/articles02.html

Chellaney, B. (1993). *Nuclear proliferation: The US-India conflict.* New Delhi: Orient Longman.

Chengappa, R. (2015). Making of the bomb. *India Today.* Retrieved 5 January 2016 from http://indiatoday.intoday.in/story/india-today-40th-anniversary-raj-chengappa-army/1/543223.html

Cigler, A.J., and Loomis, B.A. (1995a). *Interest group politics.* Washington: Congressional Quarterly Press.

Cigler, A.J., and Loomis, B.A. (1995b). Contemporary interest group politics: More than more of the same. In A.J. Cigler and B.A. Loomis (eds), *Interest group politics* (p. 8). Washington: Congressional Quarterly Press.

Clinton Speech to the Joint Session of the Parliament. (2000). *Remarks by President Clinton.* Visit of the U.S. President to India, pp. 63–67.

Clive, T.S. (1998). Interest group regulation across the United States: Rationale, development and consequences. *Parliamentary Affairs: A Journal of Comparative Politics, 51*(4), 500–515.

Clymer, K.J. (1997). *Quest for freedom: The United States and India's Independence.* New York: Columbia University Press.

Cohen, S. (2002). *India: Emerging power.* New Delhi: Oxford University Press.

Cohen, S.P. (1984). *The Pakistan army.* Los Angeles: California University Press.

Cohen, S.P. (2000). *India and America: An emerging relationship.* A Paper Presented to the Conference on the Nation-State System and Transnational Forces in South Asia. Kyoto, Japan. Retrieved 10 July 2015 from http://dspace.cigilibrary.org/jspui/bitstream/123456789/18255/1/India%20and%20America%20An%20Emerging%20Relationship.pdf?1

Congressional Caucus on India and Indian Americans. (2004a). Retrieved 12 October 2004 from http://www.usindiafriendship.net /congress/caucus/caucus.html

Congressional Caucus on India and Indian Americans. (2004b). Indian American Friendship Council. Retrieved 22 May 2004 from *http://www.iafc.us/caucus.htm.*

Congressional Caucus on India and Indian Americans. (2004c). Retrieved 14 October 2004 from *http://www.indiaus-sc.org/ccia.htm*

Congressional Quarterly. (1982). *The Washington lobby.* Washington, D.C.: Congressional Quarterly Press.

Congressional Statement. (2006). Congressman Crowley's concern over the proposed sale of F-16 to Pakistan. Retrieved 10 November 2012 from http://www.usindiafriendship.net/congress1/crowley/crowley18.htm

Contractor, H. (2002). From political apathy to activism. *Khabar Magazine, 7*(10). Retrieved 21 February 2005 from http://www.ipartlanta.net/2002.khabar.html

Conway, M.M., and Green, J.C. (1996). Political action committees and the political process in the 1990s. In A.J. Ciglar and B.A. Loomis (eds), *Interest group politics* (p. 155). Washington: Congressional Quarterly Press.

Cooperman, Alan (2003). India, Israel interests team up. *The Washington Post,* 19 July.

Crabb, C.V., Antizzo, G. and Sarieddine, L.S. (2000). *Congress and the foreign policy process: Modes of legislative behavior.* Baton Rogue, Louisiana: Louisiana State University Press.

Crossette, B. (1993). *India facing the twenty first century.* Bloomington: Indiana University Press.

Cupitt, R.T. and Gahlaut, S. (1999). Non-proliferation export controls: US and Indian perspectives. In G.K. Bertsch, S. Gahlaut, and A. Srivastava (eds), *Engaging India: US strategic relations with the world's largest democracy* (p. 172). New York: Routledge.

Dahl, R. (1950). *Congress and foreign policy.* New York: Harcourt, Brace.

Daniel, R. (1988). *Asian Americans: Chinese and Japanese in the United States since 1950.* Washington: University of Washington Press.

Dave, S. (2013). 1960s Indian American Immigrant Grandparents and the Cultural family Narrative. In A. Singh (ed.), *Indian diaspora: Voices of grandparents and grandparenting.* Rotterdam: Sense Publishers.

Davenport, C., and Barry, E. (2015). Narendra Modi could make or break Obama's climate legacy. *New York Times*, November 30. Retrieved 18 December 2015 from http://www.nytimes.com/2015/12/01/world/asia/narendra-modi-could-make-or-break-obamas-climate-legacy.html

Davenport, C., and Harris, G. (2015). Citing urgency, world leaders converge on France for climate talks. *New York Times*, November 30. Retrieved 18 December 2015 fromhttp://www.nytimes.com/2015/12/01/world/europe/obama-climate-conference-cop21.html

Dawn, 30 November 2000.

Dawn (2012). *Move to stop US aid to Pakistan.* Retrieved 10 November 2012 http://archives.dawn.com/archives/93075

Debnath, S. (2009). *West Bengal in doldrums.* Siliguri: N.L. Publishers.

Deccan Chronicle. (2015). *Hand over Zaki-ur-Rehman Lakhvi to India or international court: US Senator Royce to Pakistan.* Retrieved 22 November 2015 from http://www.deccanchronicle.com/150310/nation-current-affairs/article/hand-over-lakhvi-india-or-international-court-us-senator-ed

Department of Homeland Security. (2005). Retrieved 12 February 2005 http://www.dhs.gov/dhspublic/display?theme=11&page=3

Desilver, D. (2014). 5 Facts about Indian Americans. *Pew Research Center*, 30 September. Retrieved 6 December 2015 from http://www.pewresearch.org/fact-tank/2014/09/30/5-facts-about-indian-americans/

Dhingra, P. (2012). *Life behind the lobby: Indian American motel owners and the American dream.* Stanford, CA: Stanford University Press.

Dixit, J.N. (2003). *India's foreign policy: 1947–2003.* New Delhi: Picus.

Dutt, E. (2003). India's new lobbying firm has high connections. *Indo-Asian News Service,* 2 April.

Dutt, S. (1980). India and the overseas Indians. *India Quarterly, 3*(4), 323–328.

Eadd, E.C. Jr., and Hedley, C.D. (1975). *Transformations of American party system.* New York: W. W. Norton & Co.

Eastman, H. (1997). *Lobbying: A constitutionally protected right.* Washington, D.C.: American Enterprise Institute.

Embassy of India in the U.S. (2000). *Prime Minister Vajpayee's remarks at the India Caucus lunch.* Retrieved 22 October 2004 from http://www.indiaembasy.org/indusrel/pm-us-2000/pm-india-caucus-sep-14-2000.htm

Embassy of India, Washington, D.C. (2003). *The Indian American community in the United States.* A report.

Encyclopedia.com (2016). *Koreagte.* Retrieved 17 April 2016 from http://www.encyclopedia.com/doc/1G2-3401802268.html

Encyclopedia of Associations. (2016). *National organizations of the U.S.* Retrieved 12 April 2016 from http://find.galegroup.com/gdl/help/GDLeDirEAHelp. html

EWTN. (2004). *Chapter 126—The American media: Pro-abortion, and it shows.* Retrieved 26 June 2004 from http://www.ewtn.com/library/PROLENC/ ENCYC126.HTM

Federation for Zoroastrian Association of North America (2014). Retrieved 20 July 2014 from http://fezana.org/

Feldman, Noah. (2014). Obama takes on Cuba lobby. *Bloomberg.* Retrieved 22 April 2016 from http://www.bloombergview.com/articles/2014-12-17/ obama-takes-on-the-cuba-lobby

Feng, L. (2014). Where have all the lobbyists gone? *The Nation.* Retrieved 22 April 2016 from http://www.thenation.com/article/shadow-lobbying-complex/

Fisher, M.P. (1980). *The Indian in the New York City: A study of immigrants from India.* Columbia, MO: South Asia Books.

Fortune. (2004). *The powerful 25 top lobbying groups.* Retrieved 14 October 2004 from http://www.fortune.com/indexw.html

Friedman, T.E. (1992). A pro-Israel lobby gives itself a headache. *New York Times,* 8 November.

Galbraith, P. (1990). Nuclear proliferation in South Asia: Whose business? In S.R. Glazer and N. Glazer (eds.), *Conflicting images: India and the United States* (p. 72). Maryland: The Riverdale Company, Publishers.

Gamez-Farnandez, C.M., and Dwivedi, V. (2015). *Shaping the Indian diaspora: literary representations and Bollywood consumption away from the desi.* New York: Lexington Books.

Gandhi, S. (ed.) (2002). *The tilt: The U.S. and the South Asian crisis of 1971.* National Security Archive Electronic Briefing Book No. 79.

Ganguly, S. (1990). *U.S. Policy toward South Asia.* Boulder: Westview Press.

Ganguly, S. (2001). Behind India's bomb: The politics and the strategy for nuclear deterrence. *Foreign affairs.* Retrieved 22 April 2002 from https://www.foreignaffairs.com/reviews/review-essay/2001-09-01/ behind-indias-bomb-politics-and-strategy-nuclear-deterrence

Ganguly, S. (2014). India's pursuit of missile defense. *The Non-proliferation Review, 21*(3–4), 373–382.

Ganguly, S., Scobell, A., and Shoup, B. (2006). *US-India strategic cooperation into the 21st century.* London: Routledge.

Garamone, J. (2015). *U.S., India sign 10-year defense framework agreement.* U.S. Department of Defense. Retrieved 10 June 2015 from http://www.defense. gov/News-Article-View/Article/604775

Ghose, S. (1990). Beyond the American melting pot. *India International Center Quarterly, 17*(1), 24.

Glazer, S.R. and Glazer, N. (1990). Introduction. In S.R. Glazer and N. Glazer (eds.), *Conflicting images: India and the United States.* Glen Dale, Md.: Riverdale.

Global Terror Index. (2015). Retrieved 22 November 2015 from http://economicsandpeace.org/wp-content/uploads/2015/11/Global-Terrorism-Index-2015.pdf

Goel, M.L. (2004). *Asian Americans*. Retrieved 16 February 2004 from http://www.uwf.edu/govt/goel.htm

Gowen, A., and Bridges, T. (2015). From Piyush to Bobby: How does Jindal feel about his family's post. *Washington Post*, 23 June. Retrieved 22 April 2016 from https://www.washingtonpost.com/politics/from-piyush-to-bobby-how-does-jindal-feel-about-his-familys-past/2015/06/22/7d45a3da-18ec-11e5-ab92-c75ae6ab94b5_story.html

Gross, M.L. (1996). *The political racket, deceit, self interest and corruption in American politics*. New York: Ballantine Publishing Group.

Guha, R. (2014). How congress lost its diaspora. *Hindustan Times*, 28 September. Retrieved 3 October 2014 from http://www.hindustantimes.com/columns/how-the-congress-lost-the-diaspora/story-K8hIXsz1D7dzZFFjr41fbO.html

Gupta, A. (2004). The Indian diaspora's political efforts in the United States. *ORF Occasional Paper*, 18 September. Retrieved 18 September 2004 from http://www.orfonline.org/research/the-indian-diasporas-political-efforts-in-the-united-states/

Gupta, S. (1995). *India redefines its role*. Oxford: Oxford University Press.

Gupta, V. ed. (1983), *India and non-alignment*. Delhi: New Literature

H. Con. Res. 211. (1999). *Expressing support of congress for elections of 1999 in Republic of India*. Retrieved 4 November 2004 from http://www.usindiafriendship.net/congress/votingrecord/supportforindia.html

Haniffa, A. (2004a). *Hindu prayer: A first for congress*. Retrieved 22 May 2004 from http://www.beliefnet.com/story/42/story_4276_1.html

Haniffa, A. (2004b). *U.S. Senate India Caucus*. Washington, D.C. Retrieved 22 April 2004 from http://www.usindiafriendship.net/congress/friends/friends.htm

Haniffa, A. (2005a).Criticism aplenty of India Caucus, Reports on the First Conference to Gauge the Group's Effectiveness. India Abroad.

Haniffa, A. (2005b). Massive campaign on against Indo-US N-deal. *Rediff.com*. Retrieved 30 May 2005 from http://in.rediff.com/news/2005/dec/02aziz.htm

Haniffa, A. (2005c). Sometimes people expect a lot, says Pallone. *India Abroad*. Retrieved 10 November 2012 from http://www.usindiafriendship.net/congress1/housecaucus/haniffa-2-05062005.htm

Haniffa, A. (2006). Supporters ask senators to ignore killer amendments. *India Abroad*, 17 November.

Harrison, Salis S. (1960). *India: The most dangerous decades*. Princeton, N.J.: Princeton University Press.

Hathaway, R.M. (2000). Confrontation and retreat: The U.S. Congress and the South Asian Nuclear Tests. *Arms Control Today*, 30(1), 7–15.

Hathaway, R.M. (2001). Unfinished passage: Indian, Indian Americans, and the U.S. Congress. *The Washington Quarterly, 24*(2), 21–34.

Hathaway, R.M. (2003). The US–India courtship: From Clinton to Bush. In S. Ganguly (ed.), *India as an emerging power.* London: Frank Cass Publisher.

Hayes, M.B. (1981). *Lobbyists and legislators.* New Jersey: Rutgers University Press.

Helweg, A., and Helweg, U. (1990). *The immigrant success story: East Indian.* Philadelphia: University of Pennsylvania Press.

Government of India. (2002). *High level committee report on the Indian diaspora* (pp. Xx–xxi). New Delhi: Government of India.

The Hindu. (August 11, 2015). Top India-origin CEOs from around the world. Retrieved 10 November 2015 from http://www.thehindu.com/news/international/sundar-pichai-and-other-indian-origin-ceos/article7525835.ece#im-image-0

Hindustan Times, 30 May 1998.

Hing, B.O. (1993). *Making and remaking Asian American through immigration policy,* 1850–1990. Stanford, CA: Stanford University Press.

Hoellen, C.V. (1980). The tilt policy revisited: Nixon-Kissinger geopolitics. *South Asia Asian Survey, 2*(1), 341.

Howe, R.W., and Hott, S.H. (1977). *The power peddlers: How lobbies mould American Foreign Policy.* New York: Double Day.

Hugh, T. (1977). *The banyan tree.* New York: Oxford University Press.

Hyot, T.D. (2009). India and the challenge of global terrorism: The long war and competing domestic visions. In Harsh V. Pant (ed.), *Indian Foreign Policy in a unipolar world.* London: Routledge.

India Abroad (2002). Let Israel Sell Arrow Missile Defense System to India, Pallone tells Powell, *xxxii*(48).

India Today, 15 November 1993, "Think before you knock India." pp. 207–209.

India Today, 3 August 1999.

Indian American Forum for Political Education (2005). Retrieved 18 March 2005 from http://www.iafpe.org/html

Indian American Muslim Council (2014). Retrieved 20 July 2014 from http://www.imc-usa.org/cgi-bin/cfm/index.cfm

Indian Cuisine (2011). Retrieved 16 May 2011 from http://en.wikipedia.org/wiki/Indian_cuisine

Indian Embassy, Washington, D.C. (2014). The Indian American community in the United States of America. *Out of India.* Retrieved 12 July 2014 from http://www.outofindia.net/abroad/WashingtonDC/indian_american_community.htm

Indian Express. 28 October 1999.

Indian Express. (September 25, 1995). Parliamentarians from the parties on the Left ridiculed the Rao government for pursuing what they regarded as a misguided policy of cooperation with the United States.

Indian Express. (2003). Pallone introduces bill supporting UNSC seat for India. *Indian Express Bureau,* 28 February 2003. *Retrieved* 4 November 2014 from http://www.indiaexpress.com/news/world/200302280.htm

Indian Express. (August 10, 2004). Pak blames Indian lobby for N-check Bills US Congress.

Indo-American Chamber of Commerce USA. (2016). Retrieved 15 April 2016 from http://www.iaccusa.org//

Irish, M.D., and Prothre, J.W. (1965). *The politics of American Democracy.* New Jersey: Prentice-Hall, Inc.

Isaacs, H. (1980). *Scratches on our minds.* New York: M. E. Sharpe.

Jain, R.K. (1993). *Indian communities abroad.* New Delhi: Manohar Publishers.

Jensen, J.M. (1988). *Passage from India: Asian Indian immigrants in North America.* New Haven, Connecticut: Yale University Press.

Jha, N.K. (1995). Indian American: The growing force. *India Abroad,* New York, 3 November.

Jha, N.K. (1999). US Pokhran-II and South Asia. *India Quarterly, 55*(1&2), 1–18.

Jha, N.K. (2003). Americans of Indian origin: Bridging the Gulf between two democracies. In S.D. Singh and M. Singh (eds), *India abroad.* Kolkatta: Maulana Abul Kalam Azad Institute of Asian Studies.

Jones, K. (1999). India and Pakistan vie for US's Favor. Retrieved 18 May 2004 from http://www.wsws.org/articles/1999/oct1999/ind-o01.shtml

Joseph, L.A. (1998). It's a cleft stick. *Outlook,* 6 July.

Kamath, P.M. (1999a). *Indian nuclear policy: From idealism to realism.* Jaipur: Printwell Publishers.

Kamath, P.M. (1999b). *Indian nuclear tests, then and now: An analysis of US and Canadian response.* Retrieved 5 January 2016 from http://www.idsa-india.org/an-aug9-4.html

Kandel, A. (2010). Indo-Israeli relations in the post-Cold War period. *Blitz.* Retrieved 14 July 2014 from http://www.weeklyblitz.net/535/indo-israeli-relations-in-the-post-coldwar-period

Kanjilal, T. (1989). Outside interference in South Asia and perceptions of India, Pakistan and Nepal. *Asian Studies, 7*(4), 15–40.

Kanjilal, T. (2000). *Indian-Americans: Participation in the American domestic political process.* Calcutta: Anuradha Kanjilal.

Kapur, D. (2010). *Diaspora, development, and democracy: The domestic impact of international migration from India.* Princeton: Princeton University Press.

Keshavan, N.D. (1998). Nuclear hardsell for $750,000: Post-Pokhran, India hires four lobbying firms, two prominent US politicians. Will they deliver? *Outlook.* Retrieved 2 August 2015 http://www.outlookindia.com/printarticle.aspx?205944.

Key, V.O. Jr. (1942). *Politics, parties and pressure groups.* New York: Thomas Y. Crowell Company.

Kirk, J.A. (2008). Indian-Americans and the U.S.-India nuclear agreement: Consolidation of an ethnic lobby? *Foreign Policy Analysis, 4*(3), 275–300.

Kitano, H. and Daniels, R. (1988). *Asian Americans: Emerging minorities.* New Jersey: Prentice Hall.

Kjølseth, H.C. (2009). New kids on the block: Indian American lobby and the U.S.–India nuclear deal. *Master's Thesis*, University of Oslo. Retrieved 12 April 2016 from http://www.duo.uio.no/bitstream/handle/10852/14999/MasteroppgavenFerdig.pdf?sequence=2

Knoke, D. (1986). Association and interest groups. *Annual Review of Sociology, 12*, 1–21.

Koritala, S.B. (2014). *A historical perspective of Americans of Asian Indian Origin 1790–1997.* Retrieved 12 July 2014 from http://www.infinityfoundation.com/mandala/h_es/h_es_korit_histical.htm

Kutty, F. (2000). India and Israel: An unholy alliance. *iviews.com.* Retrieved 23 March 2004 from http://www.iviews.com/scripts/articles/stories/default.cfm?id=7288&category_id=39

Kux, D. (1992). *India and the United States: Estranged democracies.* Washington: National Defense University Press.

Lal, V. (1999). Establishing roots, engendering awareness: A political history of Asian Indian's in the United States. In L. Prasad (ed.), *Live like banyan tree: Images of the Indian American experience.* Philadelphia: Balch Institute for Ethnic Studies.

Lal, V. (2008). *The other Indians: A political and cultural history of South Asians in America.* New Delhi: Harper Collins.

Lancaster, J. (1999). Activism boosts India's fortunes. *Washington Post,* 9 October.

Leogrande, W.M. (2013). The Cuba lobby. *Foreign policy.* Retrieved 22 April 2016 from http://foreignpolicy.com/2013/04/12/the-cuba-lobby/

LePoer, B.L., Medalia, J., Rennack. D., and Cronin, R.P. (1998). *India–Pakistan nuclear test and U.S. response.* CRS Report for Congress. Retrieved 24 November 2012 from http://congressionalresearch.com/98-570/document.php?study=INDIA-PAKISTAN+NUCLEAR+TESTS+AND+U.S.+RESPONSE

Lewis, J.P. (1995). *India's political economy, governance and reform.* Delhi: Oxford University Press.

Lipsky, M. (1968). Protests as a political resource. *American Political Science Review, 62*(4), 1144–1158.

Lowi, Theodore J. (1979). *The end of liberalism: The second republic of the United States.* New York: W. W. Norton & Co Inc.

Mahapatra, C. (1998). *Indo-US relations into the 21st century.* New Delhi: Knowledge World.

Maitra, R. (2003a). India's lobby on Capitol Hill. *Asia Times,* 8 May.

Maitra, R. (2003b). Indian diaspora gains muscle in Washington. *Asia Times* 23 September 2003. Retrieved 7 February 2004 from http://www.atimes.com/atimes/South_Asia/EI23Df03.html

Malhotra, R. (2003). *Does South Asian studies undermine India?* Retrieved 10 March 2004 from http://www.rediff.com/news/2003/dec/08rajiv.htm

Martin, D. (2010). Stephen J. Solarz, former N.Y. Congressman, dies at 70. *New York Times.* Retrieved 2 August 2015 http://www.nytimes.com/2010/11/30/nyregion/30solarz.html?pagewanted=all&_r=0

Mayer, J. (2004). The manipulator. *The New Yorker.* Retrieved 22 April 2016 from http://www.newyorker.com/magazine/2004/06/07/the-manipulator

Mazumdar, S. (1984). Colonial impact and Punjabi immigration to the United States. In L. Cheng and E. Bonacich (eds), *Labor immigration under capitalization: Asian workers in the United States before World War II.* Berkley: University of California Press.

McCann, M.W. (1986). *Taking reforms seriously: Perspective on public interest liberalism.* Ithaca and London: Cornell University Press.

McCarthy, E. (1970). A senator looks at the lobbies. *The New York Times Magazine,* 19 August 1962. In L.E. Shaw and J.C. Pierce (eds.), *Readings on American political system* (pp. 200–201). Massachusetts: D.C. Heath Company.

McCutcheon, C. (2013). *Lobbying in Guide to Congress.* Washington, DC: Congressional Quarterly Press.

McMahon, R.J. (1994). *Cold War on the periphery: The United States, India, and Pakistan.* New York: Columbia University Press.

Mearsheimer, J.J., and Walt, S.M. (2007). *The Israel lobby and U.S. Foreign Policy.* New York: Farrar, Straus and Giroux.

Mellor, J.W. (1979). Conclusion. In J. W. Mellor (ed.), *India: A rising middle power.* Boulder, Colorado: Westview Press.

Min, Pyong Gap. (1995). 'An Overview of Asian American'. In Pyong Gap Min (ed.), *Asian Americans, Contemporary Trends and Issues* (pp. 22–23). Thousand Oaks, Calif.: SAGE Publications.

Mistry, D. (2013). The India Lobby and the Nuclear Agreement with India. *Political Science Quarterly, 128*(4), 717–746.

Mitra, R. (2003). Indian diaspora gains muscle in Washington. *Asia Times,* 23 September. Retrieved 7 February 2004 from http://www.atimes.com/atimes/South_Asia/EI23Df03.html

Mohan, C.R. (2003). *Crossing the Rubicon: The shaping of India's new foreign policy.* New Delhi: Penguin Books.

MTVDesi. (2011). Retrieved 10 October 2011 from http://www.mtvdesi.com/

Nasser, H.E. and Overberg, P. (2011). Census shows growth among Asian Indians. *USA Today.* Retrieved 13 July 2014 from http://usatoday30.usatoday.com/news/nation/census/2011-05-12-asian-indian-population-Census_n.htm

Nathan, J.A., and Oliver, J.K. (1982). *Foreign policy making the American political system.* Boston: Little Brown and Company.

Nayar, B.R. (1975). Treat India seriously. *Foreign Policy,* 18, 133–154.

NDTV Profit. (2012). US senator promises more L1, H1B visas for Indians. Retrieved 15 November 2012 from http://profit.ndtv.com/News/Article/us-senator-promises-more-l1-h1b-visas-for-indians-300441

NetIP Atlanta. (2002). Retrieved on 12 February 2003 from http://www.ipatlanta.net/2002

New York Times. (1987).

New York Times. (May 13, 1998). Indian's Letter to Clinton on the Nuclear Testing.

New York Times. (2000). 12 February.

New York Times. (May 19, 2001). Away from Haiti: Discovering the politics of the possible.

New York Times. (2015). *Modi and Obama at climate talks.* Retrieved 18 December 2015 from http://www.nytimes.com/video/world/100000004065489/modi-meets-obama-over-climate-change.html

Newsom, D.D. (2004). *Foreign policy lobbies and their influence.* Retrieved 12 January 2004 from http://www.cosmos-club.org/journals/1995/newsom.html

Nixon, R.M. (1988). *Victory without war.* New York: Simon & Schuster.

Nossiter, B.D. (1970). *Soft state: A newspaperman's chronicle of India.* New York: Harper and Row.

NRI Online (2014). The Indian American community in USA. Retrieved 12 July 2014 from http://www.nriol.com/indiandiaspora/indian-american-community.asp

Nurnberger, R. (2005). *Best and brightest drawn by IACPA's internship program.* Retrieved 12 March 2005 from http://www.newsindiatimes.com.2002.html

Olson, M. Jr. (1968). *The logic of collective action.* New York: Oxford University Press.

OpenSecrets.org (2016). Centre for responsive politics. *Lobbying Database.* Retrieved 22 April 2016 from http://www.opensecrets.org/lobby/index.php

Outlook. (2006). US lawmaker criticises Pak for not living up to its promises. Retrieved 14 March 2014 from http://www.outlookindia.com/news/article/us-lawmaker-criticises-pak-for-not-living-up-to-its-promises/400047

Pais, A.J. (1994). Indians with an American dream. *The Telegraph,* Calcutta, 26 June 1994, pp. 4–8.

Palmer, N.D. (1966). *South Asia and United States Policy.* Boston: Houghton Miffin.

Pandit, R. (2005). Nixon badmouthed India. *Times of India,* 17 June.

Pant, H. (2009). Introduction. In H. Pant (ed.), *Indian Foreign Policy in a unipolar world* (pp. 1–22). New Delhi: Routledge.

Pant, H. (2011). *The US–India Nuclear Pact: Policy, process, and great power politics.* New Delhi: Oxford University Press.

Parekh, N. (2000). Community must ask more of Caucus. *News India Times,* 25 February.

Perish, T. (1996). *The Cold War encyclopaedia,* 1st Edition. New York: H. Holt.

Petrecca, M.P. (1992). *Rediscovery of interest group politics: The politics of interest group transformed.* California: West View Press Inc.

Prasad, V. (2004). An Indian American election. *Frontline, 21*(14), 03–16.

Pallone, F. (2000). Now is the time' to declare Pakistan a terrorist state. *Press Release,* 4 January 2000.

Public Citizen (2016). *Public Utility Holding Company Act (PUHCA).* Retrieved 12 January 2016 from http://www.citizen.org/cmep/energy_enviro_nuclear/electricity/deregulation/puhca/index.cfm

Raj, Y. (2012). Indian-Americans top fundraisers list for Obama. *Hindustan Times,* 6 February. Retrieved 20 November 2012 from http://www.hindustantimes.com/world-news/NorthAmerica/Indian-Americans-top-fundraisers-list-for-Obama/Article1-807247.aspx

Rajghatta, C. (1997). Indian lobbying comes of age. *The Indian Express,* 6 September.

Rajghatta, C. (2003a). 200,000 NRI millionaires in U.S.: Merill. *The Times of India,* 15 May.

Rajghatta, C. (2003b). Pak-American oppose Jindal. *The Times of India,* 8 November.

Rajghatta, C. (2006). India reaches out to Hispanic, Black Legislators. *The Times of India,* 29 April.

Rajghatta, C. (2015). Indians to benefit most from sop for H1-B spouses. *The Times of India.* Retrieved 12 April 2015 from http://timesofindia.indiatimes.com/india/Indians-to-benefit-most-from-sop-for-H1-B-spouses/articleshow/46376152.cms

Raman, B. (2003). *The statement in the House International Relations Subcommittee on Asia and the Pacific and the Subcommittee on international terrorism, nonproliferation and human rights,* 29 October. Retrieved 20 January 2004 from http://wwwa.house.gov/international_relations/108/rama1029.htm

Ramer, L. (2002). Pro-Israel activists seeking allies among immigrants from India. *Forward.* Retrieved 23 March 2004 from http://www.forward.com/issues/2002/02.10.11/news9.html

Rayden, X. (1980). The nationalizing of party system. In M. J. Malbin (ed.), *Parties, interest groups and campaign finance laws* (pp. 260–262). Washington, D.C.: American Enterprise Institute for Public Policy Research.

Rediff On The Net. (1997a). *Kashmiri pandits ask US for humanitarian aid.* Retrieved 2 March 2003 from http://www.rediff.com/news/oct/16pandit.htm

Rediff On The Net. (1997b). *Kashmiri pandits find place on Clinton's agenda.* Retrieved 2 March 2003 from http://www.rediff.com/news/oct/23pandit.htm

Rediff.com (2003). *Text of ambassador Robert Blackwill's speech at the confederation of Indian industry.* New Delhi. Retrieved 12 May 2003 from http://www.rediff.com/news/2003/jul/17black1.htm?zcc=rl

Rediff.com (2004). *Bush took time out for Indian Americans.* Retrieved 21 February 2005 from http://in.rediff.com/news/2004/aug/30gop.htm

Representative Gary Ackerman, Spoken Remarks (2000). *Center for strategic and international studies, Washington, D.C.* Retrieved 22 October 2004 from http://www.usindiafriendship.net/congress/votingrecord/goodling-amendment.html

Riedel, B. (2015). Strengthening counter terrorism cooperation against growing turmoil. *Brookings.* Retrieved 24 November 2015 from http://www.brookings.edu/research/opinions/2015/01/20-strengthening-us-india-counterterrorism-cooperation-riedel

Robinson, J.A. (1967). *Congress and foreign policy-making.* Homewood, Ill: Dorsey Press.

Rosenthal, S.T. (2005). Long distance nationalism: American Jews, Zionism, and Israel. In Dan Evan Kaplan (ed.), *The Cambridge companion to American Judaism.* New York: Cambridge University Press.

Rotter, A.J. (2000). *Comrades at odds: The United States and India, 1947–64.* Ithaca, NY: Cornell University Press.

Rozen, L. (2009). India's stealth lobbying against Holbrooke's brief. *The cable—foreign policy.* Retrieved 1 August 2015 from http://foreignpolicy.com/2009/01/24/indias-stealth-lobbying-against-holbrookes-brief/

Rubinoff, A.G. (1971). *India's use of force in Goa.* Bombay: Popular Prakashan.

Rubinoff, A.G. (2001). Changing perceptions of India in the U.S. Congress. *Asian Affairs: An American Review, 28*(1), 37–60.

Rubinoff, A.G. (1992a). Congressional attitudes towards India. In H. Gould and S. Ganguly (eds.), *The hope and the reality: Indo-American relations from Roosevelt to Reagan* (p. 169). Boulder Colorado: Westview Press.

Rubinoff, A.G. (1992b). U.S. attitudes towards India. In A.G. Rubinoff (ed.), *Canada and South Asia: Political and strategic relations* (pp. 63–73). Toronto: South Asia Centre of the University of Toronto.

Rudolph, L.I., and Rudolph, S. (2008). Introduction to the regional imperative. In L.I. Rudolph and S.H. Rudolph (eds), *Making U.S. Foreign Policy Toward South Asia: Regional imperative and the imperial presidency* (p. 37). Bloomington: Indiana University Press.

S. Con. Res. 74 (*2001*). *Condemning bigotry and violence against Sikh-Americans in the wake of terrorist attacks in New York City and Washington, D.C. on September 11.* Retrieved 12 February 2004 from http://avalon.law.yale.edu/sept11/scon74_is.asp

Sahay, A. (2009). *Indian diaspora in the United States: Brain drain or gain?* Lanham, MD: Lexington Books.

Saksena, J., and Grillot, S. (1999). The emergence of Indo-US defence cooperation: From specific to diffuse reciprocity. In G.K. Bertsch, S. Gahlaut and A. Srivastava (eds), *Engaging India: US strategic relations with the world's largest democracy.* New York: Routledge.

Salisbury, R.H. (1984). Interests representation and the dominance of institutions. *American Political Science Review, 78*(1), 64–77.

Salisbury, R.H. (1996). An exchange theory interest groups. *Midwest Journal of Political Science, 13*(1), 1–32.

Sami, B. (1990). India to America, America to India. In Y.D. Prasad (ed.), *America studies in India.* Patna.

Saund, D.S. (1960). *Congressman from India.* New York: E.P. Dutton and Company.

Sayeed, K.B. (1992). American political system: A critique of its functioning. *Economic and Political Weekly, 27*(39), 21–29.

Scholzman, R.L., and Tierney, J.T. (1986). *Organized interest and American Democracy.* New York: Harper & Row.

Schroeder, M. (2011). *India aims to calm U.S. outsourcing fears.* Retrieved 12 April 2012 from http://www.internationaltraderelations.com/Article. India%20-20%20outsourcing%20(wsj%2011.13.03).html

Sen, A.K. (2004). *Indian Americans: The lobbyists.* Retrieved 26 October 2004 from http://newdelhi.usembassy.gov /wwwhspjulaug6.html

Shankar, S. (2015). What does the spelling success of Indian American kids tell us? *The Conversation,* 4 June 2015. Retrieved 9 December 2015, from https://theconversation.com/what-does-the spelling-success-of-indian-american-kids-tell-us-42459

Sharma, A. (2006). Indo-US nuclear deal: Intense lobbying. *Institute of Peace & Conflict Studies,* 24 June. Retrieved 25 June 2006 from http://www.ipcs.org/ article/india/indo-us-nuclear-deal-intense-lobbying-2049.html

Sharma, A. (2007). Retaining Indianness in America. *Pravasi Today,* July 2007, pp. 58–59.

Sharma, A. (2008a). Growing influence of Indian American lobbying on Indo-US relations. *World Focus,* July 2008.

Sharma, A. (2008b). Indo-US strategic convergence: An overview of defence and military cooperation. *CLAWS,* Paper No. 2.Retrieved from http://www. claws.in/images/publication_pdf/CLAWS%20Papers%20No[1].2,%20 2008.pdf

Sharma, A. (2009). *India's missile defence programme treat perception and technology evolution.* Manekshaw Research Paper, Centre for Land Warfare Studies. Retrieved 12 December 2009 fromhttp://www.claws.in/index. php?action=Claws%20Paper

Sharma, A. (2010). Mending ties through strategic dialogue. *New Zealand International Review, 36*(5), 21–25.

Sharma, A. (2011). Indian Americans: Migrational pattern, professional success, cultural emergence and their political activism. In A. Dubey (ed.), *Indian diaspora: Contributions to their new home* (pp. 49–82). New Delhi: MD Publications.

Sharma, A. (2012a). Counter-terrorism cooperation in the context of the Indo-US strategic partnership: An appraisal. *India Quarterly, 68*(4), 315–330.

Sharma, A. (2012b). The enduring conflict and the hidden risk of India–Pakistan War. *SAIS Review*, 32(1), 129–142.

Sharma, A. (2015a). Indo-American lobby boosted ties. *Sunday Guardian.* Retrieved 28 January 2015 from http://www.sunday-guardian.com/extra/indo-american-lobby-boosted-ties

Sharma, A. (2015b). What's behind the new U.S.–India Defense Pact. *The Conversation.* Retrieved 17 June 2015 from https://theconversation.com/whats-behind-the-new-us-india-defense-pact-42944

Sharma, A. (2016). India's soft power. *Institute of Peace & Conflict Studies,* 4 May. Retrieved 25 January 2006 from http://www.ipcs.org/whatsNewArticle11.jsp?action=showView&kValue=1946&status=article&mod=b

Sharma, A., and Bing, D. (2015). India–Israeli relationship: The evolving partnership. *Israel Affairs, 21*(4), 620–632.

Sharma, K. (2004). *Indian Americans and the 2004 election.* Retrieved 2 February 2004 from http://www.observerindia.com/publications/USElection/em041109.pdf

Sheth, M. (1995). Asian Indian Americans. In P.G. Min (ed.), *Asian Americans, contemporary trends and issues* (p. 171). Thousand Oaks, Calif.: SAGE Publications.

Shenoy, J.M. (2004). The doctor organise 'em better. Retrieved 22 September 2004 from http://www.kind.com.html

Singh, A.I. (1993). *The limits of British influence: South Asia and the Anglo-American relationship, 1947–56.* London: Pinter Publishers.

Singh, M.K. (1984). *India's defense strategy and tactics: A geographical analysis,* 1st Edition. Delhi: Shree Publishing House.

Smith, H. (1988). *The power game.* New York: Ballantine Books.

South Asian American Leaders of Tomorrow. (2012). American backlash: Terrorists bring war home in more ways than one. *A report.* Retrieved 24 March 2014 from http://www.saa-vi.org/downloads/American-Backlash-report.pdf

Sreenivasan, T.P. (2008). *Word, words, words: Adventure in diplomacy.* New Delhi: Pearson Longman.

Steele, T.L. (2002). The politics of Anglo-American aid to nonaligned India, 1962. *Electronic Journal of International History.* London. Retrieved 26 October 2012 from http://sas-space.sas.ac.uk/3394/1/Journal_of_International_History_2002_n7_Steele.pdf

Takaki, R. (1989). *Strangers from a different shore: A history of Asian Americans.* New York: Penguin Books.

Talbott, S. (2002). The day a nuclear conflict was averted. Yale Global Online, 13 September 2004. Retrieved 10 June 2014 from http://yaleglobal.yale.edu/content/day-nuclear-conflict-was-averted

Talbott, S. (2004). *Engaging India: Diplomacy, democracy and the bomb.* Washington, D.C.: Brookings Institution Press.

Thakar, M. (1999). Coping with insecurity: The Pakistani variable in Indo-US relations. In G.K. Bertsch, S. Gahlaut and A. Srivastava (eds), *Engaging India: US strategic relations with the world's largest democracy* (p. 226). New York: Routledge.

Thakur, R. (1996). India and the United States: A triumph of hope over experience. *Asian Survey, 36*(2), 574–591.

The Economist (April 4, 2015). Why the gun lobbying is winning. Retrieved 15 April 2015 from http://www.economist.com/news/united-states/21647627-prevent-gun-deaths-politicians-offermore-guns-why-gun-lobby-winning

The Hill (April 16, 1997). Dan Burton has been accused of demanding and obtaining illegal contributions from Sikh and Pakistani lobbyists.

The Hindu, 16 December 1995.

The Hindu. (September 3, 2012). Indian-Americans open up wallets for Obama; little for Romney. Retrieved 20 November 2012 from http://www.thehindubusinessline.com/news/international/indianamericans-open-up-wallets-for-obama-little-for-romney/article3853953.ece

The Telegraph. (May 17, 1997). *Senators call for better ties with India at Forum.*

The Times of India. (April 30, 2006). *Pak testfires N-capable Haft-VI missile.*

The Times of India. (February 7, 2013). *Indian-Americans' interest in lobbying for Indo-US ties wanes.* Retrieved 12 December 2015 from http://timesofindia.indiatimes.com/nri/us-canada-news/Indian-Americans-interest-in-lobbying-for-Indo-US-ties-wanes/articleshow/18381977.cms

The Times of India. (2014a). *India among most dangerous place in the world.* Retrieved 14 March 2014 from http://timesofindia.indiatimes.com/india/India-among-most-dangerous-places-in-the-world/articleshow/31357766.cms

The Times of India. (2014b). *Modi to get rockstar reception in New York: US lobby questions his credentials.* Retrieved 12 November 2015 from http://timesofindia.indiatimes.com/world/us/Modi-to-get-rockstar-reception-in-New-York-US-lobby-questions-his-reform-credentials/articleshow/43535451.cms

The U.S. Department of Commerce-Economic and Statistics Administration, Bureau of Census. (1990). *Census of the population: Asian and Pacific Islands in the U.S.* Washington, D.C.

The U.S. Embassy in India. (1999). *India–US relations.* A report.

The US Census Bureau. (2010). Retrieved 20 November 2012 from http://factfinder2.census.gov/faces/tableservices/jsf/pages/productview.xhtml?Pid=ACS_10_1YR_S0201&prodtype=table

Thomas, S. (2012). *Lululemon: Capitalizing on yoga's billion-dollar industry,* 4 May. Retrieved 1 September 2014 from http://beta.fool.com/shthomas/2012/05/04/lululemon-capitalizing-yogas-billion-dollar-indust/3036/

Tierney, J.T. (1992). Organized interests and the nation's capital. In M.P. Petracca (ed.), *Rediscovery of interest group politics: The politics of interest group transformed* (p. 207). California: West View Press Inc.

Times of India, 18 November 1999.

Tivnan, E. (1985). *The lobby*. Colorado: Westview Press.

Trikha, S. (2001). We have questions about Pakistan: Armitage. *Indian Express*, 12 May.

Truman, D.B. (1971). *The governmental process*, 2nd Edition. New York: Alfred A. Knopf.

Turner, J.C. (1982). Towards a cognitive redefinition of social group. In H. Tajfel (ed.), *Social identity and intergroup relations* (p. 15). New York: Cambridge University Press.

Urofsky, M.I. (1975). *American Zionism from Herzel to the Holocaust*. Garden City, NY: Anchor Press.

United States Census. (2010). *In security and exchange commission, Washington D.C. 20549*. Retrieved 10 September 2014 from http://www.sec.gov/Archives/edgar/data/1174824/000115752302001204/d52217_10-sb12g.htm

U.S. Census Bureau (2010). American Fact Finder. Retrieved 10 March 2011 from http://factfinder2.census.gov/faces/tableservices/jsf/pages/productview.xhtml?pid=ACS_10_1YR_S0201&prodType=table

U.S. Census Bureau (2012). *Asian Indian summary of findings*. Retrieved 15 march 2012 from http://www.census.gov/econ/sbo/

U.S. Congress, House Committee on Foreign Affairs. (1973). *Subcommittee on the near East and South Asia, the United States and South Asia*, 93d Congress, 1st session, 25 May, p. 20.

U.S. Congress, House Committee on International Relations. (1976). *Subcommittee on international organizations, hearings, human rights in India*. 94th Congress, 2nd session, 23, 28, 29 June; 16, 23 September.

U.S. Department of Defense (2015). U.S.–India joint press release on secretary of defense Carter's Visit to India. *Press Operations*, Release No: NR-214-15. Retrieved 4 June 2015 from http://www.defense.gov/News/News-Releases/News-Release-View/Article/605545

U.S. Department of State, South Asia, Office of the Historian, *FRUS, XIX*, 1961–1963. https://history.state.gov/historicaldocuments/frus1961-63v19/d138

U.S. Department of State. (1959). *The subcontinent of South Asia, near and middle east series*, (41), 6. Washington D.C: Department of State.

U.S. Department of State. (2003). *Robert D. Blackwill, "The future of US–India relations." Address at the Confederation of Indian Industry, New Delhi*. Retrieved 23 July 2003 from http://2001-2009.state.gov/p/sca/rls/rm/22615.htm

U.S. Immigration and Naturalization Service. (1977). *Annual report, 1976*. Washington D.C., pp. 86–88.

U.S. Immigration and Naturalization Service (1990). *Annual report*. Agreement Between Immigration And Naturalization Service And American Federation of Government Employees, National Immigration And Naturalization Service Council. Washington, D.C.

US Census Bureau (2010). 2008–2010 American Community Survey 3-Year Estimates.

US India Political Action Committee. (2005). Retrieved from http://www.usinpac.com/NewsContent.asp?CONTENT_ID=223&SEC_ID=14

USIA's Washington File. (1998). *Karl Inderfurth, US Chagrined to Implement Sanctions on India, Pakistan*, June 18.

US–India Political Action Committee (2012). *Indian American in new hemisphere.* Retrieved 20 November 2012 from http://web.archive.org/web/20100427163917/http://www.usinpac.com/nh/indian_americans_nh.html

Usindiafriendship.net (2004a). *Congressional caucus on India and Indian Americans.* Retrieved 14 October 2004 from http://www.usindiafriendship.net/Congress/Caucus/Caucus.htm#

Usindifriendhsip.net (2004b). Retrieved 22 May 2004 from *http://www.usindiafriendship.net/congress/votingrecord/taliban.html*

Usindiafriendship.net (2004c). Retrieved 4 November 2004 from *http://www.usindiafriendship.net/congress/votingrecord/taliban.html*

Usindifriendship.net (2004d). *Defeat of Goodling amendment: A victory for India.* Retrieved 22 October 2004 from http://www.usindiafriendship.net/congress/votingrecord/goodling-amendment.html

USINPAC-Washington, D.C. (2003). *US congress demands to know about Pakistan's role in abetting terrorism and nuclear proliferation at USINPAC's urging*, 7 May. Retrieved 10 May 2003 from http://www.usinpac.com/NewsContent.asp?CONTENT_ID=52&SEC_ID=18

Uslaner, E.M. (1996). Politics. In A.J. Cigler and B.A. Loomis (eds), *Interest group politics.* Washington: Congressional Quarterly Press.

Valero, Francis R. (1976). *South Asia: Report on Bangladesh, India, and Pakistan to the majority leader.* U.S. Congress, House Committee on Foreign Affairs, 94th Congress, 2nd session, 13.

Venkatramni, M.S., and Srivastwa, B.K. (1983). *Roosevelt, Gandhi, Churchill: American and the last phase of India's struggle.* New Delhi: Radiant Publishers.

Wainwright, M. (1994). *Inheritance of empire: Britain, India, and the balance of power in Asia, 1938–55.* Westport: Praeger.

Walker, J.C. (1983). The origin and maintenance of interest groups in America. *American Political Science Review, 37*(2), 390–406.

Washington File. (September 4, 2001). *Text: Robert Blackwill on U.S.–India collaboration on international issues.*

Washington Times (2003). *Indian Americans ascend the Hill.* Retrieved 14 October 2004 from http://www.washtimes.com/world/20031219-093705-9413r.htm

Watts, W. (1982). *The United States and Asia: Changing attitudes and policies.* Lexington, MA: Lexington Books.

Weiner, M. (1976). Critical choices for India and America. In Donald C. Hellmann (ed.), *Southern Asia: The politics of poverty and peace* (p. 65). Lanham, Md.: Lexington Books.

Weiner, T. (2013). Nuclear anxiety: The blunders; U.S. blundered on intelligence, officials admit. *The New York Times.* Retrieved 12 February 2013 from http://www.nytimes.com/1998/05/13/world/nuclear-anxiety-the-blunders-us-blundered-on-intelligence-officials-admit.html

Wertheimer, J. (1995). Jewish organizational life in the United States since 1945. *American Jewish Yearbook 1995.* New York: American Jewish Committee.

White, M.J., and Subedi, I. (2008). The demography of China and India: Effects on migration to high-income countries. *Migration Policy Institute.* Retrieved 12 July 2015 from http://www.migrationpolicy.org/research/demography-china-and-india-effects-migration-high-income-countries

Young, J. (1993). *Cold War and detente 1941–1991.* London: Longman.

Zong, J., and Batalova, J. (2015). Indian immigrants in the United States. *Spotlight.* Migration Policy Institute, 6 May 2015. Retrieved 5 December 2015 from http://www.migrationpolicy.org/article/indian-immigrants-united-states

Index

About the Author

Ashok Sharma is a Fellow at the Australia India Institute (AII), the University of Melbourne. Prior to joining the AII in May 2015, Dr Sharma was a lecturer in the Department of Politics and International Relations at the University of Auckland, where he taught "Great Power Relations" and "International Security and Conflict." He was a Visiting Academic at the University of Waikato and an Endeavour Post-Doctoral Fellow at Australian National University.

He is currently the Adjunct Faculty at University of New South Wales, Australian Defence Force Academy, Canberra; Deputy Chair of the New Zealand Institute of International Affairs, Auckland Branch; and a Fellow at the New Zealand–India Research Institute, Victoria University of Wellington.

Dr Sharma has taught Political Science at Delhi University College and worked with strategic and foreign policy think tanks based in New Delhi, namely the Observer Research Foundation, Centre for Air Power Studies and Centre for Land Warfare Studies. He did his BA (Hons) in Political Science from Ramjas College, Delhi University and MA in Political Science, MPhil, and PhD in American Studies from Jawaharlal Nehru University (JNU), New Delhi.

His broad research is in international relations and security studies with a focus on ethnic lobbying in US foreign policy, US–India relations, Indian foreign and security policy, India's domestic politics, great power relations, Asia-Pacific security, international security with an emphasis on terrorism, nuclear issues, and energy security. He has extensively published chapters in edited collections, think tank papers and articles in peer reviewed journals such as *Asian Affairs, SAIS Review of International Affairs, Israel Affairs, South Asian Survey,* and for wider dissemination in the periodicals and reviews such as *The Conversation, New Zealand International Review, Georgetown Journal of International Affairs* and *Australian Outlook.*